INCEST

INCEST
ORIGINS OF THE TABOO

JONATHAN H. TURNER

AND

ALEXANDRA MARYANSKI

FOREWORD BY ROBIN FOX

Paradigm Publishers

Boulder • London

Copyright © 2005 by Paradigm Publishers

Published in the United States by Paradigm Publishers, 3360 Mitchell Lane, Suite E, Boulder, Colorado 80301 USA.

Paradigm Publishers is the trade name of Birkenkamp & Company, LLC, Dean Birkenkamp, President and Publisher.

Library of Congress Cataloging-in-Publication Data

Turner, Jonathan H.
Incest : origins of the taboo / Jonathan H. Turner and Alexandra Maryanski.
p. cm.
Includes bibliographical references and index.
ISBN 1-59451-116-0 (cloth : alk. paper)
1. Incest.   I. Maryanski, Alexandra.   II. Title.
HV6570.6.T87 2005
306.877—dc22

2005004914

Printed and bound in the United States of America on acid-free paper that meets the standards of the American National Standard for Permanence of Paper for Printed Library Materials.

Designed and Typeset by Straight Creek Bookmakers.

10   09   08   07   06   05
1   2   3   4   5   6

To
John McLennan, Émile Durkheim, Lewis H. Morgan,
Johann Bachofen, Sigmund Freud, and Edward Westermarck,
who all shared a concern with understanding the nature and
early history of the family.

CONTENTS

FOREWORD

Robin Fox

Two casual remarks set me off on the search for the meaning of the incest taboo. When I was an undergraduate (in sociology) at the London School of Economics (LSE) in the early 1950s, we had a weekly class on social anthropology. One week the subject was the incest taboo. I was trotting out all the standard sociological explanations for exogamy and the expansion of social ties and so on when Maurice Freedman, the great expert on Chinese kinship and later professor of anthropology at Oxford, obviously bored with this recitation, interrupted me. "Why can't we have a sexual free-for-all in the family and *then* marry out of it?" I was startled out of my sociological rut and launched on a lifelong intellectual adventure.

The second significant encounter was at Harvard (the old Social Relations Department) in the late 1950s. John Whiting, the genial pioneer of culture and personality studies, observed to me that opposite-sex children who played rough-and-tumble games a lot often seemed to get very sexually excited and then dissolve in tears and anger, presumably out of frustration. It immediately hit me that this might be the foundation for Edward Westermarck's contention that siblings easily developed a "natural aversion" to sex with each other at the onset of puberty.

A few years later (1962) I worked this idea up into an article called "Sibling Incest" for the *British Journal of Sociology*. The article was much admired and its conclusions generally dismissed. The prevailing wisdom, backed by Freud, Frazer, Malinowski, and Lévi-Strauss—and most everyone else—was that it was "self-evident" that we all want to commit incest, otherwise why are there all these fierce sanctions against it? I invoked Westermarck's response: that it could be that we were so against incest precisely because we *didn't* want to do it and so were horrified by those who did. No cigar. I think the only reason my article was published is that Westermarck is one of the revered founders of sociology at the LSE; he deserved a hearing, at least.

In contrasting the two views of sibling incest I coined the terms "Freud effect" and "Westermarck effect." The former got nowhere, but the latter, as this excellent book demonstrates, has passed into the language like "inferiority complex" and "male bonding." It is hard to convey how improbable this seemed in the early 1960s. Freud dominated; you had to come to terms with him. I suppose I figured that if I couldn't lick him, I could at least hijack his theory for my own purposes. Much of what followed is spelled out in detail in this book.

Jonathan Turner and Alexandra Maryanski do a wonderful job of first summarizing the classical and modern debates on the incest taboo and then giving the debate a mighty push forward. Their command of the material across a range of social and natural sciences is almost alarmingly thorough, as is their confident weaving together of all the complicated strands. When I started the "Westermack debate" it was impossible to get sociologists to take evolution seriously or evolutionists to have any patience with sociological concerns. No one wanted to learn new disciplines. The authors here show how far we have come. I fumbled about, for example, with what little was known of ape and monkey society. Even in 1980, the year of *The Red Lamp of Incest*, it was still rudimentary. But the questions were posed, and our authors are able, with greatest sophistication, to advance the debate on the "primate baseline" and show how cladistic analysis forces us to conclude that a loose, individualistic, and low-dominance organization characterized the common ancestor of modern chimps and humans. In following the logic of the move to the savanna, I had obviously overestimated the degree to which early hominid society would have become baboon-like in its structure. I had therefore put too much "kinship" into the original mix—and too much dominance. The picture has to be adjusted. This is one example, but it shows how true science advances. My other great teacher was Karl Popper. He taught us all that our hypotheses should be vulnerable, and that we should welcome disconfirmation: it means we are indeed doing science!

There are many examples here of such welcome improvements. But I am heartened to see that the broad outlines remain intact. Turner and Maryanski demonstrate that the nuclear family was indeed a late development from the baseline and brought with it the problems that the taboo sought to answer. In one of the most significant additions to the debate, they show that as the family in industrial society becomes more isolated from the community the mechanisms of avoidance become less dependable. Mothers and sons seem to be inoculated by a "bio-program." I would follow Earl Count in seeing this as a "reverberation" of the breast suckling experience throughout life. Traditionally sons were suckled for up to three years, with, as we know, profound hormonal consequences for both partners. Since the invention of feeding bottles, in industrial societies most sons are not breast-fed at all. The bio-programs are not automatic: all need the appropriate input to be activated. Jocasta never suckled Oedipus.

The Westermarck effect is very variable, and the authors are right to stress this variability. It was there in the original hypothesis, but many since have ignored it. This is not a mechanical effect. As the age of puberty descends to the preteen levels and the years of familial dependency, with greater "privacy" for individual children, increase, so the possibility of sibling incest rises and seems to be rising. Fathers and daughters have very little natural immunity. Without community monitoring they must fall back on those evolved systems (bio-programs) of inhibition and control of emotions so ably described here. In fact most fathers enjoy positive, loving relationships with their daughters (something many feminists seem strangely reluctant to admit), and control is not an issue unless things go wrong, as they do all too often.

It has been suggested that with the advent of reliable contraception (especially the pill) the point of the incest taboo has been lost: with no genetic consequences, why bother? This brilliantly successful account by Turner and Maryanski, with its logic, its accuracy, and its impeccable data, will more than demonstrate why this is wishful thinking. The incest taboo was indispensable to that struggling ape making it into humanity, and like so much of our evolutionary heritage, we are stuck with it.

ACKNOWLEDGMENTS

We wish to thank the Academic Senate of the University of California–Riverside for supporting our research for this book. We are indebted to historian Patricia Turner for her helpful suggestions in chapter 1. We also want to thank the UCR library staff, especially Janet Moores, Maria Mendoza, Kim Noon, and Debbie Snow in Interlibrary Loan, who were somehow able to secure for us hard-to-locate texts and journals throughout the globe. We are very grateful for their help. We also extend our thanks to Julie Kirsch at Paradigm Publishers for her editorial assistance, and we want to thank Clara Dean, our friend and typist for many years, who prepared the manuscript for publication.

I
THE GOLDEN AGE OF PROMISCUITY

✌

Here lies the daughter, here lies the father, here lies the
sister, here lies the brother, here lies the wife and the
husband, and there are only two bodies here.
>   —Medieval tombstone epitaph[1]

INTRODUCTION

Humans have been fascinated by incest for all of recorded history
and, no doubt, long before ideas could be written down. When
acts are taboo, they are mysterious, frightening, and yet captivating. This combination of responses makes them topics for not just
quiet and private talk, but also for folk tales, drama, myths, and
literary works. Such has certainly been the case for the incest
taboo—the most bewitching taboo of all. Part of this attraction
stems from being forbidden, but avoiding incest reaches deep into
our humanity. Breaking the incest ban strikes at the core of the
family and society, if not the viability of the species, and people's
implicit sense of what is at stake makes this taboo especially formidable.

The word "incest" is derived from the Latin *incestum* and refers
to sexual union with a near relative. The word "taboo" comes
from Tonga via Captain James Cook's famous voyage to Polyne-
sia, where Cook observed that the Tongans employ the word

---

1. Quoted in Archibald 2001, 123. Similar double incest inscriptions are
found in many places. For detailed discussions, see Rank [1912] 1992, 296.

tabu, a variant of the more widespread Polynesian word, *tapu.* Writing in his journal in 1777, Cook noted that *taboo* has an "extensive signification" but in general denotes something that is "forbidden" (Cook [1777] 1967). The marriage of these two terms—*incest* and *taboo*—provided a label for a social interdiction that has preoccupied humans for millennia. Why should this be so? Émile Durkheim ([1897] 1963, 27) gave expression to part of the answer when he emphasized that "all repression of incest presupposes familial relations recognized and organized by society."

For contemporary Westerners, the family is typically a mother, father, and children. Yet, since a female can raise her offspring alone, it is equally plausible that the elementary family can be composed of a mother (impregnated by a visiting "father") and her offspring; and then, as Robin Fox (1967, 54) theoretically put it, "our mother-children group could settle down to a cosy little inbreeding arrangement and be totally self-sufficient for purposes of reproduction." But nobody is supposed to mate in this bundle of relationships. And among all populations, there are often explicit but always implicit understandings that the mother–son, father–daughter, and brother–sister dyads of the nuclear family are not to mate. Sometimes this understanding is expressed as an explicit ban or taboo; at other times it is simply considered so unthinkable for close relatives to mate that a rule is unnecessary (Murdock 1949). Still, as we will see, there is something worrisome about the nuclear family and we should ask, Why are people in some societies so worried about sexual relations between mothers and sons, fathers and daughters, and brothers with sisters? Is there something about the nuclear family that makes sexual intercourse more likely, and if so, to what effect?

While the incest taboo applies worldwide to the nuclear family, customs and laws often extend the prohibition to other relationships, well beyond the nuclear unit. But again we can ask, Why would this be so? Why would people make other, often remote, relatives taboo? It is not just contemporary scholars and scientists who have asked these kinds of questions; they are only following on the heels of a long Western tradition, emerging with the Greeks and Romans and running through the Middle Ages, the early modern age, and the growth of the natural and social sciences. In fact, a wide swath of individuals—from early philosophers through the papacy and literary figures to early and late scientists—have all focused on the problem of incest and the taboo. It is useful, then,

to begin our inquiry into the origins of the incest taboo by reviewing, in very broad strokes, the Western tradition of attitudes
about incest. For incest is clearly something that humans have
talked and thought about for a long time, certainly long before
literacy. But with literacy and a written record, we can now see the
varied forms such attention takes, whether these interests are recorded in the myths, legends, or narratives of the classical period
in Western history, the laws of the Christian church, or the early
speculations by the first generation of social scientists on the origins of the family and society.

THE FAMILY AND THE INCEST TABOO IN CLASSICAL TIMES (800 B.C.E.–350 C.E.)[2]

A family for Greeks *(oikos)* and Romans *(familia)* originally meant
a household, or a private domestic group composed of parents
and children, grandparents, other relatives, and even servants and
slaves. While the Greeks banned sexual intimacy between parents
and their offspring as well as lineal relatives, enforcement of this
prohibition was by public opinion alone because Greek legal codes
lacked a punishment or even a formal term for incest. Yet in Greek
society, dreams about incest were seemingly a popular pastime and
often discussed (Archibald 2001, 17), as is evident in Plato's *Republic,* when Socrates is said to have observed of some men that
"in sleep when . . . all that belongs to the calculating, tame, and
ruling part . . . slumbers . . . the beastly and wild part, gorged
with food or drink . . . seeks to go and satisfy its dispositions. . . .
And it doesn't shrink from attempting intercourse, as it supposes,
with a mother or with anyone else at all." (9.571). Yet in *The Laws
of Plato* (7.838b), the Athenian attests to the unwritten law (concerning siblings or parents and child) that "guards in a very effective way . . . against touching . . . by open or secret sleeping
together, or by any other sort of embracing. In fact, among the
many there isn't the slightest desire for this sort of intercourse"
(7.838b).

It was left to the Romans to coin the word *incestrum,* a concept
that included a variety of offenses from prohibiting incest in the
nuclear family through the lineal line of kin and even some collateral

---

2. This section leans heavily on Elizabeth Archibald's excellent study, *Incest
and the Medieval Imagination* (2001).

relations to banning sexual intercourse with a vestal virgin. However, as with the Greeks, Roman marriages (while subject to Roman law) were largely family matters, without religious or government intrusions (Archibald 2001, 12ff.; Beard 1980; Meyrick [1880] 1968, 1725–30).

The incest motif also found popular expression in ancient Greek and Roman myths, legends, narratives, and other literary works. In Hesiod's *Theogony*, the coupling of divine siblings gave life to the Olympian gods after "Kronos forced himself upon Rheia, and she gave birth to a splendid brood" (quoted in Johnson and Price-Williams 1996, 110). Yet a sharp contrast was made between gods and humans, for whom even unwitting incest invited disastrous consequences. The infamous Oedipal tale, which is usually portrayed as a Greek tragedy, is the best-known story of the consequences of even inadvertent incest on human social relations. King Laius and Queen Jocasta abandon their newborn son (after mutilating his feet) on learning that he would someday slay his father and marry his mother. He survives and is adopted by the king of Corinth, who names him Oedipus ("swollen foot"). When told of the curse, Prince Oedipus flees Corinth to avoid his destiny (because he thinks that the king of Corinth is his biological father), but when on the road, he has an altercation with and murders King Laius, thereby committing patricide. Traveling to his native city, Oedipus successfully outwits the terrifying Sphinx (a hybrid monster), winning the hand of Queen Jocasta and fathering four children. When fate intervenes to expose their incestuous marriage, Queen Jocasta kills herself and King Oedipus blinds himself and prays for death.[3] What is it that makes this tale so captivating? Is it the inevitability of fate, the parricide, or the incestuous union of mother and son? Whatever the answer, this story and a host of Oedipal-like tales are found in "family-complex folktales" that circle the globe in both literate and preliterate societies. Allen W. Johnson and Douglass Richard Price-Williams titled their fascinating book *Oedipus Ubiquitous* (1996) because the basic elements of the Oedipus narrative are familiar themes in diverse parts of the

---

3. There are several versions of this story in antiquity, although all carry the theme of patricide and the marriage of mother and son. This sketch follows Sophocles' *Oedipus Rex* (King Oedipus), first performed in Athens around 425 B.C.E. Sophocles' tragedy is the one Freud used as the focal point for his provocative Oedipus complex theory to be discussed later in this chapter.

world. And, of course, the shock of Sigmund Freud's speculation on the Oedipal triangle in the Victorian family is only an extended Western manifestation of this widespread incest tale.

Given the general attitude in classical times that incest among humans is immoral and vile (Archibald 2001, 17), it is easy to appreciate why both the Greeks and Romans enjoyed disparaging barbarians for their incestuous behaviors, with Strabo in his historical *Geography* reporting that the Persian magi "consort even with their mothers" while the "inhabitants of Ierne (Ireland) count it an honorable thing, when their fathers die, to devour them, and openly to have intercourse . . . with their mothers and sisters" ([circa 7 B.C.E.] 1930, 2:259, 7:185). Thus in the ancient world charges of incest became a convenient way to debase outsiders and enemies. Rumors connecting individuals or groups to incest also served as a common Roman device for vilifying powerful politicians, minorities, and unpopular religious groups within society. Favorite targets were early Christians, who were charged with group marriage, sibling incest, and "a promiscuous 'brotherhood' and 'sisterhood' by which ordinary fornication, under cover of a hallowed name, is converted to incest" (Apologeticus, quoted in Archibald 2001, 20, and see *The Ante-Nicene Fathers* 1908, 2:112; de Ste. Croix 1963). In turn, early Christian apologists defended Christianity and accused their accusers of scattering their "lusts promiscuously." For example, Minucius Felix writes that the "plotting of demons has falsely devised an enormous fable against us . . . (when in reality) . . . you worship incestuous gods, who have intercourse with mothers, with daughters, with sisters. . . . With reason . . . is incest frequently detected among you, and is continually permitted" (*Ante-Nicene Fathers* 1908, 4:192).

Despite the seductive entertainment in telling tales of incest, debauching enemies, and bashing outsiders with charges of incestuous acts, few Greeks and Romans ever questioned why incest rules existed or why incest was such a "wicked" thing. But there were exceptions. Well before modern times the Greek writer Plutarch (Honigmann 1976:26ff.) saw the incest taboo as a preventive measure for avoiding potential role conflict within the family (thus anticipating most sociological arguments on the origins of the incest taboo); and Plutarch along with the Roman historian Tacitus saw that the taboo created conflict-reducing alliances by forcing individuals to marry out into other kin groups and communities (thus anticipating many anthropological arguments).

THE FAMILY AND THE INCEST TABOO IN THE MIDDLE AGES (500–1500 c.e.)

When the Roman Empire splintered apart, as Germanic newcomers invaded the classical world, secular authority began to be slowly replaced by the ecclesiastical authority of the Christian church-state. And in post-Roman society, ever more aspects of sovereign family life gradually became dictated by canon law. Over time, when marriage became ordained a sacrament, and indeed as a "remedy for fornication," the early Christian fathers imposed an increasingly righteous Christian morality on husband and wife that included strict monogamy and conjugal fidelity with few grounds for divorce (or even separation), prohibitions against both polygyny and concubinage, virginity before marriage for *both* sexes, sexual abstinence during Lent and all religious holidays, and a postpartum sexual taboo between husband and wife until a baby was weaned (Gies and Gies 1987, 45ff.; Goody 1983, 37ff.; Rouche 1987).

In this new land of medieval Christendom, incest laws also operated as a tool for the Church to gain control over the family.[4] By reworking the old Roman codes of prohibited degrees of sexual relationships, the Church Fathers kept expanding the circle of forbidden marital connections, until by the twelfth century it included within Christendom all lineal and collateral relatives to the seventh degree or to a person's sixth cousin. Most in-laws were also disallowed; a man was forbidden to marry his dead brother's widow, his uncle's widow, his wife's sister, or anyone joined by a spiritual affinity to the fourth degree such as a godchild and godparent (Meyrick 1968, 1725–30; Goody 1983; Howard 1904, 287ff.). When taken to the extreme degrees, "near of kin" included all descendants of one's great-great-great-great-great grandfather, thus making it nearly impossible for anyone in small communities to find eligible marriage partners (Gies and Gies 1987). These restrictive laws naturally ensured rampant violations of such an inclusive incest taboo, resulting in clandestine unions and reported offenses that today would never be considered inces-

---

4. According to Meyrick, in *A Dictionary of Christian Antiquities* ([1880] 1968, 1092), which covers the first eight centuries of Christianity, marriage between a man and woman is "limited by a crowd of prohibitive regulations . . . having as their general object 1, the prevention of incest; 2, the prevention of evils which might accrue (a) to the state, (b) to religion, (c) to the individuals concerned."

tuous. This being so, and with a powerful papacy fixated on lust, celibacy, and stamping out "incestuous" marriages, it is not surprising that the incest motif would become a prominent theme not just in medieval religious texts and canon law but also in vernacular folklore, myths, narratives, and legends.

During much of the Middle Ages, discourse on incest was used by clerical writers to warn of the "sins of the flesh" and to bolster canon codes on conjugal duties and on proper family relationships. By using such terms as "fornication," "lechery," "sexual sin," and "unnatural act" to get their message across, the Church dramatized the "evils" of incest, a message that can still be heard today in some Christian churches. Yet, the Church's energy was directed more toward "saving souls" by doing penance rather than enforcing laws or protecting young incest victims (Archibald 2001, 5, 27); consequently, allegations of incestuous behavior could be used as a wedge to rout out sinners committing "heinous acts" and to impart to them the "gift of grace" once they confessed and did penance for their sins (and thereby accepted the guidance of the Church over their lives). Church writers were also kept busy inventing incest narratives as a means to send explicit messages to the laity. Women were often depicted as weak and as consumed by insatiable desires for sex, much like Eve who committed the first act of incest by eating the forbidden fruit that symbolized her sexual desires. By equating incestuous acts with the doctrine of original sin, the Church reinforced the belief that all humans are sinners (or at least predisposed to be) and need spiritual redemption through ecclesiastical discipline. After the sixth century, the clerics relied on Penitentials (or guidelines for various sins) to police all sexuality, even sexual intercourse between husband and wife, by prescribing light penance for deviations from Church-prescribed sexual positions to heavy penance for oral sex and masturbation. Nuclear family incest was especially horrifying to the Church. But in the Anglo-Saxon Penitential of Theodore, only penalties for mother–son and brother–sister incest were covered. Father–daughter incest is not even mentioned (see Gies and Gies 1987, 62ff.)—a rather surprising omission perhaps reflecting the patriarchy of the church (see Mead [1880] 1968, 1586–1608 for an extended discussion).

Among the laity, fictional stories of incest were extremely popular for their ability to shock audiences, impart moral lessons, and provide a ready source of entertainment. Oedipal-like tales were particularly favored. Although subjects and stories were set in a religious context, the thrust of each tale was the same, with some close cognates to the original Greek classic. *The Mediaeval Legend of Judas Iscariot,* for example, tells of a rich father who, after learning that his newborn son will someday kill him, mutilates his son's feet and pushes him from the household. But Judas is rescued, grows up, and unknowingly enters his real father's orchard in search of fruit and inadvertently commits patricide. Later when given his mother's hand, the incestuous marriage is consummated followed by the usual tragic ending (see Edmunds 1985 for a detailed discussion). Although Judas of the Bible met an ugly fate (for this villain also betrayed Christ), many mother–son incest tales had happier spiritual endings, once the sinners confessed and asked for divine forgiveness. In fact, according to Archibald (2001, 106), the Church was pleased to have Oedipus tales told in a Christian context to show how humans were mired in sin and, not coincidentally, how the Christian Fathers were there to confer the gift of grace. Other popular mother–son incest tales report on "near misses," where identities are discovered in the nick of time. However, outside of Oedipal-like tales, consummated mother–son stories are rare, except in short *exempla* when used by the clergy to buttress a moral point (Archibald 2001, 106ff.).

Incest stories during the Middle Ages were also spun around medieval kings, queens, knights, saints, and even members of the papacy. One saucy and very popular Oedipus-type story is the legend of Pope Gregory. In this tale, incest is doubled as the story begins with an incestuous relationship between two royal siblings and the birth of their baby boy. The child is put in a small boat and sent out to sea; he is rescued and later returns to the land of his birth, where he unknowingly marries his queen mother and thereby becomes a king. But unlike the Greek tragedy, a shift occurs from secular to religious values: Upon the discovery of double incest, there is remorse and confession by mother and son (husband and wife), with the devil being blamed and, amazingly, the gift of divine grace (after a seventeen-year penancy in isolation) allows Gregory to become pope. (See Edmunds 1985; Archibald 2001; and McCabe 1993 for discussions.) Why the double incest in this apocryphal myth? According to the historian Otto Rank ([1912] 1992, 271), such novelty in the medieval imagination, which approached "the limits of the humanly conceivable," simply reflects the fact that "the great repression of drives expressed in Christianity could be maintained only at the cost of a fantasy life pouring forth to the most voluptuous degree."

Father–daughter incest tales commanded the widest attention, especially in the later Middle Ages. One tenth-century poem in the *Exeter Book* (based on Genesis 19:30–38) is a riddle of jumbled family relationships:

A man sat down to feast with two wives,
Drank wine with two daughters, supped with two sons.
The daughters were sisters with their own two sons,
Each son a favored, first-born prince.
The father of each prince sat with his son,
Also the uncle and nephew of each.
In the room's reach was a family of five. (quoted in Gies and Gies 1987, 104)

Riddles spun around all types of family relationships were popular during the Middle Ages, in part because the complicated and perplexing degrees of sexual avoidance advocated by canon law fostered the invention of a more simplified forum (Taylor 1938).

For the most part, medieval tales of father–daughter incest differ dramatically from those about mother–son incest. In the latter, both individuals are nearly always unaware of their true relationship, and thus the incest is unwitting. In contrast, in tales of father–daughter incest, the father typically tries to seduce his known daughter, who is portrayed as a victim. Yet these tales often become adventure stories, as incest is averted just in time, as would be the case when the daughter runs away from her father (see Archibald 2001, 149). Unlike mother–son and father–daughter incest tales, brother–sister stories were relatively uncommon in medieval literature (although they proliferated during the early modern period). Some popular ones involve major legendary heroes, such as Charlemagne, who sleeps with his sister and thereby begets a son, Roland, who is both son and nephew to Charlemagne who, reciprocally, is both father and uncle to Roland. However, in most medieval narratives, brother–sister incest is usually portrayed as a tantalizing romance story where long separated siblings fall in love, unaware of their family ties. Oddly enough, the active medieval imagination even created an incest riddle for the birth of Christ. The Virgin Mary is the ultimate "Mother of Grace," but she is also associated with "holy incest" because she is the "mother of her own Creator, and the bride and daughter of her own Son" (Archibald 2001, 230).

In the main, few questioned the biological or sociological reasons behind the incest taboo in the Middle Ages, with notable exceptions. In the sixth century, Pope Gregory the Great (540–604) emphasized that marriage between near relatives led to fertility problems (Muller 1913, 295); in the thirteenth century, Thomas Aquinas (1225–1274) suggested that the incest taboo promoted alliances between groups by building bridges between families whose sons and daughters marry, while at the same time, the taboo worked to reduce potential conflict within the nuclear family. Thomas Aquinas also stressed that the purpose of the incest taboo was to ensure healthy children, with a deformed child being God's punishment for an incestuous act (Honigmann 1976, 46–48). And in the sixteenth century, as Robert Burton wrote, "the church and common-wealth, humane and divine lawes, have conspired to avoid hereditary diseases, forbidding such marriages as are any whit allied" (quoted from Archibald 2001, 50). Despite explicit documentation, Archibald (2001) suspects that the medieval world had a "widespread awareness" of the link between close inbreeding and deformed children. And, as we will see in this and the next chapter, virtually all of the principal scientific explanations for the origins of the incest taboo were evident, at least in incipient form, during the classical period and Middle Ages.

Thus incest tales told during the Middle Ages make an across-the-board distinction between the nuclear family and more remote relatives. Incest stories outside the nuclear family are rare, despite the Church's wide stretch of the incest rules to include many remote relatives (Archibald 2001, 221). This literary apathy is telling because it goes against the best efforts of the Church to broaden the definition of incest to a protracted array of kin; and indeed, sexual relations among any known relative was often highlighted by the clergy as a grave act of sin. Oddly enough, despite the Church's worrisome efforts to condemn incestuous acts, court records of nuclear family incest were rare. After the twelfth century, prohibited degrees of propinquity were gradually relaxed, but this relative loosening of forbidden connections ironically placed greater attention on sexual relations within the nuclear family. In addition, by putting marriage on a pious foundation with strict monogamy, the Church succeeded in its efforts at viewing mother, father, and children as the centerpiece of human society. Thus the viability of society was increasingly seen to hinge on the morality of the elementary family—a shift in perspective that was unprecedented in human history and persists to the present day in the

West, where "family values" are seen as the backbone of the "good" society.

THE INCEST TABOO AND THE EARLY MODERN PERIOD (1500–1800 c.e.)

The cultural rebirth in the Renaissance, the discovery of the Americas, and the Protestant Reformation signaled the closing of a period in Western history where the known universe was classified into "the unholy world" and the "holy church" (Howard 1904, 389). In its place a deeper and broader worldview took hold, a view characterized by religious renewal, scientific discovery, new technologies, and nation-states with secular authority. Above all, the invention of the printing press led to an information revolution by encouraging a growing literate population to read not only the Bible and religious literatures but also secular texts. And, by the sixteenth and seventeenth centuries, an ethos of secularism had taken hold, breaking down the old systems of belief and opening the door to new ideas, attitudes, and optimism (for discussions, see Chartier 1989b, 111ff.; Stone 1977; and Collins 1998). Discoveries in the physical sciences, coupled with notions of progress and evolution, began to challenge the dominant views of a "static universe," and increasingly philosophers wrote of a world in continual change. With the Enlightenment, the belief in human reason and progress was established; and so it should not be surprising that conceptions of family, sexuality, and incest would also be viewed in new ways (Bock 1956; Foucault 1986; Collins 1998).

The image of the conjugal family unit carved out during the Middle Ages stood firm, primarily because the medieval Church had relegated most kith and kin to the periphery of "the family." By focusing on the evils of incest within the nuclear family, the boundary between this unit and other kindred intensified. Moreover, the structure of kinship was undergoing significant change in England toward the nuclearization, as features more typical of the modern nuclear family gradually became apparent, including stronger conjugal ties, decoupling of sexual enjoyment from guilt and sin, and greater family privacy and autonomy (Stone 1977; Chartier 1989a). In addition, once the Church forfeited its strong moral authority, attention moved away from confession and penance for incest offenders to the consequences of incest for society at large. One late fourteenth- or early fifteenth-century example of this coming trend is the *Dux Moraud* (Duke Vagabond). The play (preserved only in fragments) is a horrific tale of an incestuous father–daughter relationship; the murder of the mother by her daughter after discovering the illicit affair; the exposure of the child born of the incestuous relationship, and the death of the father by his demented daughter (see Davis 1970, 100–11). While the father confesses his incestuous abuses to a priest and is given the normative medieval penance to "save his soul," this play also buttresses the incest taboo by highlighting the inherent role conflicts and appalling dangers of such forbidden relationships for civilized society (McCabe 1993, 116–17).

During the sixteenth and seventeenth centuries, the incest motif was amazingly popular in folk tales, literature, poetry, ballads, plays, and especially English drama (Archibald 2001; Luis-Martinez 2002; Richardson 1985). While themes of an Oedipal nature were frequent, theatergoing tastes also favored brother–sister incest. In John Ford's widely acclaimed play, *'Tis Pity She's a Whore* published in 1633, the incest taboo is upheld in a very passionate love story between two siblings, Annabella and Giovanna, who recklessly flaunt society by having an incestuous affair leading to a pregnancy, which ensures a tragic ending. Father–daughter incest also captivated early modern audiences, especially conflicts arising from father–daughter suitor triangles. For example, in Shakespeare's *Pericles* (c. 1608), father–daughter incest is revealed by the victim to her suitor in a family riddle:

> I am no viper, yet I feed
> On mother's flesh which did me breed.
> I sought a husband, in which labour
> I found that kindness in a father.
> He's father, son, and husband mild;
> I, mother, wife,—and yet his child.
> How they may be, and yet in two,
> As you will live, resolve it you. (1.1.57)

How does one fold six family relationships in two persons? The answer can only be incest. And as always, the incestuous ways of the nuclear family are key, whether the tale is tragedy, romance, or comedy and whether incest is imagined, consummated, or averted. Thus, despite major alterations in the traditional order of things after the Middle Ages, the incest motif and the centrality of the nuclear family flourished during the early modern period. However, the role relationships of the conjugal family, along with the belief that the nuclear family was the original cell of society, were seriously challenged by social scientists in the nineteenth century.

THE INCEST TABOO AND THE FAMILY IN THE NINETEENTH CENTURY

In the nineteenth century, the twin doctrines of progress and evolution began to compete with traditional Christian theology. These insurgent forces reflected a growing interest in learning about other societies in an effort to understand the dynamics of social and cultural change. While the study of alien cultures dates back to Greek and Roman times, only in the nineteenth century did scholars of the Enlightenment attempt to organize ethnographic materials with an evolutionary interpretation of history. After concluding that "ruder" societies were at different developmental stages than the societies of Western Europe, social theorists devised a hierarchal scale of progress, assigning native populations to particular stages of evolution in terms of how culturally advanced they were along the road to Western civilization. Aboriginal peoples were also viewed as "living fossils" of earlier stages of societies through which modern European societies had already passed. So-called proof of this evolutionary interpretation of history was heralded by a "doctrine of survivals" postulating that odd relics found in more advanced societies were "leftovers" from prior stages of development along the road to civilization.

Above all, what fired the imagination of early theorists was speculation on the origins of marriage, family, and the incest taboo. Until researchers took to the field, it had been taken for granted that the European family plan was duplicated everywhere. But fieldworkers soon discovered that aboriginal family life differed dramatically from the Western bilateral plan. Rules of marriage, residence, and descent differed from those in the West, as did kinship terminology. Moreover, it became evident that in many preliterate societies, kinship was the structural basis of the entire society (see Trautmann 1987). To describe these kin-based societies (what today are typically termed "horticultural" and "pastoral" societies), social scientists were forced to take up new vocabularies, with the result that terms such as "lineage," "clan," "gens," "sib," "moiety," "phratry," and "tribe" became part of the European lexicon. The discovery of alternative family forms also forced the coining of such new terms as "exogamy" (marrying outside one's group) and "endogamy" (marrying inside one's group) to describe exchange relationships and marriage patterns in many preliterate societies. And once kinship became a subject for scientific investigation, the door was opened for theories on the origins of the family and the incest taboo (for historical background, see Harris 1968; Trautmann 1987; Honigmann 1976; and Stocking 1968).

THE HORDE AS A SPECULATIVE CONSTRUCT

Johann Jakob Bachofen (1815–1887)

J. J. Bachofen, a Swiss-German professor of Roman law at Basel University, was one of the first theorists to become fascinated with the origins of the family. In 1861, after studying classic myths, symbols, and literary works, he published *Das Mutterrecht* (or mother right), a semiscientific work proposing the extraordinary hypothesis that the first human families were organized around females. For Bachofen, the matrifocal family came first and only later did a patrifocal kin structure emerge. For Bachofen (1931, 157), the study of the classics can "lead us from the known ages of antiquity into earlier periods and from the world of ideas that has been so familiar to us . . . into an older milieu, wholly unknown."

In Bachofen's evolutionary scheme, human society began with a loosely knit "horde" of unrestricted promiscuity, followed by a "gynaecocratic epoch" where females in a religious zeal created marriage and matrilineal kinship revolving around female dominance. Later, males asserted themselves and, over time, transformed kinship to a pattern of patrilineal descent. Bachofen suggested that descent through females was an "entire cultural stage" universal to all humankind and that during this stage the "maternal element" permeated every facet of life from an overriding emphasis on communal values to binary contrasts revolving around a preference for the left hand over the right, the night over the day, the moon over the sun, the earth over the ocean, the dead over the living, and the experience of sorrow over joy (Bachofen 1931, 160–61). Bachofen's stage model is more mysticism than science, but his efforts to describe the systematic development of the family as a distinct institution were insightful for their time. He was also the first theorist to explore the idea of a matrifocal and matrilineal stage of evolution in human societies.

Lewis Henry Morgan (1818–1881)

Lewis Henry Morgan a lawyer, businessman, and politician who took an interest in American Indian tribes also sought to uncover the origins of the family. Until Morgan entered the field, very little was known about the nomenclature (terms of address) that aboriginal societies used to designate relatives. Except for Western kinship terminology such as mother, father, grandfather, aunt, and cousin, Europeans did not have a vocabulary for expressing extended family ties, and indeed the Western kinship system (with its emphasis on the small domestic unit) is very limited when denoting consanguinity outside the nuclear core, especially for remote connections.[5] What surprised Morgan was that the nuclear family terms of mother, father, sister, and brother were applied by Native Americans to a much larger circle of relatives (see Tooker 1997). After sending a questionnaire around the globe asking government agents, missionaries, military personnel, and other interested parties to provide what information they could on the kinship systems of native communities, Morgan discovered that most aboriginal societies shared fundamental kinship features, suggesting a common origin. When completed, the Tables (as they came to be called) were composed of a sample of 139 kinship systems from Europe, Asia, Africa, Australia, and the Americas. These tables garnered wide attention and composed two hundred pages of Morgan's voluminous six-hundred-page text, *Systems of Consanguinity and Affinity of the Human Family* (1871). In seeking to explain why so many differences existed among societies in their naming and classification of relatives, Morgan isolated what he thought were two basic types of kinship systems—the descriptive and the classificatory. In Western societies, the kinship system is descriptive, he said, because the terms that denote husband, wife, mother, father, brother, sister, son, and daughter are discrete and distinguish the designee from all other relatives. In contrast, among American Indians and most aboriginal peoples around the world, the kinship system is classificatory because the primary kinship terms—mother, father, sister, and brother—are applied in a variety

---

5. Western kinship is a bilateral or cognatic system, a subtype of Eskimo. Common features associated with this system are a small domestic group, a kindred rather than a single-sided lineage, and an "Ego" who is equally related to particular persons on *both* sides of the family.

of ways to broader classes of relatives (i.e., both lineal and collateral relatives), with all members of a class called by the same term.[6] Morgan then used his study of kinship relationships to develop an evolutionary model of how the family originated and progressed to the modern contemporary form exhibited in Western Europe. Of special significance is Morgan's dismissal of the family as a natural social unit that had always existed. Instead, he proposed that the human family was purely invented and that even the "idea" of family is the end result of previous stages of evolutionary development, with the Western nuclear family the most recent stage.

In 1877, Morgan published *Ancient Society,* his most influential work, where he argued that the ancient family had passed through five sequential forms, with distinct marriage rules peculiar to each form. Essentially Morgan asked, How did the *idea* of the family originate and progress to the modern form? To answer this question, Morgan used the Tables as relational blueprints to reconstruct the stages of the family. During the first stage, humans lived in a disorganized horde where sexual relations were dominated by promiscuity (Morgan [1877] 1985, 500). Although neither Morgan nor anyone else had ever observed such a horde, it was the only way to conceptualize life before the family. In the second stage of development, the family took its institutional roots with marriage among groupings of brothers and sisters (who were not always blood siblings but collateral kin designated by the terms "brother" and "sister"), followed in the third stage by conjugal pairings that lasted only as long as they were pleasurable to the parties involved. In the fourth stage, polygyny (one male and several females) under patriarchal authority emerged, and in the final stage of development, the Western plan of stable, conjugal pairs arose. Thus the evolution of the family was viewed as moving from the promiscuous horde to increasing "civilization," culminating in the Western nuclear family.

---

6. Strictly speaking, Morgan's pioneering effort has a logical problem because all kinship systems merge some relatives under a single term. Western nomenclature singles out the nuclear family with such individual terms as mother, father, etc. but it lumps together other relations such as grandfather, aunt, and the catchall term, cousin. But what caught Morgan's attention was the extension of *nuclear* terms to a wider circle of kinfolk (e.g., the term "father" gets extended to all males on the father's side). Of course, this extended usage does not correspond to the European term (e.g., male parent), but nineteenth-century kinship theorists inferred the equivalent meaning.

Morgan also agreed with Bachofen that humans were first organized around matrifocal ties until paternity could be known, but
once it was established, kinship became patrifocal. Morgan's arguments are far more sophisticated than this brief summary suggests;
most importantly, his groundbreaking research laid the foundation
for the scientific study of kinship. Indeed, all scholars in the late
nineteenth century were influenced by Morgan's arguments. But
Morgan was misled because he was unaware that "classificatory"
kinship terms of address that lump together lineal and collateral
relatives (e.g., mother and mother's sisters) have a different significance than their European counterparts, nor are aboriginal people
unaware of who is related to whom by marriage and blood ties.[7]
In addition, Morgan's persuasive argument that the family was *not*
the bedrock of organized society but an invented creation brought
him such wide acclaim that he influenced an entire generation of
social scientists, including Émile Durkheim and Karl Marx.

John Ferguson McLennan (1827–1881)

John McLennan was born in the Scottish highlands, educated at
Aberdeen and Cambridge Universities, and later became a barris-
ter. When asked to write a law article for the eighth edition of the
Encyclopaedia Britannica (1857), McLennan turned to the scientific study of early law, especially ancient marriage customs and
rules. In particular, McLennan became fascinated with understanding the origin of "marriage by capture," a ritual found all over the
world in which a designated bridegroom or his friends act out a
mock kidnapping of the bride-elect by carrying her off by "force"
before the marriage ceremony. McLennan's efforts to uncover the
origins of bride capture took him on a far-reaching evolutionary
journey into the origin of the family, society, and the incest taboo.
  In 1865, McLennan published *Primitive Marriage: An Inquiry
into the Origin of the Form of Capture in Marriage Ceremonies.*

---

7. Morgan knew that sibling group marriage did not exist among any known
aboriginal populations but assumed that some aboriginal kinship terminologies
still in existence were survivals or leftovers from an earlier period. For example,
the Hawaiian terminology system, which is found worldwide but is concentrated
in areas where the Malalyo-Polynesian language is spoken, has only a handful of
kinship terms because it is intended to separate a generation of parents from a
generation of children. It forces Ego to look completely outside his kin group for
a marriage partner, rather than Morgan's hypothesized brother–sister relationship (see Fox 1967, 256).

Drawing on Greek and Roman documents as well as ethnographic data on aboriginal populations from Asia, Africa, Australia, and the Americas, McLennan concluded that the ritual of bride capture must be a survival or a "symbolic form" of some "universal tendency" during an earlier phase of human society, when "it must have been *the system* . . . to capture women necessarily the women of other tribes for wives." (McLennan [1865] 1970, 20; emphasis in the original). What forces, then, caused men to steal wives from foreign tribes during earlier stages of societal evolution? This practice could not originate, he concluded, where marriage is permitted within a family or tribe; instead, it must have emerged when customs required people to marry outside their kin and tribal groups. McLennan decided that when a kinship system had a principle of what he named "exogamy,"[8] or a rule requiring males to marry outside their group, that bridal kidnapping would be a practical option. He further hypothesized that for bride kidnapping to be necessary, not only would a rule of exogamy have to be in place but hostile relations with other tribes would also have to prevail, thereby preventing bridal exchanges as an alternative to kidnapping. What survived to the present, then, were the symbolic forms of this ancient social activity, but this symbolism gave added power to marriage rites.

The details of McLennan's argument begin with the assertion that, early in their evolution, not all human groups had a kinship system or an incest taboo; rather, people were bound together by a "bond of fellowship" and strong collective sentiments symbolized by a plant or animal (McLennan [1865] 1970, 63; McLennan [1869] 1896). Kinship must have emerged later, McLennan argued, with the "new idea of blood-relationships" among individuals, leading to a conception of *stocks* that began to substitute kinship-based affiliation for group-based solidarity. As this process ensued, totems were increasingly used to distinguish among kin groups (McLennan [1865] 1970, 64). McLennan hypothesized that kinship could not emerge as a distinct institution until a population passed through earlier stages of evolution. The earliest of these stages was a state of promiscuity that, over time, led to a

---

8. McLennan coined the terms "exogamy" and "endogamy," taking the idea from the botanical sciences, where it parallels cross-pollination or self-pollination (i.e., outbreeding or inbreeding).

system for calculating descent through the mother's blood line. Tribes must also have been combative, McLennan believed, because without hostility among tribes, there would be no reason for this system to require bride capture. Absent hostility with other tribes, individuals would simply be free to choose mates or to exchange them. This hostility led, in turn, to a premium on male survival (for defense and fighting) and a resulting preference for males over females which, McLennan argued, encouraged the practice of female infanticide. Yet female infanticide would cause an imbalance in the sex ratio, thereby forcing individuals to steal women from outside groups and tribes. A shortage of females also led to a practice of polyandry (or one female attached to several males). Eventually group-based affiliation was replaced by affiliations revolving around kinship, with totems and names now directed at family units. Hence female infanticide was the cause of both bride capture and polyandry (because of an unbalanced sex ratio). And once polyandry with one female and several males took hold, the door was opened for the beginning of kinship calculated through the male line and later the development of a patriarchal system of authority.

But how does this sequence of events cause the incest taboo to emerge? For McLennan, once the custom of stealing foreign women became established, it made sexual intercourse with women of your own group "indecent"; and as a result, rules of incest emerged to ensure that a wife would be taken from outside the kin group. After writing *Primitive Marriage*, McLennan spent time expanding this thesis, although his notions of female infanticide and bride capture attracted little attention within the academic community. However, his ideas surrounding the promiscuous horde and the emergence of female descent, coupled with his assertion that the family is not a natural human grouping but something that humans had to create, resonated with the stage models of Bachofen and Morgan who had used different approaches to come to the same conclusions as McLennan on the promiscuous horde and the invented nature of the human family. Later, in some remarkable essays, McLennan further developed his ideas on totemism (emblems or crests), stressing how they served as the primal glue that held societies together during their early stages of evolution, a line of argument that later became critical in Émile Durkheim's thinking about the origins of religion and the emergence of the incest taboo.

Émile Durkheim (1858–1917)

One of the first kinship theorists to actually focus on the origin of the incest taboo per se was the sociologist Émile Durkheim.[9] In 1898, in the inaugural edition of *L'Année Sociologique,* Durkheim published an essay titled "Incest: The Nature and Origin of the Taboo." Taking his cue from Bachofen, Morgan, and McLennan, Durkheim proposed that in the beginning, humans lived in a horde pattern of social organization, where incest was not forbidden and where promiscuous sexual intercourse prevailed. The first restrictions against incest had to wait until the arrival of clans which, for Durkheim, were the first "kind of family" revolving around a collection of individuals who shared a common emblem, or totem. Thus, much like earlier theorists, Durkheim believed that the first organizational structure, the clan, was *not* rooted in the family but in a "community demarcated by a totem." Later, when kinship was invented and solidarity began to shift to a true kinship unit, clans were matrilineal with the totem representing the mother's descent line.

For Durkheim, the incest taboo arose from rules of exogamy attached to clans. Durkheim rejects any claim that near relatives have a natural inclination to avoid each other sexually; instead, the cardinal trait of a clan is the feeling among its members that they are of one "familial blood," symbolized by a totem that reinforces this sense of shared blood. In fact, Durkheim argued that the totem represents "the blood itself." He also saw the totem as an ancestor, a god, and a protector of the group; and hence, if people see God as residing in the blood, it follows that blood is a divine thing. And if blood is divine, it must also be taboo. Anyone connected to the blood by the same totem automatically becomes sexually taboo. All clans were initially organized around matrilineal descent; hence their blood is directly connected to their totem. Women also bleed each month; therefore they should not be touched sexually by their own clan members, and hence they must mate with members of other clans. Here is the origin of exogamy, a marriage rule that made it imperative for women to be exchanged between clans. This prohibition against sex with "familial blood" continued even after clans developed into different forms of kinship, and this rule eventually evolved into the incest taboo

---

9. Few scholars realize that Durkheim was a recognized kinship theorist in his day. For a discussion, see David Maybury-Lewis 1965.

among close family members. Thus, for Durkheim, the rule of exogamy is a specific case of a more general religious emotion revolving around a taboo against sexual relations with members of a clan symbolized by a totem. The incest taboo then is nothing more than a remnant of the rule of exogamy as it first evolved in the clans of preliterate peoples.

Sigmund Freud (1856–1939)

In *Totem and Taboo* ([1913] 1950), Sigmund Freud presented a vision of the first human "horde" as patriarchal, dominated by a father who sought to keep all females for himself by driving away his sons who might seek sexual relations with his females.[10] Freud was perhaps overly influenced by Baldwin Spencer's and Francis Gillen's ([1899] 1938) summary of practices among Australian aboriginals, who at the time were considered the simplest known society (when in fact we suggest that they were former horticulturalists who had reverted to hunting and gathering after their migration to Australia and yet sustained some of the norms of the older kinship system from their horticultural ancestors). The "authoritarian father" in Freud's explanation was eventually "overthrown" by his collectively organized sons. But after an initial period of celebration, these sons were overwhelmed by remorse (just as in Oedipus the Greek tragedy), especially when they came to realize that their access to females would now be ruled by intense competition against each other. Fearful that their new-found power would be subverted by competition with one another, the sons created a compact in which they renounced claims on local women by creating the incest taboo and rules of exogamy.

Freud also argued that totems are unconscious symbols of the father, who is both feared and loved; more generally Freud felt that religion and other moral codes are ultimately fueled by the repressed sexual desires of children for their opposite-sex parent. Moreover, Freud asserted that children, especially boys, go through what had historically transpired in early "hordes" of humans be-

---

10. One of the great debates among nineteenth-century evolutionists was whether the first societies were matriarchal or patriarchal. Freud was in the patriarchal camp along with many other prominent theorists, including Fustel De Coulanges, who wrote *The Ancient City, A Study on the Religion, Laws, and Institutions of Greece and Rome* (1864), and Henry Maine, who wrote *Ancient Law: Its Connection with the Early History of Society and Its Relation to Modern Ideas* (1861).

fore they became better organized. As children are attracted sexually to their parents, the incest taboo—a kind of normative totem—forces them to repress their desires and the guilt associated with these desires. These repressed desires are carried into adulthood, where they become the unconscious motivations for supporting the incest taboo, rules of exogamy, and other moral symbols. Thus, just as guilt led to the evolution of the incest taboo and rules of exogamy in the primal "horde," so the prohibited sexual wish of each child provides a lifetime of repressed emotional energy for support of the incest taboo and other moral codes. For, when wishes and desires are repressed, they become emotional energy that supports the very taboos that prohibit what is unconsciously desired. This ambivalent emotional energy revolving around desiring what is feared and feeling guilt for these desires was also the emotional force behind the creation of totems that symbolized the group in which rules of incest and exogamy guide the actions of individuals. The totems were often animals toward whom the members of the group felt the same emotional ambivalence of fear and love as they did for their opposite-sex parent, with the result that this emotional energy directed at the totem promoted, at one and the same time, the collective solidarity of the group, the repression of sexual drives in accordance with the incest taboo, and the maintenance of exogamous patterns of mate selection.

Thus, for Freud, the incest taboo and rules of exogamy began to transform the "primitive horde" into a more organized society that could use emotionally charged cultural rules to regulate the incestuous desires of sons for their mothers. Freud later retracted some of his explanation because it offended the Victorian sensibilities of his time and even the sensibilities of his fellow therapists (especially his early belief that there had been actual sexual intercourse in the Victorian family). He added footnotes to earlier statements that qualified his argument, but the most important insight is that the nurturing relationship between parents and offspring, particularly between a mother and her son, represents a potential threat to the stability of the nuclear family and hence to society in general. As a result, it becomes necessary to develop powerful norms prohibiting sexual relations between parents and their offspring.

For Freud, there is no natural tendency for sexual avoidance between parents and children because, if there were, the incest taboo would not be necessary. To limit this sexual potential in the bonds of love and dependence between a mother and her son, powerful taboos had been created to establish sexual distance between sons and the object of their desires. In drawing this conclusion, Freud moves toward a more sociological explanation that emphasizes the disruptive effects of sexual competition within the nuclear family.

EDWARD WESTERMARCK'S (1862–1939) CRITIQUE OF SPECULATIONS ABOUT HORDES

Edward Westermarck, a professor of sociology at the University of London, also tried his hand at solving the riddle of the incest taboo. While a proponent of evolutionary theory, Westermarck in his prodigious *The History of Human Marriage* ([1891] 1922) and various shorter editions (1926) strongly criticized the notion, espoused by so many theorists of his time, that humans once lived in a state of raw promiscuity. Instead, Westermarck argued that even among the earliest humans, a pair-bond of some sort was favored over unrestricted promiscuity. Westermarck built his case on his study of the breeding habits of birds and mammals, where many species form unions "of a more durable character" and, in particular, the gorillas who live in small bands composed of one or two males and several females and their young. (We should note that Freud also used the early data on gorillas to draw the opposite conclusion that the dominant male's control of females led other males to experience hostile emotions toward the lead silverback male.) Humans and gorillas are big mammals, Westermarck argued, and cannot afford to live in large groups, making them less gregarious than the smaller, highly social monkeys. In gorillas, natural selection favored a more stable breeding pattern, and this trait evolved in humans as well ([1891] 1922, vol. 1, 34ff.; 1926, 2ff.). Thus in Westermarck's opinion the hypothesis that humans once lived in a general state of promiscuity is "one of the most unscientific ever set forth within the whole domain of sociological speculation" ([1891] 1922, vol. 1, 336).

However, it was Westermarck's take on exogamy and the incest taboo that represented a more penetrating attack on speculations about primal human hordes. Most theories of exogamy and the incest taboo assume that custom, law, or education alone prevent incest within a household, he said, although the "sexual instinct" does not easily bend to social mores. Yet, "in normal cases there is no desire for the acts which they forbid." As Westermarck ([1891] 1922, vol. 2, 192–93) tells us:

Generally speaking, there is a remarkable absence of erotic feelings between persons living very closely together from childhood. Nay more, in this, as in many other cases, sexual indifference is combined with the positive feeling of aversion when the act is thought of. This I take to be the fundamental cause of the exogamous prohibitions. Persons who have been living closely together from childhood are as a rule near relatives. Hence their aversion to sexual relations with one another displays itself in custom and law as a prohibition of intercourse between near kin.

In addition, Westermarck proposed that even unrelated children, when brought up together, show a "conspicuous absence of erotic feelings," and this phenomenon is universal. Turning the incest rule on its head, Westermarck suggests that its origins may lie in the intense dislike or disgust of sexual intimacy among individuals who are raised together. Such feelings by themselves can easily lead to "moral disapproval and prohibitory customs or laws" (Westermarck ([1891] 1922, vol. 2, 198). It is the same with other strict laws: do humans also have a propensity for prohibited acts such as bestiality, sodomy, or murdering of parents? Instead, Westermarck (1926, 91) asserts that "the law expresses the feelings of the community or the legislator and punishes acts that shock them; but it does not tell us whether an inclination to commit the forbidden act is felt by many or by few."

Westermarck (1926, 99) also pointed out that inbreeding is "injurious to the species"; animal breeders long ago discovered that close inbreeding leads to negative results. He suggested that in the case of humans "consanguineous marriages have a distinct tendency to lead to idiocy, deaf-mutism, and the eye-disease called *Retinitis pigmentosa* . . ." (Westermarck 1926, 104). Moreover, in the natural world, incestuous relations are naturally avoided by the dispersal of young, and in the case of social animals, by mating with strangers outside the natal grouping (Westermarck 1926, 102). Overall, he suggested that "natural selection has operated, and by eliminating destructive tendencies and preserving useful variations has moulded the sexual instinct so as to meet the requirement of the species" (Westermarck 1926, 107). In making these assertions, Westermarck anticipated the arguments of evolutionary biologists who were to argue that, as a result of inbreeding depression, natural selection has built into all species natural mechanisms for sexual avoidance among closely related kin.

CONCLUSIONS

From this abbreviated review of thinking about incest and the taboo, we can see that humans have wondered about this subject for a long time. Tales, myths, folklore, drama, poetry, and both canon and civil law can be seen as addressing the potential problems of incest throughout most of recorded history. We can assume, therefore, that humans were also thinking about problems generated by incest long before they could write these thoughts down. Indeed, it would not be an exaggeration to argue that the human species seems to be rather obsessed with the topic, although in modern times, narratives on incest and theories about the incest taboo are less common at the very time that rates of incest have probably increased over what they were in the distant past. But, whatever the merits of this assertion, we can ask, Why are humans so concerned about incest? And why, if Westermarck is right, do they need a taboo? Can the taboo simply be an expression of natural disinclinations for sexual contact among closely related kin? If so, Freud might ask, Why do acts of incest arouse such intense emotions and mysterious feelings that need to be expressed by a powerful taboo?

As we will come to see, the answers to these questions have been anticipated by not just early social scientists but also by religious and secular scholars from the Middle Ages to the present. We will add to their accounts more facts and knowledge about early human populations and patterns of sexual avoidance among humans' closest relatives, the primates. What we hope to substantiate is that some of the early speculations on the "horde" or life before organized society may not be as far off base as a first reading might suggest. Moreover, the contention that the nuclear family or even the human polygamous family composed of two or more nuclear families is not a natural unit among humans may not be as outrageous as it might seem at first glance. Indeed, the nuclear family, which is the foundation block for building most human kinship networks, as most historical figures seem to have recognized, forced humans to create an incest taboo. Other points made by early thinkers also contain merit. The preferred state for humans, as evolved apes, may indeed be restricted promiscuity or a loose and shifting polygyny. The evolution of the stable conjugal pair that sits at the heart of the family of mother, father, and children is not natural to those Great Apes closest to humans, and so, it probably was not a natural social formation for those early hominids who eventually evolved into humans.

It is therefore not surprising that incest and its prohibition have preoccupied humans because, without the taboo, the family as we know it contains a potential for conflict and tension associated with incestuous drives, to say nothing of the harmful effects from inbreeding depression. We believe, as Edward Westermarck emphasized, that there are natural avoidance propensities built into the human genome, but these alone are clearly insufficient to prevent all incestuous acts. The taboo surely emerged because it was needed, not because it simply expressed family members' natural propensities and preferences for sexual avoidance. While the nuclear family may not be a natural unit for an evolved great ape, it *is* a critical structure for a human hominoid that depends on collective solidarity in groups for its survival. Totems and taboos have been critical to enhancing social solidarity, as so many early social scientists recognized; and therefore it should not be seen as unusual that incest and its prohibition are so much a part of both written history and early speculations by the first generations of social scientists. For these scholars understood a simple fact: to understand the origins of the first human societies, it is necessary to explore the origins of the family and the incest taboo.

Our goal in this book is to better understand why the incest taboo exists in human societies. We believe that virtually every explanation that has been offered for its origins contains an element of the answer as to why it emerged, but we wish to do more than explain its origins. We also want to cast some light on several related questions that will help clarify and integrate contending theories. To explain why the incest taboo exists, we need to answer (1) why the taboo appears to be more prohibitive of incest in some dyads of the nuclear family than others, (2) why rates of incest vary among dyads, and (3) why incest appears to harm some victims of incest more than others. In tackling these three related questions, we can gain greater purchase on why the taboo emerged in human societies. Our answer is coevolutionary in the sense that there are both biological and sociocultural forces behind the emergence of the incest taboo and that these two sets of forces interact with each other (see Machalek and Martin, 2004, for a review of how sociologists can use evolutionary theory). But we are getting ahead of our inquiry. Before offering our explanation, we need to review in the next chapter the theoretical traditions over the past sixty years that have sought to explain the taboo. As will become evident, our explanation does not supplant but rather complements and indeed integrates existing theories.

2
AVOIDING INCEST
MORE RECENT EXPLANATIONS FOR THE
ORIGINS OF THE INCEST TABOO

↤

> The subject is incest and the fascination of incest. Why the
> fascination? Because it is forbidden? But why is it forbid-
> den—or is it always forbidden? The quick answer is—not
> always. But at the very least, the idea of it seems to make
> us easily uneasy, and at worst, downright hysterical.
> —Robin Fox (1980)

At some point in our evolution, humans and probably their hominid (or hominin) ancestors began to rely on a cultural taboo to
regulate sexual relations among family members. Before language
and culture evolved, however, humans' distant hominin[1] ancestors

---

1. The word "hominid" (a shortened form of "Hominidae") has been traditionally used to refer to the family of bipedal primates that include both humans'
direct and near ancestors (e.g., australopithecines). And strictly speaking it includes modern humans. However, this usage is currently in flux and is slowly
being replaced with a new classification system that would extend the term
hominid to not just humans (and their ancestors) but also to chimpanzees, gorillas, and orangutans. Under this new nomenclature, the term "hominins" would
then refer exclusively to humans (and their ancestors). While the new taxonomy
better captures the real evolutionary relationships between humans and great
apes, we felt it best for now to keep the word "hominid" and use it in the
traditional way of referring only to the human lineage (and near bipedal ancestors) because it is currently being used both ways in the literature. This present
double meaning might be confusing to readers not well acquainted with the
paleoanthropological literature. However, since the new term "hominins" is very
clear-cut, we decided to adopt it and apply it to anything characteristic or resem-
bling humans, using "hominid" and "hominin" as equivalent terms.

depended on other methods to prevent inbreeding between close-ly related kin; for it has now become clear that hominids were no different from other species of mammals relying on evolved mech-anisms for sexual avoidance among those sharing a high propor-tion of genes. The emergence of the incest taboo was thus a culturally constructed codification of existing tendencies for sexual avoidance, as Edward Westermarck argued, but the intriguing question remains: Why was a taboo necessary if human ancestors already had evolved devices for sexual avoidance? The answer, as we will see, lies with the invention of the nuclear family which is, by nature, a peculiar breeding and living arrangement for an evolved great ape. We are not original in making this assertion because, as we saw in the last chapter, Bachofen, McLennan, Morgan, Freud, and Durkheim came to the same conclusion. But we have the benefit of being able to document our conclusion using recent archaeological, genetic, and fossil records as well as data on Old World primates who can be used as a "distant mirror" in which our hominid ancestors are reflected. In particular, the great apes can provide us with a picture of how ancestral hominoids avoided inbreeding before the nuclear family evolved.[2] Before pursuing our argument, however, we need to review the various explana-tions by contemporary scholars on the origins of the incest taboo so that we can appreciate their contributions and to elucidate how our argument supplements existing theories. (For other interest-ing reviews, see Sanderson 2001; Wolf and Durham 2005; W. Arens 1986; and Brown 1991.)

MECHANISMS FOR AVOIDING INBREEDING

There are basically three evolved strategies for a species to reduce inbreeding. One is to limit parental investment by producing large numbers of offspring who disperse shortly after birth. Many fish, for example, evidence this pattern of sexual avoidance, with the mother releasing so many young that parental investment is im-possible, and as the young fish disperse or die off, the likelihood of closely related individuals mating is very low.

When organisms are larger and more complex, parental invest-ment increases because of the longer time needed for maturation and often because of the necessity for parental socialization. As a

---

2. Both humans and apes are members of the superfamily Hominoidea (hom-inoids).

result, parent(s) and offspring stay together for longer periods of time, frequently until the sexual maturity of offspring. Under conditions of high parental investment, then, alternative mechanisms have evolved to prevent inbreeding depression or the pairing of harmful recessive genes (Bischof 1972; Frances and Frances 1976).

One mechanism is imprinting for sexual avoidance among those who live in close proximity or are raised together with one or both parents. As we saw in chapter 1, Edward Westermarck ([1891] 1922) felt that this was the principal mechanism for human sexual avoidance among closely related kin, particularly brothers and sisters. Those raised together develop asexual orientations to one another. Similar arguments are made by many theorists.[3] This line of argument is highly plausible because chimpanzees *(Pan),* our closest living relatives, also evidence a kind of "Westermarck effect" when youngsters are raised in close proximity to each other.

Another mechanism is dispersal of offspring from their natal groupings at sexual maturity, thereby reducing the chances of sexual relations with siblings or parents. All primate species have transfer patterns. Among monkeys, males generally leave their natal group at puberty, whereas among apes, females generally transfer from their natal group or larger community at sexual maturity. And, except for chimpanzees, ape males usually depart as well. Such transfer behaviors are surely hardwired in the neuroanatomy of primates, and they greatly lessen the chances that offspring will have sexual relations with their siblings, parents, or other close kin. This mechanism is also found among most species of mammals and many birds.[4]

Sexual avoidance becomes more problematic, however, when parents and their offspring stay in close proximity for longer periods of time and way past the sexual maturity of offspring. The nuclear family, which is often considered the bedrock of human societies, thus creates a novel kind of relational structure for a primate where adult males and females form longer-term bonds, and offspring often remain within the family. Thus older transfer patterns can be delayed or even subverted, although among most studied hunter-gatherer populations females generally marry shortly after puberty and often move to another band (a human cultural

---

3. For example, Lieberman, Tooby, and Cosmides 2003; Beve and Silverman 1993; Seto et al. 1999; Mathias et al. 1999; and Fessler and Navarrete 2004.

4. For illustrative data, see Burda 1995; Paz y Miñatno and Tang-Martinez 1999; Haydrock et al. 2001; Lehmann and Perrin 2003; Cooney and Bennett 2000; Herbst and Bennett 2001; Price 1998; Takahata et al. 2002; Brook et al. 2002.

version of the female transfer pattern evident in all species of apes). Still, there is the potential for sexual relations among the incestuous dyads of the nuclear family—brother–sister, mother–son, and father–daughter—that are much less likely among apes because of female transfer at puberty, coupled with asexual imprinting.

Thus the nuclear family is not a "natural" social unit for a great ape; it seemingly emerged from adaptation pressures during human evolution—an argument that we will pursue in later chapters. In this chapter, let us turn to the more recent theoretical explanations for sexual avoidance among closely related kin that have emerged within the scientific community. As noted earlier, many key ideas are found in the nonscientific written history (and in the unwritten history of preliterate peoples), but efforts to approach the issue of sexual avoidance within the framework of science added considerable sophistication to explanations. We will begin by reviewing the evidence that has emerged on the Westermarck effect and then the data on the biological consequences of inbreeding among humans. We will finish by exploring specific types of theories, all of which include elements of Westermarck's argument and/or analyses of the harmful effects of inbreeding. Many add new ideas to account for why populations found it necessary to codify biologically programmed avoidance tendencies into a cultural prohibition.

EVIDENCE FOR A WESTERMARCK EFFECT

Data from the Kibbutz

For decades, Westermarck's argument was ignored, but studies on Israeli kibbutzim cast new light on the effects of being raised together. Melford Spiro's (1958) data from children brought up together on kibbutz Iryat Yedidim showed that children who lived, slept, played, and worked side by side did not develop a sexual attraction for each other at puberty. In fact, at about the sixth grade, girls developed hostility toward the boys and sought to distance themselves from the males with whom they had played, showered, dressed, and slept during their formative years. At about fifteen years of age, the hostility declined, with pubescent boys and girls developing more relaxed friendships as each sought sexual outlets in other groups. Spiro offers a more Freudian interpretation about repressed sexuality leading to hostility, but it is easy to interpret the sexual disinterest of children raised together in a kibbutz as support for the Westermarck aversion effect.

Yonina Talmon (1964), an Israeli sociologist, collected data on marriage patterns among a sample of kibbutz members raised together and found that none of them had married. In fact, she discovered that children raised in the same living group had never been known to have love affairs or marry each other (reported in Fox 1980, 47). The one exception was a pairing of two individuals but, on closer inspection, it became clear that one of the pair had entered the living group at the age of fifteen, long past the time that the Westermarck effect would imprint a propensity for sexual apathy.

In a more systematic effort to extend Talmon's study, Joseph Shepher (1971), an Israeli sociologist who had been raised on a kibbutz, collected data on all known marriages (some 2,769 of them) on all Israeli kibbutzim. He found only sixteen cases that would contradict the findings of Talmon, but on further investigation, he discovered, like Talmon, that in all cases one of the mates had been introduced to the living group after the critical imprinting years—seemingly from birth to around six or seven years of age. These findings are particularly impressive in light of the fact that most parents encouraged their offspring to develop romantic attachments and marry their former playmates.

Data on Traditional Chinese Marriage Arrangements

In Taiwan, a traditional practice was for poor families to give their infant daughters to more affluent couples who would raise the adopted girl as a future spouse for their son. While this arrangement was considered less desirable than regular courtship, since it was known that these marriages often had problems, it was one way to increase the life chances of daughters from poor families. Arthur Wolf (1966) studied nineteen cases of daughter-in-law adoption in one Taiwanese village. In seventeen of the nineteen cases, the children raised together failed to consummate their marriage; and in the two more successful marriages, the daughter-in-law was introduced later, between the ages of eight and eleven. These findings are remarkable because there were powerful norms pushing for marriage; once again, when housemates are raised together from a very young age, a Westermarck effect can be observed.

Later, Wolf, along with Chiehshan Huang (1979), conducted a larger demographic study of Chinese marriages over a one-hundred-year period (1845–1945). Using statistical controls, they found that wives who had been raised with their husbands had a 30 percent lower fertility rate than wives who had been raised apart from their husbands. Obviously in this study, there are more "successful marriages" than those in one Taiwanese village but there is still something lowering the level of erotic feelings between children brought up together. Wolf and Huang were reluctant to accept Westermarck's hypothesis, but after carefully analyzing the data, they concluded that the Westermarck effect offered the best explanation for their findings.

In sum, then, there is good evidence that Westermarck was correct (for more on the mounting evidence, see Wolf 2005; Sanderson 2001, 215ff.; McCabe 1983). When children are raised in propinquity, and particularly when they have physical contact in play and other activities from a very young age, they appear to develop behavioral propensities that dampen sexual interest. As the exceptions in the kibbutzim and Taiwanese villages illustrate, there appears to be a discrete time frame for this effect to be triggered. From birth to six or seven are the critical years, and each year after this period, the potency of the Westermarck effect seemingly becomes less effective.

Classic Anthropological Ethnographies

In his book *The Red Lamp of Incest*, Robin Fox (1980, 38–50) reviewed not only the data summarized above but also a number of the classic ethnographies for what they say about the Westermarck effect. Fox found wide variability in preliterate populations along two variables: the level of physical contact and interaction among siblings and the severity of sanctions for sexual play or actual incest. Children who play together and have close physical contact during the early years develop a "natural" sexual aversion to each other as they reach puberty, even if they have engaged in sexual play before puberty. In contrast, children who have had little play and physical contact and/or have been segregated by strict role definitions for boys and girls will not reveal a strong sexual aversion toward each other (indeed, often quite the opposite), and in fact these populations will generally impose severe sanctions for sexual contact between brothers and sisters. As a general rule, then, Robin Fox (1980) proposed that the more boys and girls are free to pursue close physical contact as children, the less likely are explicit incest rules to be evident and the less adults in general seem to worry about the possibility of incest (presumably because they implicitly observe the Westermarck effect); and conversely, the more children are set apart in their activities with little physical contact, the more adults worry about sexual attraction and the more severe are the sanctions for such inclinations.

Various ethnographies illustrate these generalizations. Among Morris Opler's (1941) description of the traditional Chiricascreen (Apache), strict rules against sexual play among boys and girls were enforced, especially after the age of six (before this age some realistic "playing of house" occurs). After six, boys and girls lived in somewhat separate spheres, even sleeping with dividers between their respective bed sites. Incest was equated with witchcraft, and discovery of an act of incest would lead to killing the violators. In contrast, Meyer Fortes's (1949) ethnography of the Tallensi of the African Gold Coast reveals the opposite pattern: a considerable amount of play between boys and girls in the same and extended kin groups of their lineage, coupled with no strict sanctions against incest. For the Tallensi, incest is not sinful; it is disgraceful and scandalous, reflecting of the immaturity of those involved. But the Tallensi also believed that sexual temptation between close kin did not exist. To some extent, they may be right if high rates of play and interaction among children activate the Westermarck effect.

Bronislaw Malinowski's (1932) ethnography on the Trobriand Islanders further illustrates Fox's generalization. Although the Trobriand Islanders are highly permissive about sexual activity in general, they expressed some anxiety over brother and sister sexual relations, and from Fox's prediction, brothers and sisters were kept apart socially (although they remain in close physical proximity in their lineage). As Malinowski (1932, 440) summarizes: "Brother and sister thus grow up in a strange sort of domestic paradox; in close contact, and yet without any personal or intimate communication; near each other in space, near by rules of kinship and common interest; and yet as regards personality, always hidden and mysterious." They could not look at each other or share ideas and feelings, thus making them forbidden to each other. For the Trobriand Islanders, incest in general was taboo, but they were far more concerned about brother–sister incest than either mother–son or father–daughter incest (the latter two being considered "unthinkable" but still punishable if practiced). A brother and sister caught in incest would be banished and expected to commit suicide.

While Fox summarizes other ethnographies, the conclusion is clear: a population is relaxed about incest when the Westermarck effect has been activated through physical play and contact among young children, and very nervous and anxious about incest when the Westermarck effect has not been activated because children are kept apart (either physically or socially). The irony, of course, is that the more uptight people become about incest and the more they prohibit it with taboos and severe sanctions, the more they create the conditions (separation of brothers and sisters) that fulfill their prophecy about potential sexual interest between brothers and sisters.

These data do not inform us about whether or not the Westermarck aversion operates between parents and their offspring. Given the age differences, the imprinting may not be as strong, especially for the parent but perhaps for the child as well. There may be some effect, but because a parent is past the age window so evident in the data presented above, it may not be sufficient or in force. Westermarck ([1891] 1922, vol. 2, 198) certainly held to this position. What he had in mind, he tells us, is "a feeling of aversion associated with the idea of sexual intercourse between persons who have lived in a long-continued intimate relationship from a period of life when the action of sexual desire, in its acute forms at least, is naturally out of the question." If this is the case, then the formation of the nuclear family can potentially pose problems for parent–child incest, especially since in the nuclear families of both agrarian and industrial/postindustrial societies offspring often remain in the family well beyond puberty. Keep in mind that the Westermarck effect is only one of the two mechanisms that primates reveal for sexual avoidance; primates also use transfer of offspring from their natal group at puberty to reduce inbreeding. As we will argue, the nuclear family can work against these patterns, perhaps less in hunting and gathering bands but certainly more so in industrial and postindustrial societies. But let's not get ahead of our story; now we review the effects of incestuous relations on the offspring.

THE CONSEQUENCES OF INCEST

Mechanisms to prevent incest have emerged through natural selection to maintain genetic variability within a species and to limit inbreeding depression. The more mating partners share genes, the more likely are harmful recessive genes to become manifest in the phenotypes of offspring; and since these offspring are likely to be less fit than those of mating partners who do not share a high proportion of genes, they will be selected out of the gene pool. Through natural selection, mammals have developed a combination of fitness-enhancing behavioral strategies, such as proclivities for sexual avoidance among closely related kin and dispersal from natal groups and communities of sexually mature offspring. But among humans, inbreeding among closely related kin does occur, and as will be documented below, it has very detrimental effects on offspring.

The Harmful Effects on Offspring of Incestuous Relations

The effects of inbreeding on humans are dramatic and immediate. Several reports on the children of incestuous matings document the degree of dysfunction. Morton Adams and J. V. Neel (1967), for example, studied eighteen children from incestuous matings who were placed (or soon to be placed) in an adoption facility. Twelve were from brother–sister and six from father–daughter sexual intercourse. They compared these eighteen with a control group of nonincestuous children placed in the same facility. Only seven of the eighteen offspring of incestuous unions were considered normal and ready for adoption; five others were stillborn or died early in infancy; two were severely retarded and subject to seizures; three were borderline retarded; and one had a cleft palate along with other problems. In contrast, fifteen of the eighteen children in the control group were ready for adoption at birth.

In a similar study by Eva Seemanova (1971) of a larger sample of children in a public agency in the old Czechoslovakia, 161 children were confirmed offspring of incestuous relations, 88 from father–daughter incest, 72 from brother–sister relations, and one from a mother–son mating. The control group consisted of ninety-five half siblings born to mothers from unrelated males. There were fewer reported infant deaths than in the Adams and Neel study, but other problems were prominent. Twenty-five percent of offspring from incestuous relations, compared to 0 percent in the control group, were moderately to severely retarded; another 20 percent compared to 5 percent in the control group had congenital malformation or other severe abnormalities such as deaf-mutism or epilepsy; and 6 percent (compared to 0 percent in the control group) had multiple malformations. Overall, 43 percent of the incest offspring revealed severe problems, compared with 11 percent of the control group.

Another study by W. J. Schull and Neel (1965) examined marriages among first, once removed, and second cousins in Japan (where the number of shared genes is, at best, one-eighth rather than one-half as in the above studies). Yet, even with less shared genetic material, these investigators concluded that the more unrelated the sexual partners, the more intelligent were their offspring and the less susceptible were their children to infection and congenital birth defects. Thus, even when the level of shared genes is only one-eighth (and in most cultures not considered incestuous), there are still tendencies for offspring to experience congenital problems (Bittles and Neel 1994).

Victor McKusick and his colleagues studied the Amish of Pennsylvania, who were the direct descendants of the original Amish community founded in Bern, Switzerland. The Pennsylvania Amish immigrated in the early 1700s to America. Because these Amish came from a very small founding population in Europe that had admitted few new members, married couples were genetically close. While the Amish disallow first-cousin marriages, the small gene pools of the communities in Pennsylvania make some married couples as closely connected as first cousins, who share 12.5 percent of their genes. Among the 250 married couples who were second cousins several times over and hence shared the equivalent of 12.5 percent of their genes like first cousins, their offspring revealed a number of physical abnormalities, such as dwarfism, polydactyly (more than ten digits), dystrophy, and partial harelip (see McKusick et al. 1978; for a secondary analysis, see Arens 1986, 20–22). Other studies document the same outcomes from breeding among cousins and other relatives.[5] Similar data can be found for mammals and birds.[6] Some forms of complex plant life also show the harmful effects of close inbreeding (Wang et al. 2003).

Preliterate people could easily have observed these deleterious effects on offspring from unions of closely related kin. It is so obvious and immediate, we should not be surprised that when other mechanisms like the Westermarck effect or transfer patterns were not operative, people developed rules about incest. Scientific

---

5. For example, Harel et al. 2004; Denic 2003; Fuster and Colantonio 2003; Shalev et al. 2003; Ali et al. (2003); Gustavson 2003; Lauc et al. 2003; Kumaramanickavel et al. 2002; Cook 1967; Bittles 2005.

6. For example, Janecke et al. 2004; Grant et al. 2003; Rudd and Herzberger 1999; Koenig et al. 1999; Smith et al. 1997; Dobson et al. 1997; Zumpe and Michael 1996.

knowledge about the human genome is not needed to recognize the grave effects of sexual relations between near kin, which imposed a heavy burden on traditional peoples. Thus at some point in human evolution the incest taboo was created to avoid inbreeding (Durham 2005). As Fox has emphasized, the taboo and sanctions for its violation are most intense when the Westermarck effect is not allowed to "kick in" during early childhood and, we should add, when primate dispersal patterns of the sexually mature are delayed or subverted. As we will argue in later chapters, it is the creation of the human nuclear family—a very unusual pattern of organization for an ape—that increased the probability that the Westermarck effect and female transfer would not always be operative, thus forcing people to prohibit sexual relations that would cause congenital harm to offspring.

Why Are the Effects of Incest So Dramatic and Immediate?

We can speculate that one reason for the rather dramatic harm in the first generation of offspring of incestuous relations is that the human genome reveals much less genetic diversity than that of (*Pan*) chimpanzees, our closest animal relative (Gagneux 2002; Kaessmann and Pääbo 2002). The reason for this lower level of variability seemingly stems from the relatively small breeding population from which all modern humans have descended (Watkins et al. 2003; Long and Kittles 2003; Relethford 2002), although some dispute this claim (Edwards 2003; Zietkiewicz et al. 2003). Recent inferences based on mitochondrial DNA indicate that indeed all of us are descendants of a very small mother population that migrated from Africa—one that conceivably numbered in the hundreds rather than thousands. New studies of Y chromosome markers support these findings from studies on mitochondrial DNA (Renfrew, Forster, and Hurles 2000). The population from which all modern humans evolved may have been in rapid decline in Africa, with only a relatively small deme breaking away and finding a way out of eastern Africa via shallow waters some 150,000 years ago (see Kaessmann and Pääbo 2002). This population could not move west because of the glaciers (thus saving Neanderthals from an earlier extinction), and so they moved east along the coastlines of South Asia. And, while they reproductively flourished in a more favorable habitat, eventually spreading all over the globe, the low amount of genetic diversity in this ancestral gene pool initially determined the overall degree of variation in the human genome.[7]

Whatever the explanation, the end result today is a comparatively low degree of variability in the *Homo sapiens* gene pool that, in turn, increases the likelihood that harmful recessive genes will become manifest in the first generation of offspring from closely related individuals. Moreover, it is now proposed that much of the variability in humans is also the product of "junk genes" and activation of protein sequences; and the more individuals share these, the more amplified will be their effects on offspring.[8]

THEORETICAL EXPLANATIONS OF INCEST AVOIDANCE AND THE TABOO

Sociobiological Theories

Sociobiological theories all stress the maladaptive consequences of mating among closely related individuals. As already noted, mating among close kin can lead to the pairing of harmful recessive genes that, in turn, will decrease fitness from inbreeding depression. Since virtually all mammals reveal tendencies to avoid mating among individuals who are normally genetically close (Faulkes and Bennett 2001), the incest taboo is simply a cultural elaboration among humans of an inbreeding inhibition that natural selection has hard-wired into the neuroanatomy of animals. Edward Westermarck posited, as we have emphasized, an imprinting mechanism for sexual avoidance among individuals who carry out daily rou-

---

7. This process is referred to as "founders effect" (see Mayr 1942), a form of genetic drift. Variation is reduced (from the ancestral population) because a small population does not have as many duplicate alleles as larger ones (and the breakaway population is unlikely to contain all the alleles in the original population). A small number of breeding individuals in a population can also reduce diversity. Natural selection, a directive force, can further reduce variation by weeding out less favored alleles depending on the environment. To add new genetic material to a gene pool requires the services of two other agents of evolution—mutation, a purely random and creative force, and gene flow, which results from the migration of individuals (or their genes) from another breeding population to the new "founders effect" population.

8. The "out of Africa" or recent "African origin" model discussed above enjoys wide support in the academic community. An alternative model, "multi-regional evolution," proposes coevolution of modern humans on different continents with lots of migrations allowing for gene flow between populations (see Excoffier 2002 for a comparative discussion).

tines in close proximity; but why would there be a need for a cultural prohibition if indeed a natural avoidance tendency already exists? As J. G. Frazer ([1910] 1968) argued in his criticism of Westermarck's position, "Law forbids men to do what their instincts incline them to do; what nature itself prohibits and punishes, it would be superfluous for law to prohibit and punish." As we have seen with the data on kibbutzim and traditional Chinese marriages, the Westermarck effect is presumably activated during the early years, from birth to around age six or seven. If sociocultural arrangements block this activation, then incest becomes more likely, thereby making a taboo necessary.

Yet, as we will argue in the next chapter, cultural prohibitions appear to be strongest for the incest that "nature itself prohibits"— mother–son incest. Still, the biosocial theories all make the critical point that sexual avoidance among genetically close individuals appears to be a hardwired propensity among many mammals and serves to increase fitness by minimizing inbreeding depression. Pierre van den Berghe (1980), for example, argues that not all societies exhibit an incest taboo, and in fact many people consider the act of incest ludicrous rather than heinous. Thus the key is not only to explain the taboo but, more generally, incest avoidance. Inbreeding was selected against because it reduced fitness; and as a result, humans like most mammals surely exhibited a statistical tendency for outbreeding long before a cultural ban was invented. For van den Berghe, the Westermarck effect is one example of an innate tendency for close kin to have bioprogrammers—or innate behavioral propensities—for sexual avoidance. However, van den Berghe goes on to argue that there is a fitness-enhancing value to marrying close kin because such marriages promote group solidarity, and thus selection might have favored individuals marrying kin who share only 12.5 percent of their genes (e.g., first cousins). And these marriages might have increased fitness by promoting ties and alliances among nuclear family units within or between hunter-gatherer bands. Yet, in van den Berghe's eyes, the incest taboo that forces marriage outside the nuclear family is not exogamy, as commonly conceptualized by anthropologists.

Exogamy is an entirely different form of cultural evolution that emerges among horticulturalists and pastoralists who use unilineal descent to organize larger numbers of kin into alliances (see later discussion of alliance theory). Avoiding incest was, no doubt, critical to hunter-gatherer fitness; and to the extent that this norm was codified into an incest taboo, fitness was further enhanced.

But marrying outside the nuclear family is not, van den Berghe insists, a rule of exogamy. Such rules come later in human societal development.

There are many variants among sociobiological argumenters (e.g., Crippen 1994; Lopreato 1984; van den Berghe 1980). For instance, Trivers (1972) submits that females in general will be more adverse to casual sex because the costs of sexual relations are so much greater for them than males, thus making daughters and sisters resistant to sex with, respectively, their fathers and brothers. The core argument of biosocial theories about natural selection working against inbreeding and reduced fitness is unquestionably true in its essentials; the problem is how to explain cultural taboos against incest. Are these all simply a reflection of bioprogrammers for avoidance, and if so, why are they necessary? Even if males and females have different mating strategies to maximize fitness, do these correspond to the relative strength of the taboo for different family members? There is, then, a process of coevolution between genetic selection and cultural selection for the incest taboo, but even here the various sociobiological approaches are not clear on what is biologically based and what the product of cultural evolution (Durham 1991).

Evolutionary Psychology

A more recent variant of sociobiological theories is evolutionary psychology. This approach accepts the basic tenet of sociobiology that many behaviors have a biological basis, honed by natural selection along the hominid and human line. Evolutionary psychology adds to this view the notion that the brain reveals modules for particular modes of cognition and behavior that are the result of selection processes. For example, it is assumed that "reciprocity," or the tendency for humans to exchange resources, is a hardwired propensity (Cosmides 1989; Fiske 1991). Other domains of cognition were subject to selection during hominid (ancestors near or on the human line) and human evolution (Thornhill, Tooby, and Cosmides 1997). For evolutionary psychologists, the Westermarck effect represents an evolved psychological mechanism for incest avoidance that is activated under relevant conditions (when opposite-sex children must live together). Thus with respect to incest avoidance, evolutionary psychology repeats the argument of sociobiology but with an emphasis on the brain modules (unknown at present) that activate the Westermarck effect.

We should note that much of our argument contains elements of evolutionary psychology, but not so much for explaining the biology of incest avoidance as for explaining why the incest taboo became necessary. Clearly the hominid and human brain was under intense selection pressure to enhance sociality over the past 2 million years; and in our view, natural selection worked on the emotion centers or modules of the brain to increase humans' emotional responses toward each other. But natural selection, in increasing human emotionality and attachment behavior, may have subverted older biologically based mechanisms for incest avoidance, such as the Westermarck effect and female transfer patterns that had served to limit inbreeding among primates and humans' hominid ancestors. Indeed, as the brain was being rewired for increased emotion and attachment behavior, late hominids and early humans had to create new mechanisms for incest avoidance. But these new mechanisms were not biologically based but rather based in new kinds of cultural codes.

Sociological Theories

In contrast to sociobiological theories, sociological approaches to understanding the incest taboo focus on the emergence of the taboo rather than on sexual avoidance. Why would an incest taboo emerge in the first place? While sociologists recognize inbreeding problems, they are far more likely to stress the disruptive effects on family solidarity of sexual competition among family members, a line of argument that appeared in classical and medieval thinking about incest (see chapter 1).

Malinowski's Explanation of the Incest Taboo

Bronislaw Malinowski (1927) was among the first contemporary theorists to present a fully sociological argument on the origins of the incest taboo. Malinowski believed that exogamy was an extension of the incest taboo, but the key argument is that incest would create role confusion and conflict among members of the nuclear family. He explicitly criticized Westermarck and supported Freud, at least Freud's belief that "incestuous tendencies" would cause turmoil in the family (although he did not go so far as Freud, who saw these tendencies as occurring with each generation, nor did he accept Freud's view that the attachment of son to mother was essentially sexual). The key point is that, should sexual attachments occur, they would disrupt the division of labor and roles necessary to the viability of the nuclear family.

Most sociologists have followed the essentials of Malinowski's argument. For example, Kingsley Davis (1949, 403), in the first modern introductory sociology textbook, phrased Malinowski's argument as follows: "If sexual relations between parent and child were permitted, sexual rivalry between mother and daughter and between father and son would almost surely arise, and this rivalry would be incompatible with the sentiments necessary between the two. Should children be born (from incest) the confusions of statuses would be phenomenal. The incestuous child of a father–daughter union . . . would be a brother of his own mother . . . a stepson of his own grandmother; possibly a brother of his own uncle; and certainly a grandson of his own father."

William Catton Jr. (1969, 15), while emphasizing the role strain and conflict caused by incestuous mating in the nuclear family, also advances a corollary "inertial principle": "When one has learned to interact in a given way with a particular person, it is difficult to learn a radically different relationship to that same person." He suggests that incest may be rare because "pre-established relationships of one kind effectively render subsequent relations of a different nature between the same persons improbable." For Catton, "exogamy is one result of this principle" (see also Coult 1963).

Thus sociological explanations revolve around the notion that incest would be disruptive to family relations, implicitly invoking a cultural selection argument: those societies in which the nuclear family systems did not have an incest taboo and in which incest occurred would be less fit in the sense of not adequately preparing the next generation to assume normal roles and to possess normal emotional dispositions; conversely, those societies in which the taboo emerged would ensure relatively stable family relations and socialization of the next generation to fill roles in society. Some sociologists such as M. F. Nimkoff (1947) also emphasized inbreeding depression as a force behind the incest taboo, but Nimkoff, like other sociologists, also stressed the disruption that incestuous relations would have for the normal functioning of the nuclear family (Gagnon and Simon 1967).

Parsons's Theory on the Origins of the Incest Taboo

Unlike many sociologists, Talcott Parsons (1954), as well as Parsons and Robert F. Bales (1955), adopted many elements of Freudian theory into a functionalist scheme; nowhere is this tendency more evident than in Parsons's analysis of the incest taboo. For Parsons, incestuous desires, which must be repressed to sustain harmony in the family, are a key force in the emotional growth of children and, ultimately, in the ability of children to assume extrafamilial roles in the broader society. The mother is the source of emotional support and, potentially, sexual stimulation. Consequently the mother must cut off this excitement at critical times, transmuting the son's sexual excitement into motivations to pursue success in roles outside the family. This movement of sons, and presumably daughters as well, into nonfamilial roles is essential to the smooth functioning of society, while at the same time reducing the potential for sexually charged tension and conflict within the family.

This analysis does not, however, adequately explain the origins of the incest taboo. Like so much functional analysis, there is an implicit assumption that the potential conflict within the family and the need to motivate performance in key productive roles in society somehow, through processes that are not specified, leads to the emergence of the incest taboo. Like the Freudian model, it presumes intense selection pressures to find ways to reduce sexual tension in the nuclear family and to divert sexual energy outward onto the broader society; and these selection pressures lead actors to create an incest taboo that "institutionalizes" repression of sexual desires and channels these desires into motivations to play necessary roles in society.

Thus, in contrast to Westermarck's or biological theories that view sexual avoidance as programmed into the biology of the individual through the process of natural selection, Parsons (like Freud) implicitly disputes this claim. Instead, sexual desires of children, especially boys for their mother, remain a constant pressure on society, forcing the codification of incest rules and protocols for mothers to redirect the sexual energy of their children in ways that sustain the stability of the nuclear family and the need to have motivated incumbents in the societal status-role structure.

Perhaps Parsons goes too far, as did Freud and others who make similar arguments (e.g., Rascovsky and Rascovsky 1972), but these early sociological theories provide a corrective to more biologically oriented approaches which often assume that natural selection changed the human genome so that sexual avoidance became primarily based on bioprogrammers like the Westermarck effect. While some patterns have biological components, a sociological perspective always emphasizes that norms are created to solve problems not fully managed by bioprogrammers. Indeed, if humans were fully programmed toward sexual indifference in nuclear families, the incest taboo would not be necessary. In fact, to anticipate our argument, the biological propensities for sexual aversion among closely related kin evolved *before* the nuclear family, but once the nuclear family had fitness-enhancing value, its structure and culture could potentially disrupt the Westermarck effect and older patterns of female (and male) transfer from the natal group. And so, despite the rather speculative character of Parson's approach, a theory on the origins of the incest taboo must retain one critical insight: the taboo exists because it resolves certain problems inherent in the nuclear family; and the goal of an explanation on the origins of the taboo must uncover what these problems are.

Alliance Theories of the Incest Taboo

Within anthropology, several theories explain the incest taboo in terms of a more general analysis of the emergence of kinship rules. Claude Lévi-Strauss's ([1949] 1967) arguments have exerted the most influence on what has become known as "alliance theory." For Lévi-Strauss there is no natural regularity in humans' choice of sexual partners because, he believed, there is no regularity in great apes (who are usually promiscuous; unfortunately, Lévi-Strauss ignores avoidance and transfer patterns that do indeed limit "choices" among primates and thereby reduce the probability of breeding among closely related individuals). But the more general point that the incest taboo and kinship rules are cultural is correct; and the goal of his approach is to explain the form of rules constituting a kinship system. For Lévi-Strauss there are two fundamental mechanisms by which societies become integrated: one is through redistributional systems by which scarce resources are given to members of a society, and the other is through exchange systems revolving around reciprocal gift giving. In exchange systems, it is the exchange relationship per se, rather than the "thing" exchanged, that promotes solidarity (an idea he obviously got from Mauss ([1924] 1967).

One form of exchange is the tendency of kinship systems to have rules of marriage that specify the exchange of brides among groups. For Lévi-Strauss, the incest taboo is an essential part of this exchange system because without the prohibition against marriage to close kin, it is impossible to ensure interchange among different kin units. Thus exogamy is not possible without an incest taboo that forces individuals to seek marriage partners away from immediate kin (White 1949; Hoebel 1949). If a regular pattern of bridal exchange can develop, alliances are formed among kinship units; and these alliances reduce conflict and promote integration of a larger regional population. Thus, if women of clan A are exchanged for bridal payments (known as bride wealth) from men in clan B, and conversely, if women in clan B are exchanged for bridal payments from men in clan A, an alliance is formed between the two clans. Not only are kin integrated, but the exchange relation itself promotes solidarity across clans. And if a society with many clans can reveal these kinds of regularized bridal exchanges, integration among potentially conflicting groups is achieved. A rule of exogamy works best with a corresponding rule of endogamy, which specifies the group into which one must marry.

From this theoretical perspective, then, incest rules are part of a larger unilineal descent system with rules of exogamy and endogamy; they are, in essence, the key to pushing individuals outside their natal unit in search of sexual and marital partners. The analysis of how kinship rules can work to promote broader societal integration is useful and correct for many societies, but unfortunately, as van den Berghe (1980) would emphasize, unilineal descent is typical of horticultural and pastoral societies rather than hunter-gathering societies in which humans evolved and which, at some point in this evolution, formulated the incest taboo. It is unlikely that the taboo evolved among food collectors as part of a widespread exchange system, although some contemporary hunter-gatherers reveal elements of unilineal descent (but many of these are Australian aboriginals whose ancestors, we suspect, may have been early farmers and de-evolved back to hunting and gathering after their migration to Australia). Hunting and gathering societies typically reveal bilateral descent systems, kindreds with patrilocal, bilocal, or matrilocal residence (Ember 1978). Consequently it is very unlikely that the nuclear family in the first food foraging bands revealed unilineal descent. Thus, while the arguments of alliance theorists are not wrong when examining horticultural and pastoral societies, they cannot account for the origin of the taboo; rather, they explain how it could be used, once in place, as part of a more general system of bridal exchange built around rules of endogamy and exogamy (van den Berghe 1980).

Feminist Theories

Most feminist theories do not speculate on the origin of the incest taboo; rather, they tend to emphasize patriarchy (male domination of the nuclear family) and the effects of patriarchy on rates of incest. For example, Herman and Hirschman (1977) argue that in kinship systems where women are property (as in some systems of bridal exchange), patriarchy also exists. Under conditions of patriarchy in the nuclear family, father–daughter incest is more likely than in nonpatriarchal systems because women have no bargaining power or resources to prevent male sexual advances. Women in patriarchal systems will be seen as nurturers and, hence, will try to protect their young, but this form of passivity only supports patriarchy (Herman and Hirschman 1981).

There are more Freudian feminist theories that also examine patriarchy. For example, Frances and Frances (1976) argue that men are more likely to suffer anxiety from fears of castration than females because their dominance over women and sense of masculinity are associated with the male sex organ. This anxiety leads males to impose their dominance over women, especially male sexual advances toward less mature females. As a result of this tendency, father–daughter incest and older brother–younger sister incest are more likely than mother–son incest (since the mother is more mature than her son, who, in order to assert dominance, must seek out younger and "weaker" females).

We mention these theories here because they raise an important issue that we will examine in the next chapter: the relationship among normative systems in the nuclear family. The incest taboo, where it exists, is one of several kinship rules; and the power of the taboo can be enhanced or subverted by other kinship rules. For example, in patriarchal systems, its power is reduced because of norms about a male's "right" to dominate women in the nuclear household. Conversely, when a more egalitarian set of norms prevails in the nuclear family, the incest taboo is strengthened because males and females do not have the "right" to impose themselves on others.

Demographic Theories

Mariam K. Slater (1959) proposed a demographic theory for why incest is unlikely in the hunting and gathering populations where humans first evolved. This theory revolves around the age structure of bands. By the time a child is sexually mature, she argued, the parent may be dead or past peak periods of sexual activity and child bearing. Adults age rapidly in hunting and gathering societies; and even if they live longer, they are not attractive sexual objects to their offspring; and conversely, as adults mature they have lowered sexual interest in general (hence making it unlikely that they would be sexually attracted to their children). Moreover, because hunter-gatherer women naturally space their children because of the protracted period of breast-feeding, the children will be too far apart to have sexual or marital interest in each other before the older one leaves the nuclear family in search of sexual and marriage partners.

This approach does not explain, however, why the incest taboo would ever be necessary; and Slater's notable effort to link the incest taboo to rules of exogamy is no more persuasive than the arguments of alliance theorists. Her theory also fails to explain why males would not show sexual interest in their younger daughters or siblings (as some fathers and brothers do in contemporary societies). Slater probably overstates the aging among hunter-gatherers, many of whom lived long lives and remained sexually active (just as males do today). Still, it is useful to consider the age structure of early hunter-gatherers and its potential effects on familial intimacy. Coupled with the Westermarck effect and female transfer from the natal family at puberty, the demographic patterns outlined by Slater would reduce the probability of incest. Yet the question still remains for all such explanations: Why, then, would a taboo ever be necessary?

Robin Fox's Synthetic Theory on the Incest Taboo

We have saved a review of one of the most prominent explanations on the incest taboo for last because it has many of the components of our approach. Fox (1980) synthesizes elements of virtually all approaches and adds data from primatology and neurology in a complex analysis of incest avoidance and the incest taboo. We will also seek to provide an integrative theory that looks very much like Fox's in its scope but differs from Fox's analysis in some of its conclusions.

Fox recognizes that humans, and presumably our hominid ancestors, are unique among hominoids in several senses. First, humans combine mating and kinship systems because, unlike great apes who are in the main promiscuous, humans tie the mating pairs and their offspring together for a prolonged period in the nuclear family. This combination can work against older ape patterns of transfer from the natal group at puberty (for hominoid females and, except for chimpanzees, for males as well) and places an extra burden on the Westermarck effect. In particular, it creates intergenerational potential for breeding between parents and offspring, since the Westermarck effect is more likely to work for siblings than for a parent and child. Second, humans are the only hominoid species to survive in open country conditions, where today among primates only well-organized monkeys (e.g., *Theropithesus gelada*) can live (all present-day apes live in primary or secondary forests or woodland areas that sometimes are adjacent to open country). The formation of the nuclear family was, no doubt, one of the adaptations that an open country or grassland living hominid had to make to survive where trees are few in number and predators abound. Third, in a complex set of selection effects, hominids' and later humans' major adaptation to this niche was a larger brain. For Fox, this larger brain was made possible by the organization of hominids into big-game-hunting bands that brought added protein to the diet of humans' ancestors. Big game hunting requires coordination of hunting activities by band members; and it may also have encouraged the development of kinship systems revolving around the exchange of meat (secured by male hunting) and plant foods (secured by female gathering). Larger brains also required considerably more infant dependence on caregivers and, hence, parental investment in raising the young, thus increasing selection pressures for the nuclear family in which both males and females could care for their offspring. Fourth, a larger brain involves expansion of the frontal lobe (frontal cortex and the prefrontal cortex) and the integration of these areas with emotion (amygdala) and memory (hippocampus) centers of the brain. The end result is an animal that could inhibit emotional responses and deliberate before acting and that could connect present sensory inputs with stored memories. There would be, Fox argues, selection favoring those who could think, deliberate, and bring past experiences to bear on the present; they would be more likely to survive and have higher status in bands, with the result that females would be attracted to such males because they would increase her and her offspring's fitness.

Fox also emphasizes that patterns of sexual avoidance among primates are strained with the emergence of the nuclear family. For siblings, the Westermarck effect is perhaps sufficient to reduce the probability that they will have incestuous relations, but this effect would be much less pronounced (if evident at all) for parents and their offspring. Primate patterns of dispersal are delayed or completely obviated by the formation of the nuclear family in hunting and gathering bands, thus increasing the potential for incestuous relations between adults and their children. It is the latter problem that, Fox argues, leads to the emergence of the incest taboo and its enforcement.

To explain how the taboo emerged, Fox turns to Freud, but he abstracts above the particulars of Freudian psychology and isolates the key elements of Freud's argument. In Fox's eyes, Freud's explanation for the origins of the incest taboo contains the following elements: (1) the power struggle between older males who control access to females and younger males who seek sexual relations with these females; (2) the development of restrictions on sexual relations among closely related kin that is fueled by the development of conscience and guilt when these restrictions are violated. For Freud the species went through an evolutionary phase during which the guilt over the younger males' killing their fathers or their desire to do so in order to gain access to females leads to the development of morality in general and the incest taboo in particular in human societies; and for each child born into the nuclear family, this evolutionary phase for the species is reproduced as a developmental stage, during which a child represses sexual desires and sublimates these desires into conformity to the incest taboo. Moreover, the energy of repressed sexual desire for parents leads children, when they become adults, to socialize their own children into the taboo; and in this way the taboo becomes institutionalized in society.

Fox accepts this argument in its broad outline. He emphasizes that primates—monkeys more than apes—reveal structural conditions similar to those outlined by Freud: successful and dominant males try to hoard females for themselves; younger males are left out but desire sexual access to females. To the degree that this behavioral propensity was carried out onto the savanna by humans' hominid ancestors, it posed a point of great tension in the emerging hunting and gathering band. As the brain grew and became more capable of integrating thought, emotion, and memory, new kinds of emotions such as guilt could be experienced and used to forge a morality that regularized access to females through an incest taboo and exogamous marriage rules. This morality emerged as a result of combining the mating and kin systems within the nuclear family, forcing the offspring of the mating pair to repress sexual desires for parents. They are assisted in this process by the sanctioning of parents in reference to the incest taboo and by their socialization into other kinship rules that regularize mating and marriage for offspring. These rules sustain their power across generations, Fox appears to believe, because (1) the sublimated sexual desires of the young are transmuted into emotional commitments to the incest taboo and rules of exogamy and (2) this energy continues into adulthood and is the motivation behind adult socialization of the next generation of young into the prohibitions imposed by the incest taboo and exogamous prescriptions for sex and marriage.

As will become evident, we adopt much of Fox's strategy, especially using existing primates as a basis for speculation about the behavioral propensities of humans' hominid ancestors and drawing on new knowledge on the neuroanatomy of both apes and humans to understand how emotions and thinking influence propensities for both incestuous behaviors and their prohibition. We are less convinced by Fox's adoption of the Freudian model, except in the general sociological sense of cultural selection against sexual competition within the nuclear family. And, as will be clear, we also see the nuclear family as a difficult structure for an evolved great ape, one that was clearly forced on humans and perhaps their ancestors as they sought to survive in open country conditions. In a sense we will update Fox's analysis, but we will also come to different conclusions on some key points.

CONCLUSION

The explanation that we develop in the next chapters on the origins of the incest taboo does not supplant any of the explanations reviewed in this chapter. Rather, we seek to supplement current approaches; and yet, despite the strengths of each theory that we have reviewed, none of the approaches adequately explains the research questions for which we seek answers. As we noted at the end of chapter 1, one question to address is why the taboo reveals varying levels of intensity for different dyads—father–daughter, mother–son, and brother–sister—in the nuclear family? Why, for example, is mother–son incest so much more taboo than sibling or father–daughter incest? Another question is the differential rates of incest for these three heterosexual dyads. Although the data on rates of incest are fraught with problems, clearly mother–

son incest is far less common than sibling or father–daughter incest. We need an answer to the question as to why such differences should exist. A final question is the differential effects of incest on its victims. Why would the psychological harm to sons in mother–son incest be so much greater than for the victims of sibling and father–daughter incest?

None of the theories summarized earlier can answer all these questions. Each can answer one or two but not all three, as we will explore in the final chapter of this book. In seeking answers, we are pulled into the earlier questions that scientists asked: Why did the taboo emerge? Why were bioprogrammers not sufficient, or at least were perceived by individuals as not adequate to prevent inbreeding? In developing our own explanation as to why the taboo emerged, while keeping in mind our three guiding questions, a more robust explanation of the incest taboo will emerge, or so we hope.

In the next chapter, we need to establish as "facts" the implicit claims in our questions: Is the strength of the taboo greater for mother–son than other incestuous dyads in the nuclear family? Is mother–son incest less frequent than other forms? And does incest have more harmful effects on sons than on daughters and sisters? The data, as they bear on these questions, are highly problematic, but they are all we have to work with; and so, warts and all, we need to see if we can draw some safe and reasonable conclusions from the only sources of data that are available on incest in the nuclear family today.

Even though we focus on the contemporary nuclear family in framing our three questions, our answers will take us back into our evolutionary past. We need to reconstruct how natural and sociocultural selection interacted to produce, first of all, the hunting and gathering band. For, as we will argue, the horde existed before the nuclear family. This transition from the primitive "horde" to the hunting-gathering band composed of nuclear families will occupy our attention in chapter 5. But before we can explain what transpired in the evolution of hominids, we first need to examine in chapter 4 the nature of social relations among contemporary primates to see what they can tell us about the biological and organizational baseline from which hominids evolved. Humans are evolved apes, and by looking at the anatomy, neuroanatomy, behavioral propensities, and social structures of our closest relatives, especially the common chimpanzee, we can perhaps see our hominoid ancestors reflected in a distant mirror. In chapter 6, we will examine the evolution of the nuclear family from early hominid hordes. For an evolved ape, the nuclear family encroaches on their propensities for individualism and mobility, and it confines close kin in ways that can potentially lead to incest, especially if it disrupts the Westermarck effect and patterns of transfer typical of humans' ape cousins. The potential for incest and inbreeding increased with the evolution of the nuclear family, and so there must have been intense selection pressures to create the family, even as it raised the bar for decreased fitness from inbreeding. And finally, in chapter 7, we will review our explanation for the origins of the incest taboo and compare it with the alternative explanations that we have reviewed in this chapter. From this exercise, we hope to add a few new insights into the origins and effects of the taboo in human societies.

3
FORBIDDEN ACTS
INCEST AND ITS PSYCHOLOGICAL CONSEQUENCES

↦

> We must not forget that a lack of desire, and even a pos-
> itive feeling of aversion, may in certain circumstances be
> overcome. The sexual instinct is so powerful that when it
> cannot be gratified in the normal manner it may seek for
> abnormal gratification . . . sexual intercourse with a near
> relative may be resorted to when another, more suitable,
> partner is out of reach.
>
> —Edward Westermarck (1891)

Because incest is prohibited, it remains a hidden and mysterious
act. As a result, it is difficult to get reliable data on rates of incest
in contemporary families. Yet, if we are to understand why the
incest taboo emerged, we need some sense for the relative rates of
incest among the mother–son, father–daughter, and brother–sister
dyads. Homosexual incest also occurs in families, far more commonly than once thought. In fact, mother–daughter incest is probably more common than mother–son incest, and it is increasingly
apparent that sexual abuse of males comes more from fathers than
mothers. Homosexual incest is, of course, also taboo in most
societies, but we are most interested in heterosexual incest because
its prohibition was essential to the viability of the nuclear family
during the evolution of hominids and humans.

It is not possible to draw any firm conclusions about the actual
rates of incest because of methodological problems in the data.
But it is possible to scan the enormous amount of information

collected and derive a sense for the *relative rates* of incest among the mother–son, father–daughter, and brother–sister dyads. These materials will also allow us to assess the relative psychological harm to the victims of incest.

METHODOLOGICAL PROBLEMS WITH THE DATA ON INCEST

Definitional Problems

At the outset, the first problem is the definition of incest. What constitutes incest and incestuous behavior by parents toward their children or brothers toward sisters? Definitions can be expansive, including inappropriate talk of sexuality at one pole to actual sexual intercourse at the other. As "child abuse" has become a central concern of researchers and policy makers over the past few decades, ever-more expansive definitions have been proposed for what constitutes "incest." For example, table 3.1 lists the range of behaviors defined as child sexual abuse and incest for the mother–son dyad. If incest includes all of the items on the list, or even a significant portion of them, then rates of incest increase dramatically. However, if a strict dictionary[1] definition of incest—"actual intercourse between closely related persons"—or the first item on the list in table 3.1 is used, then rates of mother–son incest are much lower. Because the field of child abuse involves moral crusading, the tendency exists to expand the list of what constitutes incest. Most clinicians would not include many of the items in table 3.1 in a definition of incest, but many policy-oriented researchers would. A somewhat less inclusive definition is provided by a clinician, Karin Meiselman (1978), who sees incest as "a very definite sexual approach, involving successful or unsuccessful attempts at exposure, genital fondling, oral-genital contact, and/or vaginal or anal intercourse, as perceived by the patient."

This definition is still rather inclusive for our purposes, and so we decided that incest will apply only to acts between forbidden heterosexual dyads in the nuclear family that involve actual sexual intercourse. We might also include explicit acts of genital contact that are deliberate and intended but we faced the immediate problem of determining *how much* contact and *how* intended. But, even if we included intended genital contact, our definition is still narrow compared to the rather broad definitions found in the litera-

---

1. *Webster's Encyclopedic Unabridged Dictionary of the English Language,* 1996.

Table 3.1 Range of Mother–Son Incestuous Behaviors Reported in the Literature

Overt behaviors

Actual penetration and intercourse between mother and son
Making the son have sex with other people
Having the son rub against the mother's genitals in acts of masturbation
Having the son insert his finger in the mother's vagina
Having the son perform cunnilingus on the mother
Having the son witness the mother's acts of masturbation
Masturbating the son by the mother
Performing fellatio on the son by the mother
Having the son fondle and suck the mother's breasts
Penetrating the son's anus with fingers and other objects

Covert behaviors

Breaking the son's privacy in the shower
Bathing the son into his teen years
Actually bathing with the son
Prolonged wiping of the son's anus long after he has bowel control
Inserting into the son's anus enemas that are unnecessary
Sleeping all night in the same bed with the son
Performing sensual massages on the son by the mother
French-kissing the son by the mother
Excessive caressing, kissing, holding, fondling of the son by the mother
Playing seductive roles in front of the son
Deliberately leaving the bathroom door open so that the son can see the mother
Dressing and undressing in front of son
Walking about the house without clothes so that son can see the mother
Allowing or forcing the son to witness the mother's sexual behaviors with other men
Exposing the son to pornographic movies
Commenting on the size of the son's penis
Making the son wear girl's clothes and treating the son as a female
Making the son feel responsible for the mother's emotional well-being

Source: Adopted from Miletski 1995, who provides a list of references on reports for overt and covert behavior.

ture on child abuse. We decided it was best, given the nature of our inquiry, to limit the term incest to actual sexual penetration while all other overt and covert behaviors were put into the category of "involving incest."[2]

---

2. Some readers may fault us for applying only the strict definition of incest, but a review of this literature requires the investigator to wade through very muddy waters. Incestuous acts are almost unlimited in type when overt and covert acts (and their multiple interpretations) are included.

Despite our effort to achieve a precise definition of incest, the reports on which we must rely for the relative rates of incest do not generally use this narrow definition. In fact, it is often unclear as to the exact definition of incest being employed in research, especially when incest is conflated with child sexual abuse in general. Thus we encounter problems with the definition of incest in surveying the literature, but as we will see, this difficulty is compounded by additional problems with the data.

Sources of Data on Incest

When an act is prohibited by a taboo, people do not generally want to talk about it. The topic is rarely put on a questionnaire, and even if it were, self-reports are not reliable. Are respondents over- or underestimating their sexual experiences? When direct questions have been asked in various demographic samples, the rates of incest are typically much higher than estimates given by clinicians and agencies working with victims of sexual abuse. For example, the original Kinsey Report (Kinsey et al. 1948) shocked Americans because of what seemed like high rates of illicit sexual activity inside and outside the family. The findings of the report were discounted, presumably because they went against people's moral sensibilities and because some thought that individuals were bragging. Other studies that poll the public also find rather high rates of sexual abuse, although disentangling data on sexual abuse from actual incest by our restricted definition is infrequently performed by researchers (Fromuth and Burkhart 1987; Fritz, Stoll, and Wagner 1981; Finkelhor and Russell 1984; Finkelhor 1984a,b; Finkelhor, Hotaling, Lewis, and Smith 1990). For instance, some reports place rates of sexual abuse at well over 30 percent for girls and women, while others push it down to 16 percent of the population. Still other data using selective definitions of incest report rates that are less than 5 percent for brother–sister and father–daughter dyads, and well under 1 percent for the mother–son dyad.

Even when adults seek professional help from clinicians, where they implicitly are admitting to sexual abuse problems in their past, they are reluctant to talk about incest; and in many cases, repression has pushed from consciousness memories of incestuous acts. People come to clinicians with other symptoms, such as generalized anxiety and depression, but they are unsure as to why they feel the way we do. While we cannot know for sure, most people who have been victims of incest never see clinicians. Even if this conclusion is incorrect, it is impossible to know what percentage of victims seek clinical help, and consequently reports by clinicians are not representative of actual rates of incest in the general population.

There is, then, an obvious problem of drawing conclusions from data that report on something people do not generally wish to discuss or that come from polling techniques where individuals retrospectively reinterpret their sexual experiences in their nuclear families. If clinical reports are our guide, then rates of incest will, no doubt, be underestimated, whereas if surveys and polls are our source of data, it is difficult to know just what they mean, especially since sexual abuse and actual incest by our definition are not generally separated. Moreover, polls do not always distinguish among members of the nuclear family involved in incest; instead, aunts, uncles, grandparents, and cousins are simply categorized as "other" family members. Thus the data do not always provide information on what occurs in the nuclear family per se.

Another source of bias is that much of the data on relative rates of incest come from governmental agencies responsible for dealing with sexual abuse—police, social workers, public health officials, school counselors, and other agencies. Those who have financial resources are probably better able to hide their acts from authorities, whereas people with few resources are less able to avoid scrutiny. People in higher social classes have alternative avenues to health care, and they can pay professionals for assistance with the outcomes of incest without alerting authorities. Those in lower social classes must often rely on state-sponsored medicine or authorities in the schools and public health systems, thereby increasing the likelihood that their incest cases will be reported. Medical ethics, to say nothing about fears of lawsuits, will keep practitioners of the affluent quiet, while public officials who deal with the poor are often obligated by law to report on cases of sexual abuse. Thus a class bias exists in reporting of cases, and it is difficult to know if rates of incest among the three dyads of the nuclear family vary by social class. For example, if the lower social classes are more patriarchal, it is likely that rates for father–daughter incest are probably higher than mother–son or sibling incest. Still, we cannot know for sure if variations in the culture and structure of the family of different social classes influence significantly rates of incest for the dyads of the nuclear family.

Biases in the Gender of Therapists

Clinicians, especially psychiatrists, are still predominately male. It is hard to determine if gender produces a bias in recognizing and reporting on different forms of incest. The greatest number of cases of incest reported to clinicians involve the father–daughter dyad, but does this "fact" reflect the relative rates of incest for the three incestuous dyads in the nuclear family? Or, does it reflect a bias in who seeks clinical help? Alternatively, does it reflect a class bias of patients, as emphasized above? Or, does it signal a bias arising from the gender of clinicians? Do male clinicians "see" some forms of incest with greater regularity than female clinicians? We do not know, but we should remain aware of the potential for a gender bias.

Psychological Concomitants of Incest: Cause or Effect?

Since we are concerned with the effects of incest on its victims, we need to be sure that the psychological outcomes of incest are indeed that—outcomes—rather than causes of incest. It is clear from the literature that there are substantially more reports of psychosis among males who have had sex with their mothers than is the case for father–daughter or brother–sister incest. For the latter, anxiety disorders such as depression and posttraumatic stress syndrome are much more common than psychotic disorders. And, for mother–son incest there are so few clinical cases reported, it is difficult to determine precisely if there is a higher rate of psychosis for sons. But, even if the rate of severe psychopathology in mother–son incest is higher, as we believe it is, the question still remains: Is a psychotic boy more likely to have sexual relations with his mother, or did the psychosis emerge as an outcome of the incest? Moreover, even when a boy has exhibited psychotic symptoms before consummated sex with his mother, these symptoms may or may not be related to earlier overt and covert behavioral acts (as listed in table 3.1) between a mother and her son that have led over time to more severe mental health problems. Even though untangling the causes of a particular set of mental health symptoms in a son is problematic (Jennings 1993), we will argue later that mother–son incest produces much more severe pathological outcomes than does either father–daughter or brother–sister incest.

Homosexual Incest

Over the past two decades, there is a growing recognition that homosexual incest is more common than once thought. The overwhelming number of cases of homosexual incest, it appears, involves a father penetrating his son as part of a more general pattern of violence and abuse in the family. These patterns of homosexual incest are less central to our argument, but they do present problems in interpreting the data. Since most of these data report on child sexual abuse in general, rather than incest in particular, increases in homosexual incest will inevitably raise rates of victimization for both daughters and sons. In many studies the gender of the abuser is not specified nor, as noted earlier, is the abuser's place in the family always reported. The result is for rates of sexual abuse to increase without the ability to determine if indeed heterosexual incest has also increased.

Gender Roles and Incest

Cultural expectations for nurturance vary for men and women. Women are expected to be loving and caring which, in turn, means that they are likely to be more physically affectionate with their children. Furthermore, they are more likely to engage in touching behaviors associated with child care, such as cleaning up after defecation, bathing and washing children, drying them after a bath, dressing and undressing them, and so on. Thus it is often hard to separate the role of mother from acts that move toward incestuous behavior; consequently, there may be significant underreporting of rates of incest for mothers (Groth 1979; Justice and Justice 1979). Children themselves will often have difficulty in distinguishing motherly acts from incestuous acts, even when actual intercourse has occurred. And there is some evidence that males may feel less victimized by the sexual acts, short of intercourse, by their mothers toward them; and there is further speculation that cultural norms about masculinity work against males expressing "soft emotions," thereby causing them to underreport incidences of female sexual abuse and incest (Bogorad 1991; Crewdson 1988; Dimmock 1988; and Finkelhor 1984a). In fact, males may view reporting their victimization as a threat to their masculinity (Lewis 1988; Maltz and Holman 1987), thus making the "other side of feminism"—hypermale masculinity—a source of injustice to male victims of sexual abuse (Finkelhor 1984a; Banning 1989).

There is another cultural bias over gender roles. It is "unthinkable" that a mother would molest her "own children"; and while this prohibition applies to fathers as well, it is considered even more "unnatural" for a woman to engage in acts that harm her children. The result of this cultural belief about females is that they are less likely than males to be scrutinized by friends, authorities, and even clinicians. Mothers are simply "too maternal" to engage in incest and other harmful acts.

Sex and Incest

The fact that women do not possess a penis is important because of its effects on reports of incestuous behavior. Sexual contact with a son will involve arousing him to the point that he will penetrate her, but up to the actual penetration, the behaviors of a woman may seem ambiguous to a son, perhaps being interpreted as being a warm, affectionate mother. In contrast, when males have sexual interest in their children or sisters, the erect penis is a clear signal of the male's intentions. Moreover, because a victim of adult male child abuse does not have to become aroused for incest to occur, as is the case with son and his mother, incest becomes more likely because the male can force sexual intercourse on an unresponsive victim. Mothers cannot "rape" their sons in the same way that brothers and fathers can coerce their victims to have sex with them. Built into the biology of men and women, then, is a bias that influences the perception of sexual advances by victims and, no doubt, their reports of incest and sexual abuse.

Patriarchy and Incest

Feminist theorists have argued that father–daughter and, to a lesser extent, brother–sister incest reflect relations of patriarchy in the nuclear family. These forms of incest are consistent with the "man's right" to dominate social relations, including sexual acts, within the family. When patriarchal beliefs and structure about male domination are compounded by dysfunctional family life and substance abuse by family members, the power of the incest taboo is greatly weakened. As a result, men may perceive that it is "their right" to have sex with the female members of the household, including daughters, especially when critical judgment is impaired by emotional problems and substance abuse. Moreover, in a patriarchal family, a wife may not feel that she has any other option than to allow a male to have sex with her daughter—thus becoming the infamous "enabler." And such enabling may be especially likely if the wife has been subjected to both emotional and physical abuse by her husband, or if she also has substance dependency problems. Thus cultural beliefs in patriarchy, as these become manifest in the structure of nuclear family relations, can increase rates of incest beyond what they might be without patriarchy.

For our purposes, this argument is less central because our view is that nearly all prohibitions against adult male–initiated incest are culturally derived and have little basis in biology, whereas just the opposite is true for siblings and especially for mothers and sons. Still, if cultural beliefs lead to an increase in rates of incest beyond what they would "normally" be in a society without patriarchy, then some of our conclusions from the data might be problematic. Humans evolved in hunting and gathering bands where patriarchy generally did *not* exist to the degree evident in later societal types; and so, using contemporary rates of incest that have been fueled by centuries of patriarchy to speculate about what happened in the distant past among hunter-gatherers may pose the obvious bias of looking at the past through present-day eyeglasses. Perhaps the rates of incest evident under conditions of male dominance simply did not exist in the past as the incest taboo emerged, thereby making any conclusions about the evolution of the incest taboo suspect.

Another key point emphasized by feminists is that patriarchy often leads to an implicit "blaming" of girl victims of incest as "little seductresses" and adult women as "enablers" to their husband's abuse (Breines and Gordon 1983; Brownmiller 1975; Herman and Hirschman 1977; Rush 1980; Westerlund 1983). When women are seen as "partly responsible" for the incestuous behaviors of males, still another source of bias creeps into reports of incest. Girls may be reluctant to report acts of incest, lest they get blamed, while mothers who have condoned it will be cautious in making reports on their spouse's or even son's incestuous acts for fear of being called an enabler.

Conflation with Child Abuse

As we mentioned, the problem of conflating child abuse, child sexual abuse, and incest runs through the literature. Indeed, as the child abuse establishment has gained a hearing with the public, academics, and governmental agencies, this fusion has become even more extensive. The result is that it is now difficult in most research reports to separate incest from child abuse, particularly as definitions of incest have been broadened to the point of being almost coextensive with child sexual abuse. And this problem is even more acute for the data that we seek: reports of *actual intercourse* between the incestuous dyads of the nuclear family.

Another kind of conflation, also mentioned above, is that the gender of the perpetrator is not always specified, nor is the relationship of the perpetrator to the victim consistently reported. Even when the perpetrator is seen as a "family member," the data often fail to make clear if this member is part of the nuclear family or an outside relative. As a consequence, the data on child abuse and, if reported, incest cannot be used in any precise way to assess the rates of incest among the heterosexual dyads within the nuclear family.

Dysfunctional Families

Child sexual abuse was for several decades on the rise, at least in the United States. Some of this increase may simply be a reflection of better reporting to officials of agencies interested in ferreting out child abuse. The more recent leveling of reported cases may now reflect the fact that agencies have gained as much purchase as they can on flushing out cases. Even with the leveling, however, child sexual abuse is apparently on the rise in the modern nuclear family; and this inflation is probably the result of an increase in dysfunctional families in contemporary societies. Drug use, alcoholism, violence, and other activities appear to be on the upswing over the past half century, although, again, this increase may simply be an artifact of stepped-up reporting of abuse in families. We do not want to portray families of the past in overly romantic terms, for they certainly revealed violence and other pathologies. Yet, it is unlikely that preindustrial families revealed as much instability as contemporary families, although we cannot know for sure.[3]

If the stability and viability of nuclear families has declined, then

3. The nuclear family in preindustrial times was more embedded in the bilateral extended family along with more tightly knit community networks. Since farming was the primary occupation before the industrial age, husband and wife were likely to have segregated (rather than joint) conjugal roles, thereby allowing each spouse considerable emotional support and resources from their own strong tie networks.

sexual abuse of many kinds may increase as a symptom of problems in the family. As a result, using contemporary data—as incomplete and varied as they are—to establish baseline rates of incest for the dyads of the nuclear family as it first emerged in human societies becomes highly problematic. The present state of the family, and the incredible pressures it must withstand in contemporary societies, is perhaps not a very good telescope for examining the past structure of the nuclear family (for a discussion see Erickson 2005).

Coupled with the growth of agencies devoted to discovering abuse in families, the combination of increased dysfunction in families and increasing numbers of agencies dealing with these dysfunctions means that reports of sexual abuse will inevitably rise. Does this rise in reported cases of incest reflect actual increases in dysfunction over the past, or just more awareness of family problems and more activism by public and private agencies to address these dysfunctions? Whatever the answers are to these questions, they affect reported rates of incest today and make comparisons with the more immediate past difficult, to say nothing of the ancestral past at the beginnings of the nuclear family. If we use present-day rates of incest to speculate about the past, can we be sure that the lenses of our telescope are not highly distorted?

The increase in homosexual incest—or, again, the reporting of homosexual incest—may further distort data of child sexual abuse and incest as it is reported in various data sets. Much homosexual incest appears to be part of a general pattern of physical abuse of sons by fathers. The same is apparently true of mothers and daughters, where reports on this form of homosexual incest have swelled dramatically as part of a larger pattern of child abuse. Thus, using reports on the trends of incest over the past thirty years as a baseline for developing our argument is fraught with the confluence of dysfunctional families, rising rates of child abuse in general, and increased reporting of homosexual incest.

Differential Reporting

As noted earlier, males appear to be less likely to report incest than females, and in some clinical studies, they may repress memories of incest more than female victims do. Part of this difference may be accounted for by the gender-centric focus of much of the literature on father violence and sexual abuse. The data reveal that males overwhelmingly commit aggressive acts of sexual abuse, but the sudden rise in reporting of female acts of sexual abuse may not signal so much an increase in actual female abuse but a concerted effort by researchers and agencies to get at the unreported abuse that had always occurred. Another part of the reason for the gender bias in reports of male sexual abuse is that male ideologies often prevent men from admitting the sexual abuse because sex is something "they are supposed to control." Moreover, for a long time, it was difficult to make officials and clinicians believe reports of female incest with sons because it was presumed that women would not do such a thing. Indeed, this problem of disbelief existed at the very beginnings of the past century and, in fact, forced Sigmund Freud to qualify his early theory about mother–son incest as the cause of clinical hysteria in young boys. Apparently his conclusion that Victorian mothers were having sex with their sons made his fellow therapists feel uncomfortable, to say nothing of offending Victorian sensibilities. Consequently Freud recast his theory and postulated that perhaps sons and mothers had "fantasies" about sex rather than actual intercourse.

These biases still exist and reflect perceptions of gendered parental roles. Added to these gender differences is the fact that most acts of incest within the nuclear family go unreported because of the strong emotional bonds between parents and children; much of the apparent increase in rates of sexual abuse in general and incest in particular may simply be an outcome of agencies dipping into a previously unreported pool of incest.

Differential reporting of incest is particularly evident for sibling incest. Parents often prefer to "deal with" the problem in the home. As a result, what may be the most common form of incest is dramatically underreported. Any increase in the rate of brother–sister incest may be a result of dipping into a formerly untracked pool, or alternatively, it might mean that the actual rate of incest has increased. It is difficult to know for sure because a large proportion of brother–sister cases of incest is hidden from authorities and even clinicians (De Young 1985).

For these and perhaps other reasons, we must be cautious in reporting rates of incest because there are no hard data on rates. Instead, we must rely on clinical reports, small-scale studies, various surveys, polling studies, and literature reviews that seek to assemble the relevant case studies and survey research. Another source of data comes from both private and public clearinghouses that assemble data on child sexual abuse. All these sources present the issues enumerated above. They are rife with problems of reporting and interpretation. Still, if we are to talk about incest at all, we must use what information is available. It can be argued, of course, that our entire argument here and in subsequent chapters is based upon faulty data, or the absence of compelling data; and to some extent, this criticism has merit. Fortunately there are discernible patterns in the data. And while these patterns might simply be an artifact of the methodological issues reviewed above, we do not think so, as we explain below.

RELATIVE INCIDENCE OF INCEST

There is a large literature on the outcomes of sexual abuse on its victims, but, as with reports on rates of incest, it is hard to unravel the effects of abuse in general from incest in particular. Despite these difficulties, we will attempt a review for (1) the relative power of the taboo for the heterosexual dyads (mother–son, broth-er–sister, and father–daughter) in the nuclear family, (2) the rela-tive rates of incest among members of these dyads, and (3) the relative psychological effects of incest on victims in these dyads. Let us begin with an assessment of the strength of the taboo on the dyads of the nuclear family.

The Relative Strength of the Incest Taboo

The taboo against incest among the dyads of the nuclear family is not universal because people in many societies cannot imagine that incest would occur, thus making it unnecessary to have a taboo for acts that do not transpire or are not perceived to occur. Yet, even though a normative taboo is not explicitly stated, virtually every society prohibits sexual relations among members of the nuclear family (Murdock 1949). The few exceptions often noted, such as those in the royal families of ancient Egypt (Middleton 1962), are just that: exceptions and confined to the ruling families. More-over, while marriage with near kin may have been permitted among elites in a few societies, we do not know if such marriages oc-curred with great frequency or if they were consummated by in-cestuous intercourse. Furthermore, there is no evidence that incest and marriage between members of nuclear families among the general populace was ever permitted. Some researchers have noted that incest was tolerated among villagers in Africa and even sub-cultures in the United States (Meiselman 1978, 2), but evidence of actual incest is scarce. In Murdock's (1949) work based on his human relations area files (HRAF), incest prohibitions are found to be universal in all 250 societies included in the HRAF at that time. Indeed, Murdock (1949, 288) emphasized that "incest taboos and exogamous restrictions . . . are characterized by a peculiar intensity and emotional quality." Some societies specified penalties, often death, for violating the taboo; and while other societies had no explicitly stated taboo or punishments, nonconjugal sexual relations among family members were so "unthinkable" that an explicit taboo and specification of punishments were unnecessary because sexual avoidance between mother and sons, fathers and daughters, and siblings had been completely internalized. In one early study by a sociologist using HRAF to explore punishment for deviations from sexual mores (J. Brown 1952), every society was found to take disciplinary action for incest when it became known, although many societies had to be excluded from the sample because they never experienced incest and hence did not need to punish what never happened. Incest was the second most sanctioned sexual deviation, right behind abduction of a married woman. The sentences specified for incest were at about the same level of severity as those for raping a married woman.

While some authors quibble over the universality of the taboo, citing examples where incest was tolerated in theory among upper social classes or where no explicit rule can be found for a preliterate population because the prohibition was so internalized that it did not have to be stated as an explicit rule, the most reasonable interpretation of these data is that prohibitions against sexual relations among mothers and sons, fathers and daughters, and siblings are universal. The taboo has probably been part of human societies since the first nuclear families of parents and children were created, and indeed the taboo was essential for a stable family. The universality of the taboo does not, however, explain apparent variations in its strength for the incestuous dyads in the nuclear family. These variations are, to some extent, a reflection of whether or not the taboo is aligned with biological avoidance patterns evident in primates and humans, but we will wait to examine this question in later chapters. Another reason for variation in the taboo is its relationship to other normative systems regulating the family, as we explain below.

The incest taboo never stands alone in a cultural environment. Other normative systems influence the relative strength of the taboo, and so we should assess how other norms intersect with the incest taboo, either weakening its power or reinforcing the interdictions in the taboo. At times, the incest taboo is amplified by more general prohibitions against child abuse; and we should expect that societies with powerful rules against child abuse, especially involving sexual relations with children, would also have strong taboos against mother–son, older brother–younger sister, and father–daughter dyads as well as homosexual relations between older and younger members of the family. Hence, mother–son and father–daughter sexual relations are more likely to be strongly tabooed because they are the most likely to involve child sexual abuse, whereas the taboo should be less strong for siblings because they are more likely to be approximately the same age. Indeed, some have argued that the taboo for siblings is so much weaker than the taboo for the other two incestuous dyads that it goes unreported by parents who prefer to deal with the problem within the confines of the home rather than alert authorities.

Norms about parental nurturance, or more generally adult nurturance of children, also intersect with the incest taboo. Nurturance norms are generally much more constraining on women than men, and hence a mother who is not warm and supportive of her children will be seen as violating nurturance norms more than a father. Such norms may increase the strength of the incest taboo against mother–son sexual relations by emphasizing the importance of a mother's role in emotionally supporting her children. If a mother had sex with her son, this act would disrupt bonds of nurturance, confusing her son and creating problems associated not only with the incest taboo but also powerful gender norms about the proper behavior of mothers toward their children. Some of the extra weight of the mother–son taboo might be accounted for by the implicit recognition that breaking bonds of maternal nurturance is especially harmful to children. The same could be argued for mother–daughter homosexual incest, which is apparently more common than once thought. As we mentioned earlier, mother–daughter homosexual incest is probably more common than mother–son incest; and by some accounts it may have more severe psychological effects on girls than father–daughter incest (Goodwin 1982; Goodwin and DiVasto 1979).

Other norms, such as a preference for marriage partners to be approximately the same age, may also influence the intensity of the incest taboo. While most cultures prescribe marriage within the same age class, these norms are generally far more restrictive for women than men. A male can usually marry someone much younger without undo sanctioning, whereas a woman is not afforded the same freedom. Such marriage and sexual partner norms put more normative weight on mothers than fathers in seeking sexual partners who are a generation younger.

Another set of rules affecting intensity of the incest taboo revolves around patriarchy. In patriarchal societies, standards allow, and indeed even encourage, men to dominate women. In this cultural climate, it is likely that rates of father–daughter and brother–sister incest would be higher than in societies evidencing more sexual equality.

Table 3.2 summarizes the directive forces at work in generating proscriptions against incest. The plus and minus signs indicate the direction of norms, either toward or against sexual relations between the potentially incestuous heterosexual dyads of the nuclear family. The incest taboo is, of course, the most powerful prohibition; and other norms either support the incest taboo or mitigate its power. For brother–sister incest, the taboo is not contradicted by any other norm that applies to sons, although patriarchal norms may diminish the power of the taboo. For father–daughter incest, the incest taboo is reinforced by norms against child abuse and norms promoting parental nurturance of their offspring, but this additive power of norms is mitigated by norms of patriarchy and norms allowing males to have sexual relations and marry women from a younger age class. Moreover, norms of nurturance often do not apply to males, and even when they do, the normative prescriptions about emotional support of children are not as strong for men as they are for women. Only for mother–son incest is the taboo supported by *all* other norms. The incest taboo appears to be stronger for the mother–son dyad than all others, and this stronger taboo is supported by norms revolving around child abuse, patriarchy, sexual relations across age classes, and nurturance. Mothers are to be nurturing toward their children, and hence the norms against child abuse are particularly powerful for women. Women are not supposed to have sexual relations with younger males. And norms of patriarchy emphasize that women are to be dutiful to the authority of their husbands and, by extension, are not to disrupt this authority relationship by placing a son in sexual competition with the patriarch of the family. Thus, by doing a rough algebraic summation of the pluses and minuses, we would expect normative proscriptions and prescriptions to add up to very strong normative prohibitions against mother–son incest, strong prohibition against father–daughter incest, and moderate-to-strong prohibitions against brother–sister incest.

Table 3.2 Incest and Other Normative Systems

Dyad	Incest taboo	Norms against child abuse	Norms of patriarchy	Norms pertaining to sexual relations across age classes	Norms of parental nurturance	Sum total of normative pressures against incest
Brother–sister	–		+			moderate to strong prohibition
Father–daughter	–	–	+	+	–	strong prohibition
Mother–son	–	–	–	–	–	very strong prohibition

+ = norm operates to increase likelihood of sexual relations
– = norm operates to decrease likelihood of sexual relations

The patterns in table 3.2 suggest that the incest taboo varies in strength for different dyads; and while it is difficult to document with the available evidence, the intensity of the taboo appears to vary. Sibling incest in probably the least tabooed. Father–daughter incest is next, and mother–son incest is the most intensely tabooed of all, often eliciting responses of horror that a mother could be so "unmotherly." For example, in American society even a hint of flirtation between a mother and her adolescent son elicits critical attention, whereas flirtatious play between a father and his adolescent daughter is usually viewed as simply what it appears to be. These varying levels of intensity for different members of the nuclear family cannot be explained by normative codification of concerns about inbreeding depression because offspring of all three dyads would evidence equally harmful biological effects (as each dyad shares 50 percent of their genes). In fact, as Meiselman (1978, 24) points out, the mother–son dyad is the least likely to produce harmful offspring because a mother is often past child-bearing age when her son reaches puberty (Slater 1959). Thus the relative strength of the taboo does not reflect biological concerns but appears to be related to how the normative systems of a culture line up, either strengthening the taboo or mitigating against some of its power.

Relative Rates of Incest

The strength of the taboo should have some effect on rates of incest in the nuclear family. Because the taboo for brothers and sisters is the weakest, we might expect higher rates of incest between members of this dyad than for mother–son and father–daughter incest. It was once thought that consummated sexual relations between brothers and sisters were rather rare, but increasingly it is evident that the incest rate between siblings is much higher than previously believed—probably even higher than father–daughter incest, although the evidence is far from conclusive. Since the taboo and other normative systems work to produce strong prohibitions against father–daughter incest, it should not be as high as brother–sister incest, but it should be more prevalent than mother–son incest, since all the normative systems reinforce the incest taboo for the mother–son dyad. The data clearly indicate that such is the case, although mother–son incest may occur more frequently than previously believed. Incest between father and daughter may violate the taboo against sexual relations but not the norms giving fathers rights to dominate women and to have sexual access to younger women. Thus some of the effectiveness of the incest taboo can potentially be reduced by norms of patriarchy that allow men to dominate women sexually and by norms sanctioning sex and marriage to younger women in different age cohorts. These two sets of norms, however, can be counterbalanced by other powerful norms, such as those associated with religion or the state as well as by the capacity of nonfamily members to monitor activities in the nuclear family (as is common in traditional societies).

While the above conclusions are, we believe, supported by the data, caution is in order because of the problems evident with all data on incest. To be sure that we have drawn the correct conclusions, we should summarize the kinds of data that are available and what they appear to say. Let us begin with sibling incest.

Brother–Sister Incest

At one time, it was thought that brother–sister incest did not occur with great frequency. Instead, a certain amount of sexual experimentation was often considered "normal" but this "sexual play" did not lead to incest. It is now clear that brother–sister incest is a much more common occurrence than once believed.[4] Some even argue that brother–sister incest is more frequent than stepfather–stepdaughter incest (Green 1988; H. Smith 1987), which had previously been thought to be the dyad with the highest rate of incest. Lindzey's (1967) and Lester's (1972) reanalysis of the Kinsey data argued that sibling incest is five times higher than the rate of parent-initiated incest. This latter conclusion may be overestimating the rate of sibling incest, especially if incest is defined as actual intercourse rather than sexual play (Russell 1988; Finkelhor 1980c). But it is now evident that brother–sister incest is common and occurs more frequently than mother–son incest and in all likelihood father–daughter incest as well but probably not as frequently as stepfather–stepdaughter incest.

Like many forms of incest, sibling sexual intercourse occurs in dysfunctional families that already exhibit high levels of violence,

---

4. Adler and Schutz 1995; Canavan and Meyer 1992; Peterson 1992; Cole 1990; Wiehe 1990; Daie et al. 1989; De Jong 1989; Finkelhor 1981; Laviola 1989; Smith and Israel 1987; Pierce and Pierce 1985; De Young 1985; Lindzey 1967; Lester 1972; Finkelhor 1980a.

drug and alcohol use, and child abuse (Wiehe 1997). In many cases of sibling incest, the father is absent for much of the time (Kubo 1959); and in other cases, the son's initiation of incest had been preceded by parental incest with children.[5] In such families, which also tend to be patriarchal, the son is often the recipient of violence and abuse, and at puberty he begins to act out his anger and engage in sexual violence against his sister. In a great percentage of cases, the son is described as a bully; and while some sibling incest emerges from sexual play, most incest involving actual intercourse is coerced by a dominating brother over his younger sister (De Young 1982a). The data on sibling incest clearly put into question Edward Westermarck's (1891) assertion that an innate predisposition for sexual indifference exists for those raised together. Perhaps in highly dysfunctional families the mechanisms for sexual avoidance hypothesized by Westermarck cannot be activated. Alternatively, the accumulated aggression in a son against his maltreatment, coupled with substance abuse and other behavioral problems, may simply overwhelm this proclivity. Indeed, Westermarck himself emphasized that "there are circumstances in which a natural sentiment may be blunted or overcome" ([1891] 1922, vol. 11, 203). Whatever the exact cause of sibling incest in contemporary families, clearly the Westermarck effect is not sufficiently powerful or fails to be activated during those critical early years.

Father–Daughter Incest

Father–daughter incest is more likely to occur in families with a patriarchal structure and with high levels of wife dependency and passivity. The fathers in such families exhibit an authoritarian personality, weak ego control, patterns of physical abuse of other family members, and alcoholism.[6] Many have argued that father–daughter incest is the most common form (Willner 1983), with

---

5. De Young 1985; Raphling, Carpenter, and Davis 1967; Eist and Mandel 1968; Magal and Winnick 1963; Weinberg 1955.

6. For reviews of the characteristics of offenders and the family structures where father–daughter incest occurs, see Anderson and Shafer 1979; T. Cohen 1983; Cormier, Kennedy, and Sangowicz 1962; De Young 1981a,b, 1982a; Herman and Hirschman 1981; Kaufman, Peck, and Tagiuri 1954; Lukianowicz 1972; Magal and Winnick 1963; Maisch 1972; Meiselman 1978; Finkelhor 1979a; Herman 1983, 1981a,b; McIntyre 1981; Renshaw 1982; Spencer 1981; Dietz and Craft 1980.

stepfather–stepdaughter incest occurring at seven times the rate of biological father–biological daughter incest. This differential between fathers and stepfathers could be perhaps explained by the Westermarck effect, although the relatively high rates of father–daughter incest clearly indicate that this effect is not sufficient to inhibit incest for this dyad, perhaps because it cannot be fully activated in fathers who are not young when their daughters are growing up. Patterns of patriarchy, coupled with other dysfunctional activities among family members, overwhelm whatever power the Westermarck effect has for adults or, as is the case with sibling incest, prevent its activation in a derailed nuclear family.

Mother–Son Incest

It is impossible to get an accurate rate of incest between mothers and sons, but by scanning some of the few available studies reporting on this type of incest, we can get a sense of its frequency compared with the other incestuous dyads in the nuclear family.[7] Kubo (1959) reports one case of mother–son incest in twenty-nine incestuous families; Weinberg (1955) discusses two cases in two hundred and three incestuous families; Lukianowicz (1972) found three cases in twenty-nine patients; Meiselman (1978) saw just two cases in fifty-eight participants in her review; Finkelhor (1979a) found that 14 percent of the cases involved a female but did not distinguish between mothers and other women, and in another review (Finkelhor 1984a), 9 percent of the cases involved abuse by a mother (without, however, fully disentangling abuse and incest by our narrow definition); Pierce and Pierce (1985) found one case of mother–son incest in twenty-five cases of child abuse reported to a telephone hotline; McCarty (1986) found that among twenty-six female sexual offenders of their children, eight had molested their sons; Vander Mey and Neff (1986) discovered no mother–son victims of incest in their review of fifteen cases, although 5 percent of the abusers were women; Condy, Templer, Brown, and Veaco (1987) note that among 349 college men and 157 inmates convicted of rape, three men of the college and three inmates had been sexually abused by their mothers; in a survey, Green (1988) found no cases of mother–son sexual abuse, while reporting that 1 percent of the sexual abuse involved a father and 15 percent a sibling in the family; Dimmock (1988)

---

7. See Miletski 1995 for an annotated review of the literature.

reports that four of twenty-five males identified as victims of sexual abuse were victimized by their mothers; Allen (1991) reports that of twenty-two female sex offenders, thirteen of the cases committed sexual acts on their sons or foster sons; Harrison reports that of the 8,663 calls in the United Kingdom to a helpline, 9 percent of the perpetrators reported were women, but only 34 percent of these perpetrators were mothers (but the sex of the victim was not reported); Sgrori and Sargent (1993) found ten cases of female sexual perpetrators of abuse, but only one case of mother–son incest was exposed; Thomas and Stamertiow (1993) note that 29 percent of cases to a child abuse hotline in Japan were victims of mother–son incest; and Trocme and Wolfe (2001) found only 3 percent of cases of sexual abuse were by females but did not distinguish between mothers and other females or clearly identify the gender of the victim.

Obviously none of these studies is definitive, but clearly mother–son incest is comparatively rare, especially if sexual abuse and actual incestuous intercourse between a mother and her son could be definitively disentangled in each study. Even among female sexual abuse offenders, the incidence of mother–son exploitation is lower than the rate of abuse by other members of the family, and even lower for actual incest by our definition. Thus, while we cannot state an absolute rate of incest, mother–son incest appears much less common than incest in the other two dyads of the nuclear family. Indeed, although incest between mothers and sons is probably underreported, it is still a rather rare occurrence (Francoeur 1991; Jones et al. 1985; Russell 1984; Shengold 1989; Ward 1984).

There is a large literature touching on mother–son incest, oddly enough because it is so rare and yet of such great interest. Mothers who initiate incest with their offspring have generally been raised in chaotic and dysfunctional families, have low self-esteem, use and abuse alcohol, evidence mental illnesses, and, within their own nuclear families, reveal considerable ambiguity of their role vis-à-vis other family members.[8,9]

---

8. De Young 1982a; Finch 1973; Forward and Buck 1978; Frances and Frances 1976; Justice and Justice 1979; Meiselman 1978; Wahl 1960; Shelton 1975.

9. For some general reviews of women as sexual abusers, including but not confined to incest, see Allen 1990; Banning 1989; Bolton, Morris, and MacEachron 1989; Finkelhor and Russell 1984; Faller 1987; O'Conner 1987; Vander Mey 1988; Johnson and Shrier 1987; and Knopp and Lackey 1987.

In sum, then, rates of incest are much higher for the father–daughter and brother–sister dyads than for the mother–son dyad, and dramatically so. It is likely that brother–sister incest is more frequent than father–daughter incest, but the data are not definitive on this score. Stepfather–stepdaughter incest is probably the most common form, despite some claims that brother–sister incest occurs more often. Thus there are differential rates of incest among these dyads, with a clear difference between male- and female-initiated incest.

The Psychological Effects of Incest

The psychological effects of nuclear family incest on the younger person in the heterosexual dyads vary. In general, boys suffer more severe psychological outcomes from mother–son incest than do either daughters or sisters. The effects on daughters and sisters appear to be about the same, increasing in intensity when the sex is coerced, when it comes early (Adams-Tucker 1982; Courtois 1979), and when it is long-term. These generalizations are, however, not without some ambiguity stemming from the sources of the data. The most detailed evidence comes from clinical settings, and there is an obvious sample bias here: a sample of individuals who are suffering to the point of seeking professional help naturally excludes all those who did not suffer adversely and/or who did not or could not seek professional help. Still, assuming that variations in the clinical data are a rough indicator of the relative severity of the psychological effects, the most reasonable conclusion is that, on average, sons in mother–son incest experience far greater psychological problems than daughters and sisters in incestuous relationships. There are some explicit efforts to compare male and female victims of sexual abuse, but these efforts generally do not employ our definition of incest as actual sexual intercourse, and so it is difficult to be sure that these data can answer our query about the psychological effects of incest revolving around actual sexual intercourse.[10]

---

10. Watkins and Bentovim 1992; Gordon 1990; Hunter 1991; DeJong 1985; Faller 1989; Farber, Showers, Johnson, Joseph, and Oshins 1984; Fritz, Stoll, and Wagner 1981; Pierce and Pierce 1985; Adams-Tucker 1982, Burgess et al. 1981; Spencer and Dunklee 1986.

Brother–Sister Incest

Because a sister is generally not in a dependent relationship with her brother, especially compared to her father, and because the taboo against brother–sister incest is not as strong as it is for the other heterosexual dyads of the nuclear family, the psychological effects of incest for sisters are seemingly less severe than for the other two incestuous dyads (Meiselman 1978). The fact that sibling incest is reported less than father–daughter incest, even though it may occur as often or even more frequently than father–daughter incest, is one indicator that the psychological outcomes do not lead to severe psychopathology for sisters. The primary effects appear to be low self-esteem, inappropriate sexual responses (Laviola 1992), trouble with establishing meaningful sexual relations as an adult, and anxiety disorders such as depression and posttraumatic stress syndrome.[11] Of course, these are hardly pleasant psychological outcomes, and they can bring about a greatly diminished quality of life for some victims, but they are not as severe as those for mother–son incest. In fact, numerous reviews of studies have reported relatively minor or no serious psychological effects on women who have been in incestuous relationships with their brothers.[12] To the degree that the incest is coerced early and is long-term, the psychological effects become more extreme, perhaps reaching the same level of severity as in father–daughter incest.

Father–Daughter Incest

The list of psychopathologies for daughters in an incestuous relationship with their father or stepfather is long: anxiety, phobic behavior, sleeping disorders, suicidal tendencies, somatic complaints, promiscuity and acting out of sex, sexual aggression, low self-esteem, depression, guilt, shame, antisocial behaviors, substance abuse, and in a few cases more serious psychotic reactions (Beek and van der Kolk 1987).[13] Some have argued through reviews of the literature and from their own studies that female victims have

---

11. Cyr et al. 2002; Mireille et al. 2002; Daie et al. 1989; Weinberg 1955; Sloane and Karpinski 1942.

12. Finkelhor 1980c; De Young 1985; Gebhard et al. 1965; Kubo 1959; Lukianowicz 1972; Magal and Winnick 1963; Meiselman 1978.

13. For a sampling of assessments on psychological outcomes for daughters, see Peleikis et al. 2004; Zlotnick et al. 2001; Chelf and Ellis 2002; Wilken 2002; Haj-Yahia and Tamish 2001; Johnson et al. 2001; Talbot et al. 2000; Ruggiero

less severe psychopathologies than male victims of incest.[14] In addition to the psychopathologies with incestuous acts, daughters in the family also experience a considerable amount of stress because they must deal with role reversals in their relationships with both fathers and mothers and because generational boundary lines become blurred. Moreover, the roles of other family members also change when mothers collude to facilitate the incest and when fathers and occasionally mothers become increasingly paranoid about outsiders discovering the family secret.[15] These behavioral changes by other family members only compound the crushing strain and anxiety for daughters.[16]

What emerges from these diverse sources of information is that daughters develop mild to severe neuroses but rarely become psychotic. In fact, we found virtually no accounts of daughters becoming severely psychotic as a result of incest with their father or stepfather. They are often unhappy, anxious, and depressed; they often have difficulty establishing and maintaining normal sexual relations with men, even their spouse; and they typically reveal more general behavioral problems that make adjustments to normal living difficult. But rarely are they unbalanced to the point of requiring institutionalization.

Mother–Son Incest

Despite the interest in mother–son incest, information on rates and outcomes is scarce, especially if we stick to the definition of

---

(note 13 continued) et al. 2000; Tsun 1999; Rudd and Herzberger 1999; Fleming et al. 1999; Alexander et al. 1998; Calam et al. 1998; Sariola and Uutela 1996; Brayton et al. 1995; Bigras 1966; De Young 1985; Knittle and Tuana 1980; Herman 1981a,b, 1977; Herman and Hirschman 1981, 1977; Justice and Justice 1979; Meiselman 1978; Westermeyer 1978; James 1977; Molnar and Cameron 1975; and Gordon 1955.

14. Yorukaglu and Kemph 1996; Koch 1980; Cepada 1978; Henderson 1983, 1972; Rascovsky and Rascovsky 1950; and Shultz 1980.

15. For statements on changes in the family that come with father–daughter incest, see De Young 1985; Eist and Mandel 1968; Gordon and O'Keefe 1984; Gutheil and Avery 1977; Heims and Kaufman 1963; Janas 1983; Justice and Justice 1979; MacFarlane and Korbin 1983; Messer 1969; Erickson 2005; Raphling et al. 1967; Rhinehart 1961; Burgess et al. 1978.

16. For more sociological treatments of father–daughter incest and its outcomes for both the individual and family structure, see Schultz and Jones 1983; Julian and Mohr 1979; Scheurell and Rinder 1973; Kubo 1959; Weinberg 1955; Davis 1949; Riemer 1940; and Erickson 2005.

incest that is guiding our inquiry. Also, in some cases of mother–son incest, the son initiates the sexual contact but typically only after a prolonged period of sexually charged behaviors (see table 3.1) by his mother. Furthermore, some mothers are very mentally ill, and as De Young (1985, 92) emphasizes, her "son is likely to later develop a serious psychopathology as a consequence of the incest." If we list the psychological outcomes by the descriptive words used in various studies on mother–son incest, we can get a sense for the psychopathologies experienced by sons who have incestuous relations with their mother: withdrawn and quiet, antisocial to the point of needing hospitalization, suicidal, borderline psychotic, fully psychotic, schizophrenic, acute behavioral problems, severe dissociative states, murder of perpetrators, narcissistic personality disorder, and sexual dysfunctions.[17] If we compare this list of psychopathologies to those for daughters and sisters, the problems are much more grave for victims of mother–son incest than father–daughter or brother–sister incest. A much larger percentage of sons involved in mother–son incest exhibit psychopathologies that can be classified as psychotic, and even problems falling under neuroses appear to be more serious. Of course, a majority of males in incestuous relations with their mothers do not become psychotic, but the percentage who do is far greater than that for other forms of incest, although some have suggested that daughters in homosexual incestuous relations with their mothers also exhibit much more serious psychopathologies than daughters in father–daughter relations (suggesting that the mother's violation of bonds of nurturance and trust cause severe emotional problems for both males and females).

Many cases report far less pathological outcomes than the list above suggests. These outcomes can be grouped under generalized anxiety disorders that are not much more intense than those evident for sisters and daughters.[18] Still, in looking over the information as it now exists in the literature, it is not an exaggeration to conclude that, on average, sons who have had incestuous relations with their mothers evidence more severe psychopathologies

---

17. These terms were pulled from the following sources: Kelly et al. 2002; Rudominer 2002; Gold et al. 1999; Mars 1992; Gabbard and Twemlow 1994; Bachmann, Moggi, and Stirnemann-Lewis 1994; Bachmann and Bossi 1993; Watkins and Bentovim 1992; Hunter 1990; Krug 1989; Shengold 1989; Kenney 1987; Lewis 1986; Kempe and Henry 1984; Meiselman 1978; Nasjleti 1980; Justice and Justice 1979; Masters and Johnson 1976; and Lukianowicz 1972.

18. For references on nonpsychotic cases, see Wilken 2002; Rudominer 2002; Margolis 1984; Shengold 1980; Catanzarite and Combs 1980; Armstrong 1978.

than either sisters or daughters involved in incestuous relationships with their brothers and fathers. Almost all of the reports on psychopathologies in the sexual abuse on borderline or full-blown psychosis are for males who have incestuous relations with their mothers. Of course, there is a potential sampling bias in these data stemming from the fact that only the severely disturbed seek clinical help or come to the attention of authorities, but this bias should be the same across all of the incestuous dyads in the nuclear family. If sons need more clinical help than sisters and daughters or if severely impaired sons come to the attention of mental health authorities more often than sisters and daughters, it is probably because the incest has had a greater psychological effect on them. Consequently the most reasonable conclusion from the literature is that mother–son incest generates more severe psychopathologies than either father–daughter or brother–sister incest. We need an explanation as to why this should be the case.

CONCLUSION

The methodological problems with the data available on incest are many. These problems begin with the definition of incest which, over the years, has become increasingly inclusive. In contrast, we have gone back to a much more restrictive definition: sexual intercourse between the mother–son, father–daughter, and brother–sister dyads. Once we move very far beyond this definition, we begin to climb up the slippery slope of all forms of sexual abuse becoming defined as incest. The relative power of the taboo on different dyads, as well as the degree to which other norms reinforce or work at cross purposes with the incest taboo, affect not only actual rates of incest but also differential reporting by males and females on their sexual experiences with other members of their family.

The information sources on incest are diverse, unreliable, and biased. Moreover, the data do not always make clear whether the effects of incest are a cause or a consequence of sexual acts. And the rediscovery of homosexual incest has further distorted the rates of incest on male and female victims, or at the very least, further embedded heterosexual incest within additional categories of child abuse. The gender of the therapists and other authorities who deal with child abuse certainly has some effect on the data, as do different expectations for the roles of mothers and fathers in the nuclear family. More general norms about how males and females should manage emotions, even those intense emotions associated with incest, lead to variations in reporting that further distort the data. The increasing conflation of incest and sexual abuse or even child abuse in general increasingly makes it difficult to unpack the data and isolate these data sets on incest per se, especially our strict definition of incest. Feminist analyses of patriarchy generated new and important insights on the dynamics of incest, but they have also confounded how the data are reported and interpreted. The biology of men and women (e.g., the existence of a penis among men and the ability to generate an erection that penetrates the female) make incest on the part of women much more difficult to determine than for men; and this simple biological fact has a considerable effect on reported rates of incest. And finally, what many see as the growing pathologies of individuals and families in contemporary societies have probably increased rates of all forms of abuse and sexual abuse, including incest.

This last fact has important consequences for our arguments on the origin of the taboo in a nuclear family structure that was, no doubt, different 150,000 years ago than it is today. Contemporary family members would seem to be under greater levels of stress leading to more psychopathologies than members of families in the distant past, and so it becomes problematic to use incidences of incest today to make inferences about tendencies toward incest in humans' evolutionary past.

It might be argued, with some justification, that these methodological problems in the data on incest are insurmountable and we should abandon our project, making this a very short book. Our analysis is speculative and perhaps doubly so given the sorry state of knowledge about rates of incest and effects of incest on individuals within the nuclear family. Yet we must use what data are available if we are to address the questions guiding our analysis. Moreover, we do not need absolute rates of incest or effects of incest; rather, all we require for our argument are *relative rates* on which type of incest is more or less tabooed, which types of incest are more common than other forms of incest, and which incestuous relationships generate more severe psychopathologies than other forms of incest. When relative assessments are made, the following seem to be the most reasonable conclusions:

1. All forms of nuclear-family incest are prohibited in every known society, but mother–son incest is more prohibited than either father–daughter or brother–sister incest, with sibling incest being the least tabooed.

2. Brother–sister incest is much more frequent than mother–son incest, and it is likely that this form of incest occurs more often than father–daughter (with the question of whether or not it transpires more frequently than stepfather–stepdaughter incest being left open). Thus, father–daughter and brother–sister incest are much more common—by a significant factor—than mother–son incest.

3. Mother–son incest generates far more serious psychopathologies than does either brother–sister or father–daughter incest. Virtually all cases of severe mental illness toward the psychotic pole come from reports on mother–son incestuous relations. Most males in mother–son incestuous relationships do not become severely mentally ill, but a certain percentage do, and this percentage is far greater than for any other form of heterosexual incest. Moreover, forms of neurosis among males who have been in incestuous relationships with their mothers appear, on average, to be more severe than those for daughters and sisters. It is an open question as to whether or not sibling or father–daughter incest generates more severe psychopathologies, but a best guess is that brother–sister incest is not as harmful to sisters as father–daughter incest is to daughters. But in all cases, mother–son incest produces the most psychological harm.

These three sets of conclusion frame the problem of this book. Why is mother–son incest more taboo than father–daughter and brother–sister incest? Why is mother–son incest significantly less frequent than all other forms of incest? And why is mother–son incest more psychologically harmful for sons than for daughters and sisters in incestuous relationships? None of the current theories on the origins of the incest taboo can answer all three questions. Our inquiry takes these questions as a challenge that must be met for a more complete explanation on the origins of the incest taboo. We should emphasize again, in closing, that our explanation does not supplant any of the ones examined in chapters 1 and 2, but it will, we trust, help to better complete the picture on the origins of the taboo.

4
A DISTANT MIRROR
APE SOCIAL STRUCTURE AND SEXUAL AVOIDANCE AMONG THE PRIMATES

↤

> Hominids wouldn't have evolved had they not once been rather like chimps, and understanding better the extant great ape (including chimp) adaptations depends on finding their elusive ancestors. And it also involves learning more about their still enigmatic cousins.
>
> —David Pilbeam (1997)

As details of "primitive" and preliterate societies came to Westerners in the nineteenth and early twentieth centuries, many thinkers felt that the basic nature of humans and society could now be discerned. Stripped of the distracting complexities of European societies, it would be possible, they thought, to discover the essence of what held society together. Most early sociologists viewed the incest taboo as keeping family members from engaging in sexual relations that would disrupt the integration of the nuclear family and hence society as a whole. As we saw in chapter 2, this "functional" view of the incest taboo is still dominant among sociologists. Yet these sociological theories as well as theories from other traditions do not explain the problems posed in the last chapter: Why does the strength of the taboo vary for different heterosexual dyads within the family: mother–son, brother–sister, and father–daughter? Why do rates of incest for these dyads vary? And why do the psychological effects on sons, sisters, and daughters diverge?

To answer these questions, it is useful to retrace the steps of early social scientists who sought to uncover the basic nature of the first human societies. But, unlike most of these thinkers, we believe that it is necessary to go back even further and see if we can discern the structure and composition of early hominid societies—or those societies of humans' distant ancestors. Anatomically modern humans emerged about 150,000 years ago, but hominids had already been around for millions of years; and so, the small bands of early humans must have been built on a structural base created by their ancestors. If the relatively few remaining hunter-gatherers studied by social scientists in the nineteenth and early twentieth centuries are at all representative of bands in the distant past, the existence of parents and offspring in these bands, whether of a single nuclear unit or occasionally a polygynous family of two or more nuclear units of parents and children, suggests that the structural core of the first human societies also revolved around the band and nuclear family; and it is reasonable to infer that the incest taboo was also present to regulate sexual avoidance.[1]

Yet this conclusion does not tell us when the family and incest taboo first emerged. Was the taboo solely an invention of *Homo sapiens* or did it originate earlier with ancestral hominids as they became ever more intelligent? No definitive answer can be given to this question, but we can make some reasonable inferences if we engage in a comparative analysis of the societies among humans' closest living relatives: apes and specifically chimpanzees. In essence, humans are evolved apes; thus looking at ape social structures can provide a mirror in which we can gaze and derive an image of what our ancestors were like some 6 million years ago. Our pursuit will begin, however, by looking into an even more

---

1. We are not proposing that contemporary hunter-gatherers are living fossils of Pleistocene band societies. However, the structural characteristics found among most studied hunters and gatherers point to shared traits associated with a food collecting lifestyle that include an emphasis on self-reliance and individualism, an ethic of egalitarianism, a principle of reciprocity, little political leadership, ancestor respect and animism in religion, and, most importantly, a strict sexual division of labor with kinship and marriage patterns that facilitate rather loose-knit network structures. Indeed, the food collecting mode of fission/fusion with lots of mobility within a larger "big band" community range is (in purely organizational terms, of course) not that far removed from contemporary chimpanzee communities. For overviews on hunting and gathering societies, see Nolan and Lenski 2004; Ember 1978; Maryanski 1994; Maryanski and Turner 1992; Bicchieri 1972. For an interesting comparative study viewing humans as primates, see Bailey and Aunger 1989.

distant mirror in an effort to find the necessary preadaptations that shaped the evolution of apes and hominids.[2] As evolved apes, humans have some hardwired behavioral propensities that we carry from our primate ancestry. To be sure, these propensities have been altered by our species' adaptation to an open country habitat, but by seeing how natural selection might have altered these propensities so as to make hominids and then humans more fit to survive in a new ecological habitat, we can begin to explain the origins of the incest taboo. In so doing, we can answer the questions that guide our inquiry.

THE STRUCTURE OF APE SOCIETIES

The Social Network Approach

There is now a large literature from field studies of primates. Such long-term research has documented that monkeys and apes are highly intelligent, undergo a long period of socialization, and live a long time. Nearly all primates also live in year-round societies (much like humans), and this living arrangement naturally creates a variety of age and sex classes that follow a human organizational pattern where individuals are divided into an assortment of infants, juveniles, adolescents, and adults. And like humans, infants are born one at a time, and their high intelligence facilitates rapid learning but long dependence on mothers. This ability to learn allows primates to be flexible in adapting to changing circumstances as they mature, but this flexibility is not infinite. Phylogeny clearly plays a role in restricting and regulating the behaviors of individuals, especially with respect to the attachments formed among different age and sex classes and to who stays and who leaves the natal group after puberty.

Primate social structure can be viewed in terms of (1) the behaviors and attributes *of* individuals or (2) the relationships *among* individuals (Hinde 1983, 1976). Much of the primate literature, however, has a behavioral bias because it is focused on the recording of such attributes as age, sex, and status or on the attributes typical of these classes of individuals. And while the attributes described vary, the emphasis is still on individuals and their social

---

2. The concept of preadaptation refers to selection pressures for a trait at one point in time, with this same trait later utilized to serve another function or to provide the foundation block for further selection in a future habitat.

behaviors. The other way to view a primate social structure is to consider the pattern of social relationships or *structure of relations* that emerges from the social behaviors of individuals. Here the emphasis is on the regular and persistent configurations of social ties among individuals. Thus, while social behaviors remain the building blocks of any primate society, a network approach points to the patterned and stable bonds linking individuals. True, some personal attributes are ignored with a network methodology, but the beauty of network analysis lies with its ability to uncover the underlying relational structure of a population, a configuration that can be difficult to detect when the focus is primarily on the behaviors or social traits of individuals or classes of individuals. It is the regularities or habitual patterns of relationships making up a social structure that interest us because we are seeking clues about the societies among humans' distant ancestors (for discussions of network analysis, see Freeman 2004; Wellman and Berkowitz 1988; Wasserman and Faust 1994).

One way to get at the patterns of relationships among individuals, or social structure, is to ask questions about the social bonds of primates in their natural habitat. These questions revolve around such matters as, Who likes to be with whom? What is the intensity of the relationships or ties between what classes of individuals (Hinde 1983)? By answering these kinds of questions for ape societies, it becomes possible to generate a relational blueprint of the baseline social structure from which human hunting and gathering societies were ultimately derived. True, all contemporary primates are themselves the end result of evolution, and so, we should caution that the social structure of present-day great apes can only give us a fuzzy image of what early hominid societies were like. However, even though the forest belt has shrunk with cooler climatic conditions (which led to the opening of a new niche for hominids), it has otherwise remained relatively stable since the Miocene epoch, which began some 25 million years ago. Niche theory would predict relaxed selection with little pressure for organizational changes among forest dwelling animals, such as primary-forest apes (Simonds 1974). Moreover, once we assemble and compare the relational networks among species of present-day apes, we can utilize the tools of *cladistic* analysis to reconstruct the *last common ancestor* (LCA) population of all living hominoids, which will then give us more confidence in making inferences about the structure of early hominid societies.

What Is Cladistic Analysis?

In disciplines such as historical linguistics and textual criticism, the historical comparative method, called cladistic analysis in biology, is a standard tool for reconstructing the past (Platnick and Cameron 1977; Andrews and Martin 1987; Jeffers and Lehiste 1979; Maas 1958). This procedure basically involves the identification of a group of entities that are believed to be the end points or descendants of a developmental or evolutionary process, with the idea that the original source or the last common ancestor (LCA) can be reconstructed through the uncovering of shared diagnostic characters among these entities (Hennig 1966; Andrews and Martin 1987). What matters here is that such nested resemblances or "evolutionary novelties" reveal a clear-cut evolutionary or developmental connection. For example, in historical linguistics one could take the linguistic units shared in common by a modern language group and then use these characters to reconstruct the speech form of the original mother tongue from which all daughter languages evolved. Or, in textual criticism one could compare alternative forms of the same book with the aim of reconstructing the original manuscript from which subsequent ones were later copied. And in cladistic analysis one can reconstruct evolutionary connections by evaluating taxa, or categories of related species, on the basis of shared diagnostic characteristics. Thus the methodology we will use here is common to many disciplines and has the utility of reconstructing from present-day sources ancestral patterns—whether for a dead language, a lost manuscript, or a prehistoric social structure (Forey et al. 1994).

Two essential assumptions guide the logic of all cladistic analysis. One is the *relatedness hypothesis,* which assumes that any similarities found in a class of objects, such as social tie formation, are not due to chance but are the outcome of descent from a common ancestor. The other assumption is the *regularity hypothesis,* which assumes that modifications from the ancestral form to the descendant forms are not randomly acquired but show a clear systemic bias that links these descendants to each other and to their last common ancestor (Jeffers and Lehiste 1979, 17ff.).

To assess the plausibility of the relatedness and regularity hypotheses, it is useful to employ a "control group" consisting of a sister lineage to the focal lineage—in our case, ape taxa. As can be seen in figure 4.1 on page 90, the closest sister taxon to

Hominoidea is *Cercopithecoidea* or the Old World monkeys, who diverged from apes some 25 million years ago (Maclatchy 2004; Goodman et al. 1998). Old World Cercopithecoid monkeys share many traits with apes but if representatives of this sister taxon do not possess novel or derived characteristics found among ape taxa, then we gain confidence in the conclusion that the unique features of ape social organization come from a common ancestor *after* the separation of monkeys and apes, thereby lending credibility to the relatedness and regularity hypotheses (Hennig 1966). Thus our goal is to isolate out the distinctive features of contemporary ape social structure even as these descendants have adapted to different ecological niches.

Human and Ape Primate History

As primates, humans belong to an order of mammals that originated about 60 million years ago when a small rodent-like mammal clawed its way up the trees and began to adapt to an arboreal habitat (Gingerich 1990; Szalay and Delson 1979). In this three-dimensional environment, primates developed some peculiar features for mammals. A most important change was the alteration in the dominant sense modality of most mammals. Most mammals are olfactory dominant, with the visual, haptic (touch), and auditory senses subordinate to the sense of smell. Exceptions to this pattern include bats who are auditory dominant and use echolocation to move about in their environment and higher primates who became visually dominant, with the other senses subordinated to the vision (Campbell 1985a,b; Forbes and King 1982; Rodieck 1988). It is easy to see how visual rather than olfactory sensing would facilitate survival because an animal that must smell, feel, or hear its way about the forest canopy is at a sensory disadvantage. Visual dominance was achieved by rotating the eyes forward so that the eyes are in a particular geometrical relationship to each other, thereby giving rise to stereoscopic perception. This ability to perceive the depth of objects represents an extraordinary advancement in visual acuity over the basic two-dimensional monocular vision of most mammals. In addition, selection also favored specializations that included color vision and a finely tuned fovea, an adaptation that gives primates the ability to detect fine detail, especially when near to the eyes. These traits made the visual sense so powerful that visual sensations are not only paramount for spatial orientation and for location of objects in space but also for social communication among group members in the form of visual gestures and body movements (Simonds 1974, 136). Along with these elaborations, the brain was rewired, setting into motion complicated neurological changes so that vision would dominate, with the haptic, auditory, and olfactory senses becoming subordinate to vision. For example, if a higher primate hears, feels, or smells something, it will immediately turn to look in the direction of these sensory inputs and integrate these other sensory inputs with what it sees. These functional changes also involved creating association areas in the brain that, as we will see, appear to have prewired or preadapted the brains of apes with a rudimentary capacity for language (Geschwind 1985, 1965a,b,c; Savage-Rumbaugh et al. 1993, 1988; Maryanski 1997, 1996b; Geschwind and Damasio 1984).

More immediately, a gradual shift to visual dominance was part of other body changes that enabled higher primates to move about rapidly in the forests. Monkeys and apes all have grasping (or prehensile) hands that reveal both strength and sensitivity for feeling the properties of branches (Napier and Napier 1985; Tattersall et al. 1988; Conroy 1990); and coupled with a generalized skeletal structure, movement through the trees was further enhanced. Teeth and jaw structure also changed with adaptation to new diets (Haile-Selassie, Suwa, and White 2004). Overall, higher primates are smarter, controlling for body size (which is correlated with brain size), than most other mammals who live on the ground in a stable two-dimensional world. The tree living adaptation of monkeys and apes thus required a larger neocortex to foster survival and reproductive success (Turner 2000; Jones 1990; Mesulam 1983; Maryanski 1997, 1996b; Stephan, Baron, and Frahm 1988).

In figure 4.1 a classification of living primates is outlined with a special emphasis on hominoids (apes and humans). The primate order is composed of the suborders of Prosimii and Anthropoidea. Prosimians or lower primates (like lemurs and lorises) are descendants of the first primates, and as a consequence, their locomotion patterns, anatomy, sensory traits, and other habits are considered less evolved than those found among monkeys, apes, and humans. In turn, the anthropoids or higher primates are divided into three superfamilies: Ceboidea or New World monkeys, Cercopithecoidea or Old World monkeys, and Hominoidea or hominoids, a taxa that includes all extant species of apes and humans. Ceboidea are called New World monkeys because they live in South and Central America, whereas Cercopithecoidea are called Old World monkeys

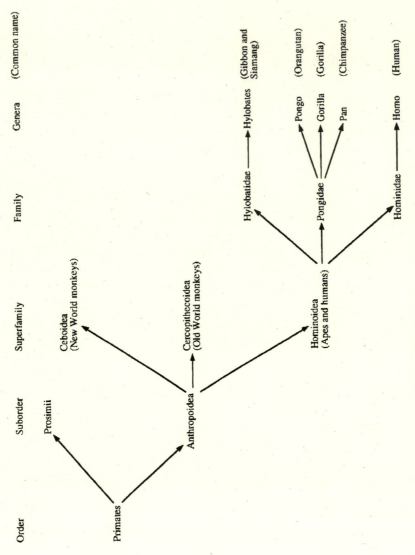

Figure 4.1 Simplified Family Tree for Primates

because they live in Asia and Africa. The superfamily Hominoidea is composed of three Old World families—Hylobatidae, Pongidae, and Hominidae—which have genera that in turn encompass different species. The Hylobatidae, or the family of gibbon apes, is composed of a number of species that all live in Asia (although genera status is currently in flux; see Roos and Geissmann 2001; Geissmann 2002). Pongidae, or the great ape family, has three genera: *Pongo pygmaeus,* a single species of orangutan that lives only in the Asian forests of Borneo and Sumatra; *Gorilla gorilla,* a single species of gorilla that lives in Africa's equatorial rainforest but primarily in secondary or montane forests; and *Pan,* a genus with two chimpanzee species, *Pan troglodytes* (the widespread common chimpanzee) and *Pan paniscus* or bonobos (sometimes called pygmy chimpanzees), both of which live in Africa's equatorial rainforest or in mature woodlands or forest-savanna mosaic regions; and *Homo sapiens,* a single species (and the only extant hominid) who lives worldwide. All Hominoidea are originally Old World primates, as fossil data clearly point to Africa as the home of the hominids.

While Cercopithecoidea and Hominoidea are both higher Old World primates that once shared a common ancestor, they are put into separate superfamilies because of many biomolecular and organismal differences that include striking variations in their anatomy and locomotion patterns. The skeletal structure of Old World monkeys is functionally adapted for a pattern of locomotion known as arboreal quadrupedalism, where both hindlimbs and forelimbs are relatively short and similar in length, with a tail being used for balance. This equipment is what gives monkeys the ability to trot along so nicely on the tree limbs or to run on the ground. In contrast, apes and humans (Hominoidea) lack a tail and share a morphology where limbs are long and of unequal length, a locomotor adaptation that originally relied on forelimb flexibility, an orthograde posture, and wide joint movement in all directions to move through arboreal space. This anatomy allows all apes and humans to brachiate or to use a "hand-over-hand" movement to swing from branch to branch (or to perform acrobatic feats at the Olympics). It is perhaps because of this unique locomotor adaption that the neocortex of apes initially expanded. The ability to assess the strength and distance of branches and to weigh alternative routes in the more hazardous areas of the trees would be adaptive for an animal that could easily die from the power of gravity. As we will come to see, once monkeys and apes separated from a common ancestor, ape evolutionary history turned topsy-turvy with novel adaptations that included not only major deviations from monkeys in anatomy and locomotor patterns but also in evolutionary trends toward much larger body size and new organizational structures that would eventually lead to hominid societies and the human nuclear family.

Thus the primate order today includes nearly two hundred species grouped into prosimians, monkeys, apes, and humans. Nearly 70 percent of all living primate species are monkeys; 25 percent are prosimians; and a mere 5 percent are apes and humans. This handful of hominoids comprise the little gibbon/siamang (with about nine species), the great apes or pongids, which comprise one species of orangutan and gorilla as well as the two species of chimpanzee, and the family of hominids with humans the only living representative. For our purposes, we can stick with this simplified and time-honored classification. However, we should emphasize that hominoid taxonomy and nomenclature are in flux, as new kinds of data force researchers to reassess older schemes of classification. Why the need for a new classification? In essence, the problem turns on clarifying ape and human evolutionary kinship. As can be seen in the cladogram in figure 4.2, biomolecular data reveal that gorillas, humans, and chimpanzees are genetically closer to each other than any are to the orangutan (yet the great apes are all in the same family, to the exclusion of humans). What is more surprising is that humans and chimps are genetically closer to each other than *either* is to the gorilla. In fact, on the basis of accumulating evidence from DNA, Wildman et al. (2003, 781) concluded that "we humans appear as only slightly remodeled chimpanzee-like apes." But how to reclassify apes and humans is a thorny issue. On what attributes should this classification rest? Should it rest on overall physical likeness (a phenetic taxonomy) or should it rest on phyletic closeness which would warrant placing them in the same family or the same genus? Whatever the outcome of these debates, it is clear that if we want to know about early hominid societies, it is chimpanzees who can provide us with the best sense of what early hominid ancestors were like.[3] But our first task will be to compare the social networks among all *living* ape genera and look for sets of nested resemblances (or shared

---

3. For recent molecular evidence and current debate, see Lockwood et al. 2004; Page and Goodman 2001; Mikkelsen 2004; Wimmer et al. 2002; Wildman et al. 2003; Gagneux and Varki 2001.

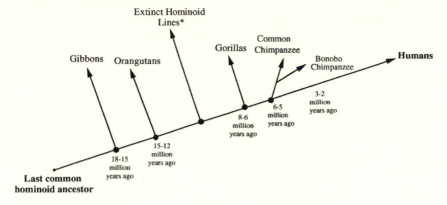

Figure 4.2 Cladogram of Hominoids

Sources: Fleagle (1999:258); Relethford (2003:36); Falk (2000); Page and Goodman (2001).

*All along the cladogram, species of hominoids were going extinct. This arrow simply draws attention to this fact, although the decline of hominoids accelerated during the late Miocene and continues to the present day where both the orangutan and mountain gorilla are threatened with extinction in their natural habitats.

derived traits) in their social structures that can inform us about the last common ancestor (LCA) to apes and humans and, more recently, to chimpanzees and humans.

In figure 4.2, a cladogram or phylogenetic tree is shown, which is based on molecular data. Here the ancestral lineages of modern apes and humans, plus one extinct lineage (to represent the many extinct lines), are arranged in a time sequence as they branched away (or underwent cladogenesis) from the last common ancestor population (LCA). About 15–18 million years ago the ancestral gibbon line diverged. About 12–15 million years ago the ancestral orangutan lineage broke away. Then about 6–8 million years ago, the gorilla lineage differentiated from the stem line. Finally, after remaining intact for at least another million years, the ancestral chimpanzee/hominid lineage branched into two lineages about 5–6 million years ago (later the chimp lineage further branched into the bonobo line around 2–3 million years ago). By knowing the clad, we are now ready to proceed. First, we need to go back and reconstruct the proto-hominoid society that served as the root social structure for all ape organizational patterns; then, in the next chapter moving closer to the present, we will speculate on the root or stem society common to chimpanzees and hominids.

The Organization of Contemporary Ape Societies

To use cladistic analysis to reconstruct the patterns of social organization among the last common ancestor to apes and humans, we can use network methodology to describe the structure of social ties among apes to see if they reveal certain commonalities across all taxa and to determine if there is a systematic bias in the later modifications in tie structure of all apes, despite adaptations to diverse ecological niches. Before presenting the tie structure of present-day apes, it is useful to summarize some of the more general features of social organization that organize tie structures among apes. These features include the general organizational form of ape societies, the transfer and migration patterns of apes, the relatively muted dominance hierarchies among apes, the diverse niches of apes in the arboreal habitat, and the variations in mating strategies of apes.

General Organizational Forms of Ape Societies

Let us begin with the various species of gibbons and siamangs (a larger gibbon-type ape) that deviate somewhat in their patterns of social organization from the other apes. Gibbons and siamangs are lesser Asian apes who are organized into rare isolated "family units" with a modal size of about four individuals. In this tightly knit two-adult group, a male and female (and sometimes dependent offspring) fiercely guard a small, stable arboreal territory from encroachment by other gibbons. Left only to themselves, gibbon partners turn to each other for companionship and engage in such relaxed joint activities as sunbathing at the tops of trees and singing morning duets.[4] Thus the conjugal pair constitute the backbone of gibbon and siamang societies, a pattern which is unique among present-day apes.

What is remarkable about other apes—with the exception of the distantly related gibbons—is the fluidity of their social structures. Orangutans (which means in native tongue "person in the forest") are organized around a fragmented and widely scattered society where about fifty semisolitary individuals live an arboreal lifestyle within a two-mile-solid block of Asian rainforest. The only stable group is a

---

4. For detailed field studies of gibbons, see Leighton 1987; Groves 1984; Ellefson 1974; Gittens 1980; Chivers 1984; MacKinnon and MacKinnon 1984; Tilson 1981; Tuttle 1986, 249–55; Geissmann and Orgeldinger 2000.

mother and her dependent offspring. While males and females socialize when a female is sexually receptive and while some individuals
congregate together for brief intervals (especially when trees are load-
ed with fruit), orangutans typically ignore each other. As a result,
enduring adult attachments are virtually nonexistent.[5]

Gorillas, in contrast, move about mostly on the African forest
floor where four or more gorilla groups known as bands (each
with an average size of about twelve individuals), along with a
number of lone, wandering males, share a solid block of secondary
or montane forest of about ten square miles. Each residential
gorilla band has a lead "silverback" male, who is often the sexual
partner for the adult resident females, but females breed with
other resident males or even a lone, single male. In a gorilla
group, members are tolerant of each other and easygoing, but
most adults are phlegmatic and engage in few overt social interactions. Adult females seldom interact with each other, although
they may remain in propinquity for many years. Even bonds between the leader male and resident females are unstable, being
linked to the status of a male and a female's maternal responsibil-
ities. Indeed, a female will typically attach herself to a leader male
only if she is successful in giving birth and if he can be relied on
for "baby-sitting services." When her offspring mature or if her
youngster dies, bonds typically weaken, and a female may simply
depart and join another band.[6]

Finally, our close cousins, the common chimpanzees, inhabit a
block of African forest that ranges from eight to eighty square
miles, living in what primatologists call a "community" level of
organization. Within each community, up to 130 chimpanzees
travel about alone or freely join and depart from a changing mixture of temporary social groupings or "parties" that can last just
minutes or a few hours. Although chimpanzees clearly behave as
though they share a "sense of community," even guarding its
borders from incursion by males from other communities, rarely
do community members cluster together at one time. The only

---

5. For detailed field studies of orangutans, see Tuttle 1986; Rodman 1973;
MacKinnon 1971; Rodman and Mitani 1987; Sugardjito et al. 1987; Galdikas
1995, 1988, 1985; Rijksen 1975; Knott 1999; Wich et al. 1999; Schaik 1999.

6. For detailed field studies on gorillas, see Watts 1991; Dixson 1981; Fay et
al. 1989; Weber and Vedder 1983; Fossey 1976, 1972; Gatti et al. 2004; Harcourt et al. 1976; Yamagiwa 1983; Schaller 1962; Harcourt 1981, 1979a,b,c,
1977; Robbins et al. 2004; Stewart 1981; Stewart and Harcourt 1987; Stokes
2004; Bermejo 2004; Goldsmith 1999; Sicotte 2001.

stable grouping is a single mother and her dependent offspring who spend up to 70 percent of their time wandering about alone. In contrast, adult males are more social, with each adult male enjoying his own particular set of friends.[7]

Migration Transfer Patterns among Apes

The "fission–fusion" nature of group structures among apes (with the exception of gibbons and siamangs) promotes overall weak tie social networks. These loose-knit networks, in turn, enable the great apes to be self-reliant, individualistic, and mobile in space. But it is the transfer or migration patterns that are critical to understanding the nature of ape societies (compared to our control group of monkey societies to be discussed shortly). Among all apes, females emigrate from their natal unit at puberty, a proclivity that is rare among Old World primates (and mammals in general). Once daughters depart, they seldom (if ever) spend time again with their mothers as adults (their fathers, because of ape promiscuity, cannot be known, again except for gibbons).[8] Among gibbons, orangutans, and gorillas, sons also depart at puberty (which is typical for primates), but adult male chimpanzees remain in their natal community, either wandering about alone, joining friends in social parties, or visiting their mothers and younger siblings. Thus in chimpanzee society, the vast majority of adult females in a community are relative newcomers (or temporary visitors who

---

7. For detailed field studies on chimps, see Herbinger et al. 2001; Mitani et al. 2000; Wilson and Wrangham 2003; C. Jones and Sabater Pi 1971; Tuttle 1986; Goodall 1996, 1986; Goodall-Lawick 1975; Halperin 1979; Nishida and Hiraiwa-Hasegawa 1987; Takahata 1990a,b; Wrangham 1987, 1980; Wrangham and Smuts 1980; Nishida et al. 2003; Boesch and Boesch-Achermann 2000; Lehmann and Boesch 2004; Gagneux et al. 1999.

8. At first glance one might assume that gibbon and human organization are similar. Both hominoids share the rare mating pattern of small, stable nuclear family units composed of a bonded pair and offspring (monogamous pair bonds are rare among primates and mammals in general). However, gibbon family units are distinctive because each nuclear family is isolated from all other families. Living high in the treetops and fiercely defending their territory, a male and female lacking other social relationships must rely on each other and on bonds with their offspring. Yet gibbon parent–child bonds break down as the young mature until at puberty both male and female offspring leave to resettle in another territory. What is special about human nuclear families is that offspring typically live or stay near their parents throughout their lives.

have immigrated from other communities); whereas all the males are lifetime locals, a fact that will have relevance for understanding the incest taboo among humans.

Dominance Hierarchies among Apes

Another structural feature of ape societies is the weak to moderate dominance hierarchies. Among gibbons and siamangs, there is no hierarchy as males and females are codominant, living in scattered nuclear families high in the trees. Among orangutans, a dominance hierarchy is difficult to sustain since they so rarely socialize together in groups. Gorilla adult males reveal a dominance hierarchy, with a leader silverback male directing band activities or trying to limit access of other resident males to females (typically unsuccessfully). Chimpanzees also appear to have a dominance hierarchy (Boehm 2004, 1999; de Waal 1996), although there is some controversy over how much actual dominance behavior occurs. But it does appear that a chimpanzee male, sometimes in partnership with other males (particularly his brother), will exert some control over other members in a group. But there are limits to how stable this hierarchy can be under free-ranging forest conditions when males are joining and then leaving temporary parties in which a particular male may show some dominance. If a male does not like being subordinate, he can simply go off on his own or join another social party within his community.

Habitat and Niches of Apes

There are variations in the ecological niches occupied by apes. All living apes live in the forest habitat; the orangutan and gibbon occupy an arboreal habitat, and the gorilla and chimpanzee are terrestrial. The gorilla spends most of its time on the forest floor, while the chimpanzee spends half of the day in the trees and the rest on the floor.

Mating Arrangements of Apes

A variety of mating arrangements are evident among apes. The pair-bonded gibbons and siamangs occupy one end of the continuum with their conjugal fidelity. The loosely polygamous gorillas, where females move freely from band to band, stand in a middle position with some degree of lead silverback–adult female attachment (that is often violated and easily abandoned). And the promiscuous orangutans and chimpanzees, who reveal no permanent bonds between adult males and females, occupy the other end of the continuum.

The Structure of Ape Social Networks

We might expect some variation in the structure of ape social networks in light of varying organizational features, such as migration patterns and mating strategies. But in accord with the relatedness hypothesis—that apes all share a common ancestor with distinct characteristics—the network data reveal considerable similarity in patterns of social ties among apes. Table 4.1 summarizes the network structures among gibbons and siamangs, orangutans, gorillas, and chimpanzees. Present-day species of apes are listed across the top of the table, while the strength of the tie between sex and age classes is recorded. An o indicates a weak or null tie; a + denotes a strong tie, and an o/+ signals a weak to moderate tie.[9] At the far right of the table is the reconstruction of the probable ties among age and sex classes for the last common ancestor to all of the species of apes. From table 4.1, we can see that gibbons have strong ties between the conjugal pair and dependent offspring. All other adult–adult ties are null (because gibbon pairs are isolated and widely dispersed in space). Gibbon parental relations with their adult offspring are also null since offspring disperse at puberty. For the near solitary orangutans, all same-sex adult ties are null, and adult male–female ties are weak, although a male occasionally stays with a female for several weeks. Ties between orangutan mothers and dependent offspring are strong but, like the gibbon, this tie dissolves when males and females disperse after puberty. Among gorillas, most adult ties are

---

9. Constructing ape (and monkey) tie patterns required two consolidation procedures: (1) Social bonds are assumed to be symmetrical and overall positive; (2) social bonds are coded using a simple scale of tie strength: dyads with null ties rarely or never interact; those with weak ties do so only occasionally; those with moderate ties affiliate for a time but this tie lacks emotional intensity or endurance (at least for adults); and dyads with strong ties are in close physical contact (e.g., grooming), elicit strong social support for each other, and evidence very stable bonds over time. Ties were coded for strength based on a comprehensive review of the primate literature, using a simple ordinal scale to accommodate the diverse methods used by researchers. Long-term field studies on primate social bonds made this process relatively simple as researchers typically agree on "who likes whom and to what degree."

Table 4.1 Strength of Ties among Extant Ape Species[†]

	(Hylobates) gibbon	(Pongo) orangutan	(Gorilla) gorilla	(Pan) chimpanzee	Last common ancestor
Adult-to-adult ties					
male–male	o	o	o	o/+	o*
female–female	o	o	o	o	o*
male–female	+	o	o/+	o	o*
Adult-to-child procreation ties					
mother–daughter	+	+	+	+	+*
mother–son	+	+	+	+	+*
father–daughter	+	o	o	o	o*
father–son	+	o	o	o	o*
Adult-to-adult procreation ties					
mother–daughter	o	o	o	o	o*
mother–son	o	o	o	+	o*
father-daughter	o	o	o	o	o*
father–son	o	o	o	o	o*

o = weak or null ties
+ = strong ties
o/+ = weak or moderate ties
[†]All primates have preferential relationships within and between age and sex classes (Cheney, Seyfarth, and Smuts 1986; Hinde 1983). For primates, the strength of social bonds is assessed on the basis of social grooming, food sharing, aiding and protecting, continual close proximity, embracing (excluding sexual contact), alliances, and the length and intensity of a social relationship. This table focuses on the structural regularities in the patterning of relations among conspecifics and the emergent properties that characterize these relationships.

weak or null, although the tie between a silverback male and a resident female can be weak to moderately strong depending on the male's ability to protect and help care for her offspring. Gorilla mother–offspring ties are strong but they normally dissolve when both sexes leave the natal band at puberty. Finally, among common chimpanzees, adult female–female ties are weak to null or what Jane Goodall describes as a "neutral relationship," being neither friendly or unfriendly (Goodall 1986, 17).[10] In contrast,

10. In this analysis, the network ties of the widespread common chimpanzee were used. *Pan paniscus,* which as shown on the cladogram as branching away from the ancestral chimp line about 2–3 million years ago, is a small, isolated

chimpanzee male ties are weak to moderate, resting primarily on individual "friendships" although brothers have strong ties that last a lifetime. Adult male–female ties are weak. Mothers and their dependent daughters have strong ties until puberty, but the daughter then leaves her natal community and breaks this tie. Sons, in contrast, leave their mother's side after puberty but they remain in the natal community, and as a result, adult sons usually maintain a strong lifelong tie with their mothers.[11]

The Cladistic Reconstruction of the Last Common Ancestor

With this information on the relative strength of ties, we are in a position to perform cladistic analysis. First, we can begin our cladistic analysis by scoring the regularities in hominoid ties that are evident in *all* apes, or 4/4 match tie patterns for the four sets of genera. Here we can see that adult female–adult female ties are all weak or null in gibbon, orangutan, gorilla, and chimpanzee. Mother–daughter and mother–son ties are all strong during childhood among the gibbon, orangutan, gorilla, and chimpanzee. Mother–adult daughter ties are all weak or null and father–adult daughter ties are all weak or null among gibbons, orangutans, gorillas, and chimpanzees.

Second, let us summarize and review the 3/4 matches, where three of the four present-day apes share a tie regularity. Adult male–adult male ties are weak or null among gibbons, orangutans, and gorillas. Father–daughter and father–son ties are weak or null

---

(note 10 continued) population that lives in the Zaire River basin. While bonobos share a community organization and female dispersal at puberty, their network ties vary somewhat from common chimpanzees. More importantly, the peculiar female habit of genito-genital (or GG rubbing) where females rub up against each other's genitals presents a problem for coding strength of affect bonds. Although GG rubbing seemingly functions to promote sociality, it is not an affect tie so much as a stress-reducing exercise to "reduce tension among unrelated females" (see White 1989, 162). Indeed, Kano considers it "comparable to copulation between female partners" and unique among the two hundred species of primates (1992, 190–92). Seemingly, selection favored it as a mechanism to promote greater network density in the bonobo habitat by using sex as a bonding ploy for female–female tolerance. To evolve such an oddball and truly unique social behavior, selection pressures must have been intense to create greater cooperation between adult female dyads.

11. For discussions of social relations among apes, see references in footnotes 4–7, and see Maryanski 1996a, 1993, 1992, 1987; Maryanski and Turner 1992 for data sets on ape social networks.

during childhood among orangutans, gorillas, and chimpanzees. Mother–adult son ties are weak or null in the gibbon, orangutan, and gorilla.

Third, for evenly split ties, or a correspondence of two out of four or 2/4 tie regularities, we have moderate or strong ties in adult male/adult female among gibbons and gorillas. Weak or null ties between adult females and males are evident for orangutans and chimpanzees.

Drawing from these tie patterns among living genera of apes, we can infer the social structure of the last common ancestor, as is done on the far right of table 4.2 (an asterisk denotes a reconstructed form). Given that among the adult male–adult male ties, three of the apes have weak to null ties (with the male chimpanzee the only exception), we can assume that a weak to null tie pattern existed in the LCA population. We can make the same inference for females since adult female–adult female ties are weak to null across the board. Adult male–adult female ties are split evenly, but since the gorilla tie between a lead male and a resident female is linked to her reproductive status, we can conclude with reasonable certainty that weak ties prevailed between the sexes in the LCA population. Mother–child ties are strong, a pattern common to all mammals, whereas father–child ties are weak to null (with the exception of the gibbon), a fact that strongly points to a similar tie pattern for the LCA. Mother–adult daughter ties are weak to null across the board. Mother–adult son ties are weak to null, with the exception of the chimpanzee. And father–adult daughter and father–adult son ties are weak or null across for all apes. Thus looking at our relational blueprint of the LCA population, the case can be made that social ties were mostly weak or null for the common ancestor of all present-day hominoids. There were, then, very few strong ties for the last common ancestor to apes and humans.

Is this LCA reconstruction plausible? After all, social relations do not fossilize, and our cladistic reconstruction might seem overly speculative. Certainly, caution is always in order when dealing with past events, but it is at this point that we can put to work the strict procedures of the cladistic method to further guide our analysis. To assess the credibility of our conclusions, we first need to entertain the null hypothesis that the shared ties depicted among all present-day apes were not inherited but were evolved independently *after* each genera branched away from the LCA population. To assist us here, we can turn to our control or "sister group" of Old World monkey societies. By sketching the organizational arrangements among monkeys and then comparing monkey with ape social networks side by side, we can gain further confidence in our reconstruction of the LCA.

Old World monkeys often live in close proximity with apes, but they reveal dramatically different traits from their ape cousins in terms of sociality, physical form, migration patterns, feeding, and reproductive behaviors. Moreover, compared to apes, monkey organizational arrangements are more consistent across species, with most species living in discrete groups that typically move about in a rather synchronized fashion within a defined ranging area. Their breeding patterns are also fairly uniform as most species follow either a true polygynous mating plan of one male and a number of females, or a promiscuous multiple-male and multiple-female mating plan. Monkey social networks also reveal a common form, with males normally leaving their natal unit at puberty and with females remaining in their natal unit and forming cliques of tight-knit matrilines.[12]

Monkey living arrangements are reflected in their bonding patterns, as is delineated in table 4.2. If we begin with monkey adult male–adult male ties, they tally out as four out of four, or a 4/4 match, of weak or null ties. This pattern (with rare exceptions) is ubiquitous among all Old World monkeys and is clearly associated with male-biased dispersal at puberty. Other across-the-board monkey ties include the strong mother–child ties (again, characteristic of all mammals), null or weak father–child ties (which continues in adulthood), weak or null adult mother–son ties, and strong ties between adult mothers and their adult daughters. Adult male–adult female ties are also generally weak, although there are exceptions. While it is true that counting monkey ties does not seem all that different from those among apes, the absolute number of ties is not what matters here. What is critical is whether a strong tie *can serve as a recruitment block* for extended networks. In ape societies, adult daughters transfer from their natal group at puberty, whereas in monkey societies, adult daughters remain with their mothers for a lifetime, as do sisters, grandmothers, aunts, cousins, and other related female kin. Thus the mother–daughter

---

12. For detailed reviews and field studies on Old World monkeys, see Falk 2000; Whitehead and Jolly 2000; Schultz 1970; Fleagle 1999; Fa and Lindburg 1996; Jolly 1985; Glenn and Cords 2002; Napier and Napier 1985; Strum 1987; Goosen 1980; Smuts et al. 1987; Pusey 1980; Pusey and Packer 1987; Greenwood 1980; Andelman 1986; Fedigan 1982; Cheney and Seyfarth 1990; Cheney et al. 1986; Wrangham 1980.

Table 4.2 Strength of Ties among Some Well-Studied Terrestrial Species of Monkeys*

	Gelada	Patas	Macaque (most species)	Baboons (most species)
Adult-to-adult ties				
male–male	o	o	o	o
female–female	+	+	+	+
male–female	o	o	o/+	o/+
Adult-to-child procreation ties				
mother–daughter	+	+	+	+
mother–son	+	+	+	+
father–daughter	o	o	o	o
father–son	o	o	o	o
Adult-to-adult procreation ties				
mother–daughter	+	+	+	+
mother–son	o	o	o	o
father–daughter	o	o	o	o
father–son	o	o	o	o

o = weak or null ties

+ = strong ties

o/+ = weak or moderate ties

*The absolute number of ties shown here is not of great significance. What is significant is whether a tie can serve as a building block for extended networks. The mother–daughter bond is the focal center in monkeys for generating both large and tight-knit kinship cliques and for providing continuity through intergenerational time.

bond is the center of what are called "female-bonded" monkey societies because this tie serves as an operative way for constructing matrilines that can include as many as four generations of blood-tied female relatives (see Wrangham 1980; Jolly 1985, 123ff.).

Another key aspect of monkey social structure is its staying power. Thus, for our control group of geladas *(Theropithecus);* patas *(Erythrocebus);* macaques *(Macaca);* baboons *(Papio),* and most other Old World monkey species, perpetuation of the group rests on a permanent nucleus of female relatives. This reliance on the strong adult mother–adult daughter ties as well as ties to other female kin is even greater because males leave the group at puberty, thus destroying the ability to build social ties along the male line. In contrast, for gibbons, orangutans, and gorillas, there is no abiding kinship lineage for intergenerational continuity because the females *and* males leave at puberty. For the promiscuous chimpanzees, female dispersal alone has much the same consequences. Thus, for gibbons, the nuclear family dissolves with the death of the mated pair; for orangutans, their solitary ways preclude continuity; and for gorillas, a band typically dissolves with the death of the lead male (with females dispersing to other bands).

The exception among apes is for chimpanzee males to remain in their natal community. For kinship recruitment, however, a mother–daughter bond compared to a mother–son bond leads to very different social structures. For a society to be organized around matrilines, stable mother–daughter ties are essential, whereas for a society to be organized around patrilines demands stable adult male–adult female ties and paternal investment in their offspring. Lineage recruitment for chimpanzees is limited to a mother, her sons, and brothers, but since mothers and sons do not have sexual intercourse with each other (with very rare exceptions), this dyad is reproductively speaking a dead end. Thus, despite their lifelong tenure, the best connections that chimpanzee males can muster is to share a "common fellowship" and a "sense of community" with each other (which is, of course, just what they do).

On the face of it, the *relatedness hypothesis* that living apes have descended from a common ancestor is supported because it appears that apes, when compared with monkeys, have a clear systematic bias of female dispersal that triggers disruption of the structural continuity generated by the mother–daughter bond which, in turn, produces a social structure consisting mostly of null and weak ties. Since all four ape genera are predisposed toward this rare organizational pattern, we can be reasonably confident that this trait is an "evolutionary novelty" or a distinct derived trait in ape evolution that was retained from the LCA population. In contrast, to support the null hypothesis, we would be forced to conclude that such a rare pattern of female transfer was independently evolved in each ape genera after separation from the LCA, a very unlikely possibility.

A next step in our cladistic analysis is to hypothesize the LCA mating arrangement, although we must caution here that mating patterns evolve to the requirements of a particular niche in a specific habitat. Yet, in looking over the breeding habits of apes, we can probably dismiss the gibbon's monogamous pattern as a candidate for the LCA population, as it is highly specialized, rather inflexible, and otherwise a very rare pattern for primates and mammals in general.[13] Instead, the best candidate for the LCA population is a flexible, promiscuous pattern because it is found among both orangutans and chimpanzees. Indeed, even the sexual habits of gorillas lean toward a semipromiscuous profile, given that a band can have several adult males along with a number of females with each resident female free to transfer by herself out (a transfer pattern *never* seen among monkey harem females).[14] An open "horde-like" breeding strategy also corresponds well with the surmised weak ties of the LCA population and the dispersal of both males and females at puberty. What we conjecture, then, is that the LCA population was a fluid, shifting collection of individuals with both males and females dispersing at puberty and with the mother/child bond the only strong and stable dyad—a tie that was, however, broken at puberty.

Why Did the Last Common Ancestor Have Weak Ties?

Why did the social structures of Old World monkeys and apes take such divergent paths? Why is it that living apes do not share the strong mother–daughter bonds, coupled with male dispersal that is so characteristic of monkeys, prosimians, and many other social mammals? The regularity hypothesis requires us to demonstrate that the structural modifications away from the ancestral form reveal a systematic bias for each descendant lineage that branched away from the last common ancestor population. While fossilized "weak tie networks" obviously do not exist, we do know that the LCA of present-day hominoids lived sometime during the Miocene epoch (a timeline of some 5–25 million years ago), and the overwhelming consensus is that all living apes are connected to this LCA by ancestor–descendant sequences through time, with the gibbons, orangutans, chimpanzees, gorillas, and humans forming a monophyletic grouping or clade. Hence, to validate the

---

13. Scholars are now questioning the credibility of gibbon lifelong monogamous units, seeing more variability in some grouping patterns (see Fuentes 2000). Falk (2000, 265), in discussing recent data on gibbon units, suggests that monogamy is maintained by adult same-sex aggression and the "fact that monogamy requires such vigilant regulation suggests that it might not be as inflexibly ingrained as traditionally believed. . . . If hylobatids weren't guarded by their mates, they would mate with outsiders."

14. When a monkey group (or troop) gets too large, some males with some female lineages break away to form a new social unit. Monkey females stay with their kinfolk and move only as a matrilineage. In striking contrast, ape females usually set out alone when moving from one social unit to another.

regularity hypothesis that the networks among apes reveal a systematic bias inherited from a common ancestor, we need to step back in geological time and link weak tie networks to specific events in hominoid evolutionary history. These data, we believe, will not only provide support for the regularity hypothesis but also cast light on some crucial hominoid preadaptations that paved the way for the origin of the human family and the incest taboo. However, in order to set the scene, a quick background sketch of the geological timescale and early primate evolution will be helpful before turning to the Miocene and early hominoid evolution.

As mentioned earlier, the earliest primatelike mammals are found in the Paleocene epoch about 65 million years ago. Then, in the Eocene epoch beginning about 55 million years ago, a huge radiation of prosimians, who looked much like contemporary lemurs and lorises, occurred. The Oligocene epoch followed about 34 million years ago, and with it came a large radiation of primitive anthropoid forms such as *Aegyptopithecus* and *Propliopithecus* who were basically tree-living quadrupedal primates. We should emphasize that Oligocene anthropoids are not Old World monkeys or apes but, instead, "primitive catarrhines" with a mixture of both monkey and ape traits (*catarrhine* means downward-facing nose, a characteristic of all living Old World monkeys, apes, and humans; Fleagle 1999, 397ff.; Wolpoff 1999; Maclatchy 2004; Goodman et al. 1998). Then, about 23–25 million years ago at the Oligocene–Miocene boundary, the ancestral mother lineage of both Cercopithecoids (monkeys) and hominoids (apes and humans) split into two new lineages that eventually lead to the evolution of modern Old World monkeys and hominoids (Nei and Glazko 2002; Pilbeam 1997; Kumar and Hedges 1998).

About 23 million years ago during the early Miocene epoch came a number of changes, including a warmer and dryer climate, a landscape with much volcano activity in Africa, and a shifting of the earth's plates as India slammed into Asia creating the Himalayas (see Fleagle 1999, 453 for a discussion). The early Miocene was also a golden age for hominoids, a time when apes proliferated, taking over a large swatch of niches in the huge African forest habitat. Then, by the middle Miocene, species of apes stepped up both their diversity and their ranging habits by migrating over to parts of Asia and Europe. In contrast, monkey species were scarce.

But after the middle Miocene, the fossil record reveals a dramatic reversal in the respective fortunes of apes and monkeys. Species of apes had begun a decline to the small handful of apes

that survive today, while species of monkeys had begun to prolif-
erate and occupy many of the niches previously occupied by apes
(Benefit 1999; Ungar 1996; and Andrews 1992). As this decline
in the number of species of apes occurred, monkeys and apes
became increasingly differentiated from each other (Conroy 1990;
Ungar 1996; and Andrews 1992).

During the early Miocene, apes and monkeys were not nearly as
distinctive as they are today. An ape known as *Proconsul* (a genus
that includes a number of big and small ape species) was, for many
years, viewed by researchers as the exemplar of these early apes
because it lacked a tail like all apes but compensated for this lack
of a tail for balance with enhanced forelimb abilities (Kelley 1997;
Campbell and Loy 2000). Otherwise, it revealed a body plan that
was clearly designed for "monkey-like" locomotion above branches (leaping and running along branches, as present-day monkeys
do). Monkeys had tails and different dentition from apes, but it
was assumed that their respective modes of locomotion were similar, walking and running quadrupedically in the arboreal habitat
(Ward 1993; Conroy 1990).[15] But as ape numbers declined during the later Miocene, their recovered body parts began to show
a dramatic alteration from a monkeylike torso for walking on the
tops of branches to an anatomy that suggested a shift to vertical
climbing and more forelimb-dominated movement such as sus-
pensory hanging and swinging. The restyled apes also evidenced a
short and wide chest, shoulder joints capable of allowing the arm
to rotate, stronger and more flexible hands and wrists, stronger
and more sensitive fingers (perhaps, like living apes, revealing ridges
or "fingerprints" for increased sensitivity), no tail, and arms much
longer than legs (Napier and Napier 1985; Corruccini et al. 1975;
Holloway 1968; Maryanski 1996b; Ward 1993). All of these novel
features suggest that apes had moved to the terminal feeding areas
of the arboreal habitat, where their locomotor activities revolved
around vertical climbing, underbranch suspension, and swinging

---

15. All Old World monkeys and apes have thirty-two teeth (distinguishing
them from prosimians and New World monkeys with 36 teeth), but they differ
in dental traits such as cusp patterns on their lower molars. Monkeys have four
cusps arranged in two pairs, each linked by a loph giving them a bilophodont
four-cusp pattern; whereas apes and humans have five cusps separated by a Y-
shaped fissure giving them a Y-5 cusp pattern. In phyletic relationships, dental
anatomy looms in importance because teeth are normally under strict genetic
control, and they are the most likely part of an organism to be preserved in the
fossil record.

from branch to branch. Selection also favored greater intelligence to allow apes to remember routes through the more hazardous portions of the arboreal habitat and to assess the relative strength of limbs and branches. The signs are clear, then, that these morphological features among apes evolved to enhance fitness in the precarious three-dimensional niches of the arboreal habitat (Napier and Napier 1985; Tattersall et al. 1988; Conroy 1990; Turner 2000; Jones 1990; Mesulam 1983; Stephan, Baron, and Frahm 1988).

Until recently, the most plausible explanation for the changes in apes' morphology was that monkeys had gained a strategic advantage over apes, pushing them to the marginal feeding areas of the arboreal habitat, while monkeys took over the core and more verdant niches of this habitat. The leading hypothesis was that monkeys appeared to have developed dietary specializations, as reflected in their teeth and specialized digestive tracts (found in some Old World monkeys today) that allowed them to tolerate and digest the toxic compounds of raw fruit. These specializations enabled monkeys to secure food earlier and more efficiently than apes, thus pushing apes to parts of the arboreal habitat where they could secure the ripe fruit that monkeys could not reach (see, for discussions, Andrews 1996, 1981; Galili and Andrews 1995; Temerin and Cant 1983; and Kay and Ungar 1997). The ancestors of the present-day gibbon and siamang were often considered to be representatives and exemplars of the evolution away from the more monkey-like *Proconsul*. Adding to this line of reasoning, we had concluded in earlier work that once apes were pushed to the edge feeding areas of the arboreal habitat, they could no longer support large forging parties, leading to the male and female transfer patterns that break group continuity among all apes (Maryanski and Turner 1992; Turner 2000). This conclusion follows from the fact that foraging strategies, morphology, and organizational patterns reveal a complex, though patterned, cause-and-effect relationship with each other (Tattersall et al. 1988; Napier and Napier 1985).

More recent fossil findings suggest that this line of argument does not represent the whole story as to why apes developed unique specializations in not only their morphology but in their network structures, as summarized in table 4.1. A new fossil, *Morotopithecus bishopi*, coexisted with *Proconsul* some 20 million years ago, but it does not reveal the latter's monkey-like features for quadrupedal movement on the tops of branches. Instead, *Morotopithecus* is much more like a present-day ape, with an anat-

omy geared toward vertical climbing and forelimb-dominant locomotion (Maclatchy 2004). What this finding suggests is that during the great radiation of apes during the early Miocene some
20–24 million years ago, many different kinds of apes evolved as
most niches in the arboreal habitat were exploited. Long before
monkeys gained their selective advantages, some species of apes
like *Morotopithecus* were already pursuing food foraging strategies
in the more difficult-to-reach niches of the arboreal habitat. And,
we can presume that if these vertical climbers pursued these niches, they may well have had to change their patterns of social
organization to accommodate the fact that few individuals can be
supported in these endpoint feeding areas of trees, much like
gibbons and siamangs today must disperse and spread out in the
forest canopy, or as the large, virtually solitary orangutan does.

The other fascinating feature of *Morotopithecus* is that this was
a big animal. It was not gibbon-like in size (15 lbs.) but more in
the range of a contemporary chimpanzee, standing at 100 pounds.
Large size, coupled with foraging in the extremities of trees and
the undersides of branches, would place even more pressure on
this primate to reduce the size of the group and keep it small and
flexible as resources varied.

How, then, is the story of ape evolution changed by the discovery of *Morotopithecus*? First, the differentiation of apes from monkeys may have occurred *before* monkeys gained their dietary or
some selective advantage. Second, the radiation of early Miocene
apes involved exploitation of more niches in the arboreal habitat
than previously believed, with some like *Proconsul* foraging in the
core branches of trees, and others like *Morotopithecus* moving out
to the ends and undersides of branches. Third, this differentiation
in the locomotion patterns among apes indicates that the initial
competition for resources leading to the distinctive morphology of
present-day apes occurred perhaps by virtue of competition *among
apes* rather than between monkeys and apes. Fourth, if network
structures changed as a result of adaptation to the more tenuous
niches of the arboreal habitat, the weak tie structure of apes
may have evolved alongside of a tie structure among other apes
that somewhat resembled that of present-day monkeys, as is reported in table 4.2.

Thus, as monkeys displaced apes in the core niches of the arboreal habitat, the only apes that remained were those with a morphology designed for underbranch feeding. This niche placed
further selection pressures, we hypothesize, for the weak tie network

structure evident among present-day apes. Long before monkeys were becoming ascendant in the late Miocene, the structure of ape societies may have already been in place, with all extant apes descending from the relatives or descendants of apes like *Morotopithecus*. This conclusion argues that the distinctive weak tie network structure of apes, as generated by female transfer from the natal group or community at puberty (and, except for chimpanzees, males as well) is very old. It has long-term phylogenetic inertia, and it posed a problem for all descendant apes who later in time sought to develop stronger ties and more stable group structures, including the hominid ancestors of humans.

Thus, lacking the ability to create matrilines, the touchstone of Old World monkey societies, apes had little choice but to forge very unconventional ties for a primate. These novel network linkages discussed earlier exist in every living ape social structure because they can enhance hominoid social tendencies in the face of female migration. And today as in the LCA, all apes remain self-reliant and autonomous and evidence weak tie networks. Hence there is strong evidence for both the *relatedness hypothesis* that weak tie networks were inherited from a distant Miocene ancestor and the *regularity hypothesis* that, even with wide variations in niches and mating strategies, the basic network structure among all species of apes converges, revolving around female dispersal and the inability of apes to form the matrilines so evident among monkeys, and even perhaps those early monkey-like apes who went extinct and were displaced by monkeys during the Miocene.

The relatedness hypothesis is upheld because living apes are clearly a monophyletic group or clade with shared evolutionary novelties of weak tie networks and female dispersal at puberty. Thus there is only a very remote possibility that such atypical traits were independently evolved after each ape lineage split from the last common ancestor. In turn, the regularity hypothesis places the onus on us to demonstrate that the organizational changes or modifications from the LCA population were not randomly acquired but reveal a systematic bias or show characteristic patterns. Today the living apes are far removed in time from their LCA; and new adaptations by their lineage ancestors to different ecological niches should produce some modification in the organizational arrangements of living apes. Gibbons and orangutans are arboreal in the forests of Asia; gorillas are primarily terrestrial in the forests of Africa; and chimpanzees are both arboreal and terrestrial. They also evidence different mating strategies—monogamy among gibbons, a loose polygyny among gorillas, and promiscuity among orangutans and chimpanzees. Yet, if the retention of female dispersal at puberty is truly a part of ape evolutionary history, there should be some telltale signs that harbor this bias. And there are. All present-day apes have had to construct social relations that circumvent female dispersal at puberty. Natural selection created in gibbons the rare monogamous pair bond to structure a unit that could persist after female (and male) dispersal at puberty. For gorillas, the lead male and female-with-offspring tie enabled some degree of continuity in structure in the face of female (and male) dispersal. Among chimpanzees, the rare mother–son bond, coupled with male bonding and a general sense of community or home range, generated a structure that could get around the stumbling block created by female dispersal from their natal group and community. Only the orangutan—the ape with the least continuity of structure—appears to have retained the behavioral propensity of the LCA, where females and males disperse, along with near solitary ways among adults. Thus all extant apes have worked around female dispersal and, except for the chimpanzee, male dispersal as well. Consequently the structures of ape societies and, in the case of the orangutan, the very lack of structure attest to the phylogenetic power and persistence of dispersal of females (and, again except for chimpanzees, males as well); and this persistence lends credence to the regularity hypothesis.[16]

THE TALE OF THE TEETH AND THE CONSEQUENCES OF LIVING IN THE SLOW LANE

Did Old World monkeys really acquire a selective advantage over apes during the later Miocene? As noted above, the fossil record makes it clear that ape species began to go extinct about the time monkeys began taking over what had been ape niches in the arboreal habitat. Since both monkey and ape dietary habits were large-

---

16. Our construction of the LCA population is in line with other researchers who used methods different from our social network/cladistic analysis but came to similar conclusions. In two classic papers, Richard Wrangham (1987) views the lack of adult female–female bonds and female dispersal at puberty in apes as an ancestral suite of traits inherited from the LCA population; whereas Foley and Lee (1989) argue in their reconstruction of early hominid social structure that the lack of adult female–female alliances in living apes suggests that the social anchor for early hominid societies rested on enhanced adult male–male bonds and a stabilization of male–female bonds.

ly centered on fruit (rather than foliage), any advantage in monkeys' ability to digest fruit at earlier stages of ripening instead of waiting for fruits to fully ripen (as apes and humans still do today) might well be decisive. In addition, new research on the life history traits among contemporary Old World monkeys supports the conclusion that monkeys enjoyed other advantages that continue to make Old World monkeys the most successful family of primates today. In contrast, contemporary apes have been labeled as "atypical relict forms" or worse, as "evolutionary failures" because of their small numbers and specialized habitats (Corruccini and Ciochon 1983, 14; Andrews 1981, 25; and Temerin and Cant 1983).

An analysis of life history traits can include many features, but the primary focus is on species developmental characteristics, such as the length of gestation, weaning age, speed of maturation, age of sexual maturity, rate of reproduction, interval of time between births, and length of life (Kelley and Smith 2003). For example, a comparison of human and chimpanzee life histories would highlight some dramatic differences since they last shared a common ancestor. Yet the usefulness of the life history approach is not limited to the study of living animals; the approach can also be used to reconstruct the lifeways of early hominids (to be discussed later), as well as the living patterns of extinct hominoids. In applying this approach, one key issue in primate paleobiology is to explain why living Old World monkeys and apes diverge so dramatically in their life history features. All higher primates mature slowly and live longer than most other mammals, but contemporary Old World monkeys and apes are, respectively, on a fast and slow lane. For example, as shown in table 4.3, an adult male

Table 4.3 Comparison of Life History Traits of Two Primates

	Adult male baboon (monkey)	Adult male chimpanzee (ape)
Average weight	50 lbs.	115 lbs.
Gestation	175 days	228 days
Nursing	420 days	1,460 days
Infancy	1.6 years	3.0 years
Juvenile phase	4.4 years	7.0 years
Adult phase	23 years	34 years
Spacing of births	1.7 years	5.6 years

Sources: Wolpoff 1999, 97; Falk 2000.

baboon (an exceptionally big monkey) has a mean weight of about 50 pounds, a gestation phrase of 175 days; a nursing phase of 420 days, an infant phase of 1.6 years, a juvenile phase of 4.4 years, and an adult phase of 23 years, with 1.7 years between births. In contrast, an adult chimpanzee has a mean weight of about 115 pounds, a gestation period of 228 days, a nursing phase of 1,460 days, an infant phase of 3 years, a juvenile phase of 7.0 and an adult phase of 34 years, with 5.6 years between births. Why is there such a difference in their living histories? Larger animals usually mature more slowly, but this fact alone does not fully explain the disparity between monkeys and apes. In point, the 15–pound male gibbon is smaller than many monkeys and dramatically smaller than the baboon but has a gestation phase of 205 days, a nursing phrase of 730 days, an infant phrase of 2 years, a juvenile phase of 6.5 years, and an adult phase of 23 years, with 2.7 years between births (all demographics drawn from Falk 2000; Wolpoff 1999, 97). These figures tell us that gibbons are "phyletic dwarves" (Maclatchy 2004) because this lengthening of ape life history is reflective of not just an increase in body size among most apes compared to monkeys but also a derived trait or "evolutionary novelty" *built into* the hominoid line. But how can we know if hominoid life history patterns reflect a phylogenetic trend in hominoid evolution?

One way to answer this question is to collect the fossilized teeth of young apes who died as their first molar cusps were erupting. By determining the age that each specimen died, these molars (which are entirely under genetic control) can be used as a broad measure of other life history traits. This methodology is appropriate because life history features are usually packaged as a *system* of features such that species with a long gestation phase will also have a long nursing interval, a long maturation period, a long infant phase, a long juvenile phase, and a longer adult life (see Kelley 2002; Kelley and Smith 2003 for details). To date, this technique has only been applied to two Miocene hominoids, *Afropithecus turkanensis* from the early to middle Miocene (c. 17.5 million years ago) and *Sivapithecus parvada* from the middle to late Miocene (about 10 million years ago), but nonetheless the results are already impressive. The dentition of these fossil hominoids reveals that the eruption of their molars falls *outside* the range of living Old World monkeys and well *within* (or above) the mean of living chimpanzees. In particular, the finding that the life history of the early Miocene ape, *Afropithecus,* was within the chimpanzee range is especially significant because as Kelley and Smith (2003, 326) tell us: "This . . . (finding) . . . is compatible with the hypothesis that there was a shift to the prolonged life histories that character-ize extant apes early in the evolution of the Hominoidea." These researchers also propose that the maturation trends in monkeys and apes are reversed, with apes running in the "slow lane" in such traits as maturation and reproduction and with Old World monkeys running at an accelerated pace in the "fast lane."

What, then, accounts for such life history differences between monkeys and apes? While we cannot know exactly why early Mi-ocene apes evolved a slower maturation rate, Maclatchy (2004) suggests that slower maturation and reproduction is an evolution-ary "luxury" and is usually matched with a low mortality rate. When food is plentiful and when there is little competition for resources, animals can become large and mature slowly. The life history of *Morotopithecus* is still unknown, but we can reasonably surmise that such a large-bodied ape (the size of a chimpanzee) also participated in this developmental trend. Maclatchy (2004) further suggests that in the early Miocene, a stable rain forest environment, coupled with little predation for large-bodied apes, might have fostered a slowing of their life histories. In addition, the fossil data suggest that in the early Miocene the ecological scene was a comfortable time for apes because monkey species were scarce until the middle Miocene. It is certainly plausible that monkeys' later advantage may have included both a dietary edge *and* an accelerated life history edge of shorter gestation and more rapid development to maturity. If so, this edge would make it difficult for a large-bodied ape to compete with a smaller monkey who is able to forage for fruit sooner, eat less, and reproduce faster.

Whatever the explanation, the fossil record clearly documents that, by the late Miocene, ape habitats had become problematic for hominoids. It is a plausible hypothesis that during this time monkeys had acquired selective advantages to displace species of apes. However, the LCA population of all living hominoids sur-vived these catastrophic events, bestowing to its descendants the "evolutionary novelties" of weak tie networks, lowered sociality, individualism, self-reliance, and life history for much slower mat-uration and reproduction. These traits are pronounced in all con-temporary hominoids—from the little gibbon to large-bodied humans. In fact, this trend in life history was subject to further selection in hominid evolution, especially the period of childhood dependency, which has been greatly lengthened in humans. While these traits seemingly served to limit the survival and reproductive success for most hominoid lineages, they were to serve as necessary and, in fact, crucial preadaptions for the survival and reproductive success of the hominid lineage as the brain grew, thereby forcing early birth and longer maturation.

THE STRUCTURE OF SEXUAL AVOIDANCE AMONG PRIMATES

Basic Strategies for Sexual Avoidance

The behaviors of animals in zoo captivity as well as the selective breeding of animals by humans have given a somewhat skewed view as to what occurs among animals in their natural habitats. In their natural niches, most species of animals reveal mechanisms for limiting inbreeding, as we emphasized in chapter 3. As we noted then, there are several basic ways that sexual avoidance is achieved among animals. One is for the mother to produce many offspring who reach maturity rapidly, and in whom parental investment is minimal. As a result, it is very unlikely that inbreeding can occur, and even if by some remote chance inbreeding did transpire, it would not decrease the fitness of a total population. The other strategy is for females having fewer young spread out over their lifetime. This strategy is most likely among animals that take a long time to mature and in whom considerable parental investment is necessary. This strategy is also accompanied by innate sexual avoidance bioprogrammers or, lacking such programmers, transfer patterns that limit the chances of closely related kin having sexual intercourse.

Among intelligent animals like primates, only one offspring is born at a time, and bonds of attachment enhance fitness until an offspring reaches maturity. In these kinds of settings, two mechanisms appear to have evolved. One is the propensity for parents to push their offspring from their natal home at sexual maturity, thereby decreasing the likelihood of mating between parents and offspring as well as between siblings. As we noted earlier, primates have developed a variant of this mechanism through transfer patterns of offspring when they reach puberty. The other mechanisms, common among birds that live together, is for asexual imprinting on those who are raised together, leading them to seek mates that are not closely related to them. As we will see for both monkeys and apes, there appears to be something like the asexual imprinting or some proclivity for blocking sexual relations among mothers and sons and to a lesser extent brothers and sisters in both monkeys and apes.

In order to reduce inbreeding depression, evolutionary pressures work on behavioral propensities of animals to reduce the chances that two related individuals will mate. These pressures are more intense for animals that have relatively fewer offspring in their lifetime and that must invest a great deal of parental time and energy in raising offspring. Primates meet both of these conditions because a female will have just a few young in her lifetime, and she will expend a great deal of energy caring for them until they reach puberty. To have combinations of harmful recessive genes reducing the chances of their survival would, over time, reduce the overall fitness of the species.

Sexual Avoidance among Monkeys

Let us begin with monkeys and see how inbreeding is avoided. For most monkeys (and prosimians), mating patterns fall into two basic types: (1) a relatively stable arrangement between a male and one or more females who form a one-male group (or a harem arrangement) and (2) an arrangement of multiple males and multiple females in a group with nonexclusive and unstable mating patterns (A. Jolly 1985; Smuts et al. 1987; Falk 2000, 48ff.). In the single male–multiple female group, a male might have access to not only a mother but also her daughters, and if fathers had consistent sexual relations with their daughters, problems associated with inbreeding depression could emerge. Although a "harem holder" normally has sexual rights to adult females, his tenure is typically relatively short, lasting only a few years at best (often only a single year), and thus he is not likely to be around when his daughter reaches puberty. In the multiple male–multiple female group, the presence of so many individuals (sometimes numbering in the hundreds), the absence of a stable heterosexual bond, and the relatively open mating practices serve as an effective strategy against inbreeding depression. Thus, while monkey mating arrangements do not wholly preclude possible inbreeding depression, the chances are substantially reduced by term limits on harem holders and the size and promiscuous nature of heterosexual groups.

For mother and son as well as siblings, inbreeding is avoided by the dispersal of males at puberty in most monkey (and prosimian) groups. In addition, as A. Jolly (1985, 241) points out, "Adult sons seem to specifically avoid mating with their own mothers." This finding has been well documented in long-term and detailed studies on free-ranging monkey groups but it is especially worthy of notice that even under laboratory conditions when mother and son are together for years in the same cage, mother–son sexual avoidance is still evident. In fact, Takahata et al. (2002, 406), recently reported that among Japanese macaques close kin dyads up to the third degree of consanguinity "strongly avoid matrilineal inbreeding" (and see Pusey 2005 for a review). Thus, among all known monkey populations, there is an active avoidance of intrafamilial matings (Itani 1972; Demarest 1977; Pusey and Packer 1987; Pusey 2005; Greenwood 1980; Andelman 1986; Sade 1968; Rhine and Maryanski 1996).

Sexual Avoidance among Apes

In ape societies, transfer patterns once again reduce the chances of sexual contact among mothers and sons, fathers and daughters, and siblings. Let us review how transfer reduces the probability of sexual relations for each genera of ape. For the monogamous mating arrangement of gibbons/siamangs of Asia, both daughters and sons are pushed from the natal unit at puberty and are forced to take up residence in other territories. This severing of ties between parents and offspring effectively cuts off sexual contact not only between parents and offspring but also between siblings who migrate to different areas in search of mates. Among orangutans, the other Asian ape, an open mating pattern and the lack of any local groupings revealing continuity over time reduces the chance that lone males or females will mate with their offspring. "Fathers" are not likely to encounter their daughters; and the same is true for mothers and sons, although it is likely that there is a hardwired mother–son avoidance pattern running through all primates, including orangutans. Transfer patterns further decrease these chances of inbreeding among siblings since males and females leave their mother at puberty, often migrating to another area of the forest. Thus the combination of relative isolation of individuals and the dispersal of males and females away from the mother at puberty greatly reduces that probability of intrafamilial matings between siblings. Gorillas do reveal stability in a band structure, composed of a lead male, a number of females and their young, and sometimes several other adult males. But again, female transfer precludes the likelihood that a father will have sexual relations with his daughter. At puberty, daughters generally emigrate to another band, and this migration is also an effective block on brother–sister matings. In addition, sexual encounters between siblings are also unlikely because of male dispersal at puberty and because of long birth intervals between siblings. On top of these obstacles, Dian Fossey tells us that adolescent brothers are already looking elsewhere, seemingly practicing "bride capture" by approaching other groups and flirting with unrelated females (quoted in Demarest 1977, 331). In turn, gorilla mothers and sons follow the monkey pattern of showing a strong disinterest in intrafamilial matings (Pusey 2005).

Among chimpanzees, the transfer of females to another community at puberty shuts off sexual relations with fathers, who are not known because of female promiscuity. Moreover, there is a constant mixing of genetic material as females leave their natal community, and new immigrants from other communities take their place (Gagneux et al. 1999). Sexual encounters between brothers and sisters are thus rare (A. Jolly 1985, 240ff.). Yet, because males stay in their natal community and remain emotionally close with their mothers, transfer patterns cannot ensure that sons will not have sexual relations with their mothers, especially since mothers are promiscuous. How, then, is sexual avoidance achieved? One chimpanzee ritual is illuminating: During those times when a female is receptive to "hoi polloi" sexual relations, males will line up and patiently wait their turn to have sex with this female. But one male is conspicuously absent from the lineup: the receptive female's son. Sons clearly refrain from sexual relations with their mothers, and so we can conclude that natural selection wired into the neurology of the chimpanzee brain a bioprogrammer for sexual avoidance between a son and his mother—just as it appears to have done for monkeys and other apes as well.

Thus the human cultural taboo prohibiting sex between mother and son is likely to be a cultural manifestation of a hardwired behavioral propensity in apes; and this fact, we believe, helps explain the questions that we have raised about the incest taboo among humans. But let us not get ahead of the argument just yet. Clearly transfer patterns operate to prevent inbreeding depression, but in addition, natural selection appears to have installed in both apes and humans hardwired propensities for avoiding mother–son and brother–sister matings (Demarest 1977; A. Jolly 1985). And in particular Donald Sade (1965) in a summary of his research on Old World monkeys, concluded that an innate mechanism evolved among all higher primates to prevent mother–son incestuous matings: "We may now speculate that a preexisting condition became invested with symbolic content during hominization; the origin of at least the mother–son incest taboo may have been the elaboration of a phylogenetically older system, a system which can still be observed operating at the monkey level of organization" (quoted in Demarest 1977, 327).

In table 4.4, the patterns of sexual avoidance among monkeys and apes are outlined. Within the structure of ape and monkey societies, natural selection found a way to decrease the chances of inbreeding, primarily through transfer patterns of offspring at puberty. If transfer alone was not fully up to the job, other mechanisms evolved. For example, in harem-like groups of monkeys where females remain in the local group, the potential for harem-holding males having sex with their daughters is reduced by the short tenure for males. And the most important example is the wiring of sexual avoidance between mothers and sons as well as siblings, in both the monkey and ape lines. And this avoidance is particularly noticeable for mothers and sons among chimpanzees, where members of this dyad typically enjoy an emotionally close relationship for a lifetime.

Thus, if those apes that were to become hominids were anything like present-day chimpanzees (and the genetic evidence says that they were), natural selection had probably already wired sexual avoidance between mothers and sons by caretaking and between brothers and sisters if something like the Westermarck effect could be activated by close physical contact early in life between siblings. The big challenge to natural selection, then, would be to find a way to achieve sexual avoidance between father and daughters as the nuclear family began to emerge in the bands of hominids. The Westermarck effect is likely one such mechanism that was hardwired, but as we will argue, this mechanism alone for humans is not adequate to the task of incest avoidance. We will need to look elsewhere, but before doing so, it is necessary to see how the loose chimpanzee-like structures of humans' hominid ancestors could be transformed into a more organized and cohesive structure of social relations that would facilitate survival, especially on the African savanna. For, as we will argue, the more natural selection generated new mechanisms to increase hominid sociality and solidarity in the group, the greater would be the potential for inbreeding as old transfer patterns that had assured a high degree of sexual avoidance were contradicted by new mechanisms for enhancing sociality—a sociality that eventually led to the nuclear family.

Table 4.4 Mechanisms of Sexual Avoidance among Primates

Dyads among apes and Old World monkeys	Transfer patterns		Dominance patterns	Long maturation	Group patterns		Biological patterns
	Female transfer at puberty	Male transfer at puberty	Periodic succession of dominant male		Mobility from group to group	Lack of group structure	Hardwired sexual avoidance
Monkeys							
mother–son		x			x		x
father–daughter			x^1		x		
brother–sister	x	x					x^3
Apes							
Gibbon/siamang							
mother–son		x					x
father–daughter	x						
brother–sister	x	x					x^3
Orangutans							
mother–son		x				x	x
father–daughter	x					x	
brother–sister	x	x		x^2		x	x^3
Gorillas							
mother–son		x			x		x
father–daughter	x				x		
brother–sister	x	x		x^2	x		x^3
Chimpanzees							
mother–son							x
father–daughter	x				x		
brother–sister	x			x^2	x		x^3

[1] This avoidance mechanism applies only to one-male-multiple-female monkey groups. A harem-holder typically keeps his dominant status for less than two years.

[2] The Great Apes have high mortality rates (up to 50 percent) during the first year of life coupled with three or four years of nursing before an offspring is weaned and birth intervals of at least four years.

[3] Data support a Westermarck-like effect operating between brothers and sisters, although the data are not without gaps and ambiguity.

CONCLUSION

Humans are evolved apes. This fact has important implications for how we go about studying behavioral propensities and sociocultural arrangements that predate history. Cladistic analysis gives us a glimpse at how humans' ultimate hominoid ancestors were organized. What characterizes the LCA population and all present-day great apes is a weak tie social structure, composed of fluid groups. Early scholars often speculated on proto-human groups, and some termed this early structure the "horde," as we saw in chapter 1. This notion of the horde was obviously a crude way of denoting a form of prehuman society, buried in human evolutionary history that lacked the nuclear family as a core structure. Great ape social structures come very close to this conception of the proto-hominid society because apes do not reveal a kinship institution as we know it. Present-day apes and the ancient apes from whom we all evolved were probably organized, at best, at the community level with highly fluid groups in which membership was constantly changing. It is possible, of course, that this distant ancestor was more like present-day orangutans and near solitary. However we portray these ape societies, they were typified by weak ties among adults, high levels of individualism, and mobility among loosely organized foraging parties.

This organizational base was not very conducive to survival, once early hominids left the forest for more open ranging areas on the African savanna where tight-knit group structures would increase fitness in foraging and in fighting off predators. The hominid ancestors of humans somehow beat the odds and became better organized, moving from the horde-like structure of ape societies to hunting and gathering bands composed of nuclear families. As this transition occurred over several million years, the problem of incest and inbreeding became more and more salient. As maturation was prolonged and as individuals bonded together and as fathers, mothers, and their children galvanized into the nuclear unit, transfer patterns were probably not enough to assure that inbreeding would not occur. We have already seen that natural selection created among chimpanzees a hardwired sexual avoidance between mothers and sons. If the ancestors of humans were anything like present-day chimpanzees, then mother–son avoidance was already hardwired into the neuroanatomy of hominids. And this propensity of males to stay close to their mothers would give natural selection something on which to select in order to forge more cohesive groups, as would the fitness-enhancing friend-ships that develop among adult males and brothers. Enhancing these behavioral propensities evident among chimpanzees might have given the ancestors of humans just enough edge to survive until more complex and longer-term neuroanatomical changes could be forged by natural selection. The original proto-human horde may thus have emerged from natural selection working with pat-terns of male bonding and male attachment to mothers.

Females could not serve as the structural core of this chimpan-zee-like horde, as they do in monkey groupings, because of the retention of the hardwired proclivity for female transfer from the community at puberty. But, at some point, sexually mature fe-males delayed leaving their natal group and migrating to another community, and perhaps some never left their natal community. The evolution of the nuclear family would require stronger and longer-lasting bonds between females and the rest of the members of their family; and these new, emotionally laden bonds may have begun to disrupt more ancient bioprogrammers for transfer and even for sexual avoidance in the mother–son and brother–sister dyads. And, for the father–daughter dyad where no obvious bio-programmers exist for sexual avoidance, delaying or eliminating a daughter's transfer to another community could lead to inbreed-ing between this pair. As this transition occurred, the incest taboo as a cultural force supplemented biologically based avoidance pat-terns. This will be our story, but first we need to go back to the beginnings of the hominid line as "the horde" moved from the trees to the African savanna.

5
THE HORDE
SOCIAL ORGANIZATION BEFORE
THE NUCLEAR FAMILY

-⊖-

> The bulk of the evidence from studies of behavior and the paleontology as well as genetics indicates that human ancestors were probably very much like chimpanzees.
> —John Fleagle (1999)

Early speculation on the origins of the family, the incest taboo, and society often used the metaphor of the "horde," as noted in chapter 1. It is easy to see this concept as a quaint and misplaced conceptual mistake, born of ignorance if not ethnocentrism about the superiority of Western culture. Yet the notion of the primitive horde makes an important point: the nuclear family did not always exist. It was preceded by a society not based on the family, as Westerners saw it. Instead, as Franklin Giddings, an early American sociologist, tells us in *The Elements of Sociology,* published in 1900, early humans likely lived in "a mere horde in which family relations were irregular and unstable" (255). Moreover, for some analysts, the notion of the horde allowed thinkers to emphasize that the nuclear family had to be "invented," which suggests that it is not such a "natural" part of human social organization as is commonly assumed. We believe that early scholars were thus onto something with the concept of the horde, and our goal in this chapter is to revisit the notion of the horde, or society before the nuclear family, in order to see what it can tell us about the origins of the incest taboo. But first we will conclude our story of the Miocene apes and then sketch the key players and events that occurred in the evolution of our own species.

MUSICAL CHAIRS AND THE SWINGING MIOCENE APES

The long Miocene epoch began about 25 million years ago and ended approximately 5 million years ago. The early Miocene in Africa was the heyday of apes, beginning with *Proconsul* (the quadrupedal walker) and *Morotopithecus* (the hanging ape), with ape taxa favoring a habitat of deeply wooded forest. The fossil record also documents the later migration of apes into parts of Eurasia about 15 million years ago and, overall, registers a remarkable abundance and variety of apes, from smallish ones to enormous creatures such as the 650-pound *Gigantopithecus* (an Asian ape who some believe is the ancestor of the conjectured Bigfoot). Moreover, the fossil record reveals the continued existence of monkey-like quadrupedal apes alongside such newly discovered species as the 12–13-million-year-old European *Pierolapithecus* with a mosaic mixture of modern and primitive ape traits (Moya-Solà et al. 2004), the intriguing *Oreopithecus* and *Dryopithecus,* also of Europe, and the 14-million-year-old *Kenyapithecus,* an African ape whose skeletal features resemble modern apes (McCrossin 1997) and who, as a consequence, is floated as an LCA ancestor of humans, chimps, and gorillas. However, during the late Miocene the music stopped for most apes, while for monkeys it had just begun, with monkey species taking up residence in former ape niches. Soon all the above-branch monkey-type apes disappeared forever from the fossil record, leaving only the under-branch swinging apes sitting on the hominoid family tree. And eventually one of these swinging ape taxa was to beget the last common ancestor of chimpanzees and hominids (for discussions, see Campbell and Loy 2000; Gibbons and Culotta 1997).

A SKETCH OF HOMINID EVOLUTION

The First Hominids

Both the molecular and fossil data agree that the LCA population of chimpanzees and hominids lived between 5 and 7 million years ago, although this mother ancestral lineage remains elusive. Currently fossil hunts seek to find (1) the earliest hominid species (or hominin) and (2) the hominid lineage that ultimately lead to *Homo,* our own genus, which appeared about 2.5 million years ago. What is clear is that the hominid tree is not a stately and graceful one with a main trunk and a handful of soft, billowy branches; instead, it is a thickly branched stumpy tree with most ends becoming terminal twigs except for the branch leading to *Homo*. In figure 5.1, a simplified branching tree of the Hominidae is shown, highlighting most of the central players in hominid evolution. We should caution, however, that scholarly debates over hominid phylogenetic positions are particularly fierce and combative right now; and for the earliest hominids, a virtual war of words is being played out in the journals over whether or not some specimens even warrant status in the hominid clade.

At this point it is useful to ask, What criteria are used to determine hominid membership? Of course, there is no "the missing link," where an ape mother gives birth to a hominid child. Instead, human evolution is punctuated by an evolving mosaic of hominid traits, with different traits evolving at different rates. While cranial, dental, and other derived traits (or "modern-looking" traits) are used to assess membership, *the* cardinal trait for hominid status is habitual upright walking, although for the earliest hominids who are extremely ape-like, any feature that even hints at bipedal walking is enough to warrant a fossil hominid consideration. As shown in figure 5.1, there are three leading contenders for the title root hominid. Reading up from the bottom on the right side, this first grouping begins with *Sahelantropus tchadensis*, a 6–7-million-year-old late Miocene taxa that is a relatively new entry on the hominid clade. Hominid status for this genus is inferred from facial and dental characteristics associated with more modern hominids, but its bipedal status is in question, with some scholars arguing that it is not a hominid at all but a female gorilla.[1] The second late Miocene taxa, *Orrorin tugenensis* at 5.8–6.0 million years old, is viewed as a more viable nominee because such diagnostic traits as the shape of its thighbones suggest bipedality, and if so, it would be the earliest upright walker on the hominid clade.[2] Finally, *Ardipithecus kadabba* at 5.2–5.8 million years old and *Ardipithecus ramidus* at about 4.4 million years old of the late Miocene–early Pliocene are also in the running. These taxa are believed to be on the same line, with *Ardipithecus kadabba* revealing intriguing dental characteristics that place it close to the split

---

1. For more on this debate, see Wolpoff et al. 2002 and Brunet 2002; for discussions of *Sahelanthropus*, see Dalton 2002; Beauvilain and Beauvilain 2004; Begun 2004; Brunet et al. 2002; Haile-Selassie et al. 2004; and Vignaud et al. 2002.

2. For discussions of *Orrorin*, see Begun 2004; Galik et al. 2004; Haile-Selassie et al. 2004; Coppens et al. 2002.

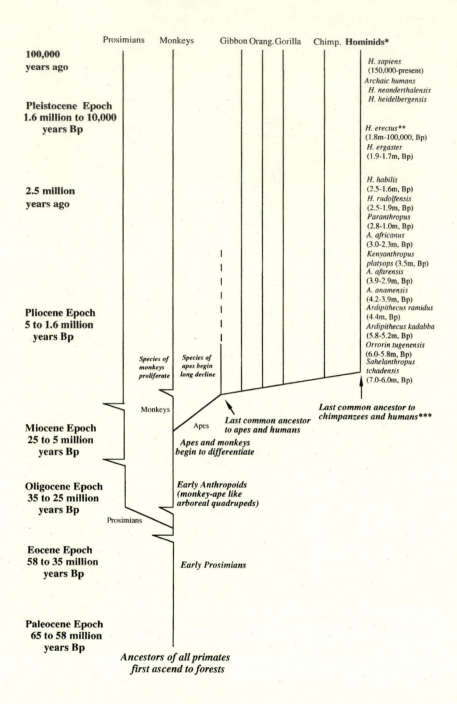

Figure 5.1 The Hominid (Hominin) Line through Time

*All fossils attributed to a taxa fall between the ranges indicated.

**H. erectus fossils are found throughout the Pleistocene and as late as 50,000 years ago in Indonesia. The newly discovered H. floresiensis, who died some 18,000 years ago, may be a decendent of H. erectus (see Gibbons 2004).

***This provisional listing of hominids after the split from the last common ancestor of present-day chimpanzees and humans is constantly being revised. Our listing summarizes the data as they stood in early 2005.

Note:
Fossils are dated with a variety of methods. Absolute dates rely upon radiometric techniques, such as radiocarbon dating (14C), potassium-argon dating (K/Ar), and fission track dating, that date within a probability range. Relative dates (or dates by association with something else) rely upon such methods as faunal correlations and paleomagnetism.

Key:
m = millions of years

Bp = before present

Figure 5.1 *(continued)*

between chimps and hominids, but leaning toward the hominid line.[3] Which of these evolving lineages will be crowned *the* basal hominid and which (if any) is connected to later hominids is now up for grabs and rests on the recovery of more of these enigmatic specimens. What we do know is that these taxa lived during a time of shrinking forests in response to a cooler climate, a trend that was evident by the late Miocene. All of these contenders for basal hominid lived near the time (in geological terms) of the last common ancestor of chimpanzees and humans. We can also assume that, through the process of Darwinian descent with modification, all of these incipient hominids inherited the long-standing ape proclivity of weak ties and female dispersal, along with the morphological, neurological, sociological, and life history preadaptations that emerged during the 15 million years of hominoid evolution during the Miocene.

During the Pliocene epoch, which began about 5 million years ago, the African fossil record reveals a large variety of upright walking genera and species (some coexisting at the same time). As shown in figure 5.1, the oldest is *Australopithecus anamensis* at 3.9–4.2 million years, followed by the gracile hominids that in-

---

3. For discussions of *Ardipithecus,* see Haile-Selassie et al. 2004; Haile-Selassie 2001; Begun 2004; Harcourt-Smith and Aiello 2004; Gibbons 2002a; Fleagle 1999; Semaw et al. 2005.

clude *Australopithecus afarensis* at 2.9–3.9 million years old, *Ken-yanthropus platyops* at 3.5 million years (a new guy on the block), and *Australopithecus africanus* at 2.3–3.0 million years. There is no doubt that these "Australopiths" (their informal name) and the new entry, *Kenyanthropus* (who was living at the same time as *afarensis*), were all habitual bipeds, although controversy exists over their modes of bipedal gait. In looks, they had ape-like jaws, faces, and teeth (although their canines were reduced). In stature, they were relatively short with females in the range of 3.3 to 3.8 feet in height and about 55 to 66 pounds, whereas males were in the range of 4.5 to about 5 feet and 90 to 154 pounds. Their brains were in the range of living chimpanzees at about 400 cc (cubic centimeters) to 500 cc in size; and overall, their dental, cranial, and skeletal traits are more ape-like than human-like (although later forms show a more modern-like transition; see Campbell and Loy 2000). In eating habits, their dentition points to dietary preferences for soft foods such as fruits but a shifting trend toward harder, gritty foods that wear down teeth. Reconstruction of their habitats points to a preference for well-watered, woodland environments (with some earlier hominins in more heavily wood-ed areas). Yet, despite their bipedal ways, the Australopiths slept at night in trees (as their limbs retain grasping features), probably near the forest fringe. While social structure is difficult to recon-struct from fossils, the early hominids show a significant level of difference between males and females in body mass. In Old World primates, a high degree of sexual dimorphism is normally associat-ed with polygynous or promiscuous mating patterns, with Lock-wood et al. (1996) suggesting that the high levels of sexual dimorphism in early hominids was probably a retained trait from the LCA population of African apes and humans. The evidence from living apes suggests that early hominids were promiscuous, although it is difficult to know for sure (Campbell and Loy 2000, 269). On a stronger foundation, Fleagle (1999, 523–24) notes that the maturation traits or life history features of early hominids (associated with their molar development) also correspond to the ape pattern of longer-term maturation discussed in the last chap-ter.[4] Thus, during the early and middle Pliocene, the portrait painted

---

4. The composite picture of early hominid traits, lifeways, and paleoenviron-ment was drawn from Walker 2002; Harcourt-Smith and Aiello 2004; Leakey et al. 1998; Ward et al. 2001; Campbell and Loy 2000; Strait et al. 1997; Fleagle 1999; Wolpoff 1999; Foley 2002; Reed 1997; Lockwood et al. 1996; Lockwood and Tobias 2002; de Menocal 2004; Bobe and Behrensmeyer 2004.

of early hominids depicts a highly successful variety of ape-like upright-walking taxa who were well adapted to their forest and woodland environments and who seemingly had few selective pressures for change over millions of years. Yet the trend toward harder foods suggests that Austropiths were beginning to venture out to more parkland environments, perhaps because of the expansion of grasslands that came with the major global cooling trend during the Pliocene epoch. However, the lifestyle of the gracile looking Austropiths ended when they all went extinct in the later Pliocene, leaving it up to another group of hominids to exploit the new foods in a more open habitat.

The Appearance of Homo

The genus *Homo* emerged in Africa about 2.4 million years ago during the later Pliocene and early Pleistocene epoch (the latter epoch lasted from 1.6 million to 10,000 years ago). Taxonomic debates over early *Homo* are centered on how many early *Homo* lineages coexisted and which ancestral stock through cladogenesis gave rise to the *Homo* genus, with *Australopithecus afarensis* (of which the famed "Lucy" is a member) and the recently discovered *Kenyanthropus platyops* (who is seen to have more modern dental and facial features) currently favored. We do know that early *Homo* coexisted for some time during the late Pliocene and early Pleistocene with some rugged and very robust *Australopithecines* by the names of *Paranthropus aethiopicus, robustus,* and *boisei* (with *aethiopicus* first appearing about 2.8 million years ago in the fossil record). Reconstructions of their dietary habits and paleoenvironment suggest a movement to more grassland ecosystems, and a diet of harder and more abrasive vegetable foods, such as seeds and tubers (which was facilitated by their huge grinding teeth). Then, about a million years ago *Paranthropus* went extinct.

In the middle of figure 5.1, *Homo habilis* and *Homo rudolfensis* (collectively known as early *Homo*) are featured. What is visually evident in the bones of *Homo habilis* is a gradual transition toward a more modern form but with some features that harken back to its *Australopithecine* ancestors (e.g. longer arms and shorter legs). Nonetheless, although not much bigger in size or weight than the Austropiths, *habilis* and *rudolfensis* have larger brains than Austropiths, with cranial capacity for *habilis* in the range of 509 cc to 674 cc and for *rudolfensis* (who also has more modern frontal lobes) in the range of 752 to 810 cc (the modern human range is

1200 to 1600 cc [Campbell and Loy 2000; McHenry and Coffing 2000]). In addition, the jaw of *habilis* is more modern (a more parabolic shape), its dentition is smaller, and its bipedal stride is more human. Moreover, there is less sexual dimorphism between the sexes. In reconstructing their paleoenvironment, there is a dramatic shift in habitat for these hominids with species of the *Homo* genus seemingly now occupying "a complex mosaic of environments" including open woodlands, shrublands, and dryer grassland habitats (Bobe and Behrensmeyer 2004, 415). Indeed, *habilis* fossils are now found in association with terrestrial open country baboons *(Papio),* who remain the most widespread and successful Old World monkeys on the African savanna today (see Bobe and Behrensmeyer 2004). In their interpretation of early *Homo*'s adaptive strategy, Wood and Strait (2004, 150) argue that "unstable or changing environmental conditions in the late Pliocene may have driven early *Homo* species to reduce their reliance on arboreal resources and yet maintain a broad diet. As a result, species consolidated their adaption to bipedal locomotion while expanding their exploitation of terrestrial food items." This dietary shift may have included a greater reliance on meat, perhaps facilitated by the fact that *habilis* or the "handyman" was making stone tools. Thus, with *Homo habilis* we have the first real expansion of cranial capacity from the Australopiths and chimpanzee-size brain, the earliest record of lithic technology, and the adaptation of *habilis* to a complex range of open country habitats.[5]

The next hominid grade—*Homo erectus* (and *Homo ergaster*)—is shown near the top of figure 5.1. Here, at 1.8 million years, we come face to face with a true open savanna dweller with smaller teeth and jaws. More revealing, *Homo erectus* reveals from the neck down a human-like body, although its limbs are more robust than modern humans. What is so striking about *erectus* is the large increase in body size, with some individuals nearly six feet tall! Equally important, accompanying this bigger body is the size of the brain (even controlling for body weight) from a range of 700 cc to at least 1100 cc. As the earth grew steadily cooler, *Homo erectus* was the first hominid to become a long-range traveling biped who extended its range to Europe and Asia. In fact, *Homo*

---

5. This composite of early *Homo*'s features, lifeways, and evolutionary ecology is drawn from Wood and Strait 2004; Cela-Conde and Ayala 2003; Fleagle 1999; Wolpoff 1999; Campbell and Loy 2000; Foley 2002; McHenry and Coffing 2000; Bobe and Behrenmeyer 2004.

erectus reached China by 1.5 million years ago, carrying along sophisticated tool kits for colonization of many parts of both Europe and Asia. Given that a big brain is costly to maintain, there is no doubt that this large-bodied and big-brained hominid needed more food and higher-quality nutrition. It is surely no accident that *erectus* is associated with a large increase in the consumption of meat; and whether a scavenger or a hunter of game animals (Anton 2003), *Homo erectus* needed more protein to support its large brain.

By 700,000 years ago, brain size in these advanced hominids had expanded again in an unfolding continuum of increased cranial enlargement, a trend that is the hallmark of human evolution. While controversy exists over whether or not *Homo erectus* is a single gradually evolving species or is the ancestral stock for later hominids such as *Homo heidelbergensis* (known collectively also as *Archaic sapiens*), there can be no disagreement of the importance of *Homo erectus* in the scheme of human evolution. For surely, *Homo erectus* stock gave rise to later *Homo*; and during the reign of *erectus,* the hominids underwent major cognitive and organizational changes. It is difficult to reconstruct social structure from the fossil record, but *Homo erectus* was probably the first major contributor to the archaeological record. This taxa left its artifacts all over the African, European, and Asian continents; and these artifacts tell us about the tools, simple housing shelters, and butchering of animals. Thus *Homo erectus* originated in the late Pliocene and lived during most of the Pleistocene epoch, and in all likelihood, *erectus* was the ancestral stock of later forms of *Homo*. During the middle Pleistocene, populations of *Archaic sapiens* appeared.[6] Neanderthals are shown in figure 5.1 as a divergent lineage that went extinct in the late Pleistocene. By this time, brain size was fully in the human range and facial features had softened with smaller teeth. The overall robustness of the body was greater than modern humans. Finally, modern looking humans make their appearance about 150,000 years ago.

Thus the story of human evolution is a strange tale of evolved apes who carried into a series of mixed environmental niches the morphological and neurological characteristics of animals who had

---

6. This composite of *Homo erectus* and *Archaic sapiens* was drawn from Potts et al. 2004; Lee and Wolpoff 2003; Schwartz 2004; de Menocal 2004; Wood and Richmond 2000; Bobe et al. 2004; Stringer 2002; Reed 1997; Finlayson 2004; and Anton 2003.

evolved in an arboreal habitat. This tale began with early hominids who acquired a bipedal gait and who began to forge for new resources outside the forests, slowly migrating from the dense canopy forests to the well-watered forest edges. This initial shift in habitat probably resulted in little disruption to hominid lifeways because present-day chimpanzees forage about either in primary forests or on forest edges, moving about mostly on the ground to get from one fruiting-bearing tree to another. By nightfall, however, chimpanzees are comfortably situated in their makeshift beds in nearby trees, much like the hominids who had moved to the forest's edge. Dental features, like thick enamel (for tooth protection), suggest a gradual dietary shift from mostly ripe, soft fruits to harder tubers and more abrasive foods, a shift indicating that the Austropiths were experimenting with new foods by forging at times in more open woodlands. With the arrival of *Homo habilis,* there was a clear shift away from primary forests to secondary forests, bush lands, and arid grasslands terrain. And, as late Australopiths such as the robust *Parapithecus* along with *Homo habilis* ventured even further away from the safety of forests, they must have confronted greater predation risks, surely triggering a need for better organized foraging groups which are the key to survival in an open country environment where predators abound. Of course, other factors affect organizational arrangements, but as Stanford (2001, 753) points out, despite the risks, "animals must often spend time exposed to predation in order to forage for needed or highly desired foods or water." In a closed canopy forest, the safety of trees helps minimize risk, whereas in open, flat grassland savanna, where an animal can flee but not hide from predators, organization becomes essential. The better organized is a species on the savanna, the greater are its chances for survival. Thus, as primates moved from the protection of the forests to the dangers of open country grasslands, social organization would have enormous survival value. For most Old World monkeys, survival on the savanna would not be as problematic with their existing matrilines and hierarchies of dominance; selection would have much to work on in enhancing organization among savanna-dwelling monkeys. In fact, many present-day savanna dwellers march across the open country in military-like formation, with larger monkey males flanking smaller females and young. Indeed, predators face a well-organized phalanx of males who are ready to defend the troop (Rhine et al. 1985).

The fossil record tells, as we mentioned earlier, that species of *Homo* and *Papio* baboons coexisted in open areas of the savanna during the Plio-Pleistocene, but we also know that most apes who ventured into the open country went extinct. It is not difficult to see why such a "mass extinction" would occur because apes are not well organized, revealing weak tie networks and highly fluid group structures. Monkeys had behavioral propensities on which natural selection could work, whereas apes did not have these same propensities. And so it is important to ask: How did early *Homo* and eventually *Homo sapiens* become better organized in a parkland or open country habitat environment?

One hypothesis to entertain is that since monkeys and early *Homo* both faced similar adaptation problems (e.g., getting food, sleeping sites, predator protection), the solution was for natural selection to forge a social structure among hominids that more resembled "female-bonded" monkey groups. Yet such matrilocality and matrilineality can only exist *if* mothers and daughters remain in spatial proximity; and given that female dispersal exists in every living ape species, it is likely that *Homo* also inherited the legacy of female dispersal at puberty from the LCA of chimpanzees and hominids. Although the question of whether dispersal rates were higher for females or males in human history is currently being debated using DNA variation on mitochondrial DNA and the Y chromosome, it is true that in most preindustrial societies today, a strong bias after marriage still exists for patrilocal residence (for discussions see Pennisi 2001; Gibbons 1997; Wilder et al. 2004; Fox 1967; Murdock 1967; and Ember 1978). Thus, for *habilis*, given its ape legacy of fluid and loose-knit ties with female dispersal at puberty, adaptation to an open habitat must have presented a formidable challenge. For as G. L. Stebbins (1966, 103–4) emphasized, all sophisticated animals are richly designed with highly complex and precisely programmed patterns of gene and gene products that must be integrated with any new adaptive responses. Indeed, given that early *Homo* was already a highly complex and sophisticated end product of 20 million years of ape neurological and anatomical evolution, it is difficult to see how radical or dramatic mutations could play a major role in its adaptation to a new habitat; for, as R. A. Fisher has argued, "the probability that individual mutations will contribute to evolution is in inverse correlation to the intensity of their effect on the developing phenotype" (quoted in Stebbins 1966, 104). Instead, while changes due to random mutations surely had some evolutionary effect, most of the burden, we believe, was on the directed force of natural selection to elaborate, extend, or alter *Homo*'s already existing tendencies from its hominoid legacy. Thus, regardless of the selection pressures operating on hominids when they shifted to a parkland or semiarid savanna habitat, it would have taken an act of evolutionary gymnastics to convert such a long-standing hominoid social structure into a monkey-like matrifocal arrangement. Instead, our best bet is to return to the relational blueprint of humans' closest relative, the chimpanzees, and search for some clues into the likely social structure of hominids. Then, we can move to other biological characteristics that might also have been subject to selection among early open country hominids.

THE HOMINID HORDE

Today we can do much better than construct a purely speculative hypothesis about the ancient "horde." True, a certain amount of speculation is still involved, but we are on a much firmer empirical footing than early thinkers who offered highly conjectural portraits of "the horde." In particular, we can begin by returning to the network ties among living chimpanzees who represent our best view of what those apes who became hominids were like. Thus, using the tie structure among contemporary chimpanzees as our best template for *Homo,* we can begin with a population of up to 120 individuals who live within the boundaries of a community or regional population where they are free to move about alone or join temporary foraging parties within a defined block of forest. Let us now consider the core ties among living chimpanzees (see table 4.1, page 99) to see which might best serve as the organizational building blocks for a more tightly knit hominid social structure. These core ties are summarized below:

1. Mother–prepuberty male offspring ties are strong
2. Mother–prepuberty female offspring ties are strong
3. Mother–adult daughter ties are broken at puberty
4. Mother–adult son ties remain strong
5. Adult female–adult female ties are weak or null
6. Adult male–adult male ties are weak to moderate
7. Adult male–adult female ties are weak

Turning to ties (1) and (2), the strong ties between a mother and her dependent offspring certainly have potential for enhanced structure. In (3), however, adult mother/daughter ties are severed when daughter leaves for another community. In (4), the strong ties between mother and her son certainly qualify for a strong dyad structure, although they cannot serve as a *reproductive building block* for lineal kinship ties since this dyad avoids sexual intercourse. A social structure resting on (5) would be fundamentally unstable since most adult females, while tolerant of each other, exhibit neutral relations, having arrived as strangers from outside communities. Adult male ties in (6) can serve as a potential building block because unrelated males enjoy a common fellowship and share a "sense of community," while brothers enjoy strong ties. Finally, the weak adult male–adult female ties in (7) also have potential as a structural building block; indeed, strengthening the male/female dyad would increase the strength of ties in general, while building a stable, reproductive pair bond. As a result, this tie would have the potential for establishing intergenerational continuity through time. Thus, among contemporary chimpanzees, given the pattern of female dispersal at puberty, the following ties could be subject to selection that would strengthen hominid social structure:

1. The already strong ties between mothers and adult sons
2. The weak-to-moderate ties among adult males
3. The weak ties between adult males and adult females

Male chimpanzees also show some tendencies for dominance (Boehm 1999), although many observations of this propensity were made on chimpanzees that have been pushed together in unnatural circumstances. For example, Jane Goodall's (1986) famous chimpanzees at Gombe were habituated and fed by investigators, with the result that the density and competition among individuals for food probably increased dominance behaviors. Other studies documenting high levels of dominance among chimpanzees have also been conducted in zoos or other relatively confined spaces, where competition for resources is more intense and, no doubt, contributes to dominance hierarchies (de Waal 1996, 1992, 1989, 1982). One could argue that the dominance patterns that have emerged from these studies are very much like studying humans in prisons where dominance behavior is very pronounced in the inmate subculture—far more than in the broader culture. Yet, even if we assume that dominance is indeed a behavioral propensity among chimpanzees and, by inference, hominids, selection on these behavioral tendencies would be an ineffective way to increase solidarity without matrilines among females. Moreover, as Boehm (2004, 1993) has argued, the first hunter-gatherers sought to limit dominance, creating the egalitarian societies composed of nomadic gatherers and hunters who shared food.

But let us assume a time in the distant past, when selection worked on dominance tendencies as a strategy for creating more social order among the individualistic hominid ancestors of humans. It is not too far fetched to imagine a dominant male trying to control unrelated females from other communities or attempting to bring them together into a harem when, in fact, these females possessed only weak ties, if not some hostility and tension, among themselves. This male would probably exhaust himself to no avail and would, as a result, not promote fitness-enhancing solidarity in the group. Since there may have been propensities for dominance hierarchies among early *Homo* populations who ventured onto the savanna, natural selection may have taken this route and enhanced dominance behaviors, but without the matrilines to order female relations, this path to solidarity was probably a dead end, causing an extinction curve on those species where dominance had been selected and enhanced.

Furthermore, dominance by itself does not generate high levels of social solidarity. Rule by might alone creates resentments, conflict, and defection from the group, especially if those who are dominated do not have built into their neurology bioprogrammers for submissive behavior when confronted by a stronger male. Such was not likely to have been the case for adult males who would become our hominid ancestors. Indeed, Boehm (2004) may be correct in his view that the most fit nomadic hunting bands were typified by egalitarianism and sharing of resources, a pattern of organization that was made viable by males forming coalitions against any male who sought dominance. Thus, even with tendencies for dominance, successful hunters created systems of social control that worked against inequality as a strategy for group formation and, instead, opted for the higher levels of solidarity that arise from equality and sharing of resources. Moreover, as the sexual division of economic labor evolved, the exchange relation in food sharing between males and females (meat for plant food) would generate not only positive emotions but also considerations of justice and fair exchange—just as all exchanges among humans do today.

Thus the original "horde" was probably composed of associative ties that could be subject to solidarity-enhancing selection.

Whatever the merits of Boehm's argument, clearly fitness could only be enhanced by ties promoting solidarity among the members of the protosocial formations that would eventually evolve into hunting and gathering bands composed of nuclear families. Since natural selection can, of course, only work on what is available, we believe that the most parsimonious way for early *Homo* populations to reorganize once they made the transition out to more open country or savanna terrain was to begin the process of strengthening *any* social bonds readily available for selection to work on (for random mutations might never arise). Thus the first stage of *Homo* reorganization under savanna conditions, we believe, was the creation of a social arrangement that social scientists in the nineteenth century termed the horde.

The initial horde, we believe, revolved around the mother–son, adult male–adult male, and brother–brother relationships that typically form in chimpanzee communities. Thus the early *Homo* horde was not built around a nuclear family but rather around a mother and her sons, friendships among males, and females who had migrated from another community. To the extent that egalitarianism would promote solidarity, selection may have even worked to reduce the tendencies for dominance among humans' early *Homo* relatives.

Since chimpanzees reveal a hardwired propensity for sexual avoidance between a mother and her son, inbreeding depression would not occur and thereby decrease fitness. It is likely that female transfer from the group at puberty persisted, thus eliminating potential inbreeding between the father–daughter and brother–sister dyads (indeed, a pattern that was evident for the majority of preliterate societies, where patrilocal residence rules and exogamy sent females out of the band or village). Selection probably worked to enhance male solidarity and mother–son bonds because the fleeting and unstable parties known among chimpanzees would not be viable in an open country habitat.

This path would be the easiest route for natural selection to take if pressures to get organized were intense and evolution was punctuated. Problems of sexual conflict over mates would be minimal, since females would still be promiscuous, while at the same time, potential incest would be avoided as females migrated to new communities and as the mothers and sons continued to avoid sexual contact, just as present-day chimpanzees do.

For this basal society to evolve into a band composed of nuclear families, however, more extensive changes in behavior would be required. Males and females would have to form more stable pair bonds, while offspring would stay within the group for a longer period well beyond puberty, as did the offspring of many hunter-gathering populations among humans. To create behavioral propensities for establishing the bonds typical of nuclear families, much more drastic alteration of hominids' neuroanatomy would be necessary; and changes in the wiring of the brain would take much longer, especially changes that generated behavioral propensities that went against tendencies among apes for weak ties and female transfer to another community at puberty. Moreover, as the horde was transformed into the band organized around small groups of closely related nuclear families, the problem of incest avoidance would become more acute especially for the father–daughter dyad. While some Westermarck effect was possible, what would be needed was cultural prohibitions against incest that could be the functional equivalent of the hardwired sexual avoidance evident for the mother–son dyad and the full-blown Westermarck effect in brothers and sisters. Thus creating the rudimentary horde was only a first step in getting hominids better organized. Many more modifications in the hominid genome would be necessary; and the more socially inclined hominids became, the more incest and inbreeding needed to be regulated as old transfer behaviors—which had worked to limit the potential for inbreeding for millions of years—were altered.

NATURAL SELECTION AND ENHANCED SOCIALITY

To address the question of how increased solidarity was achieved among early *Homo* hordes—especially a solidarity that would eventually revolve around nuclear families in the band—we need to break down the question into two parts. First, how did natural selection rewire the hominid brain so as to create behavioral propensities for stronger social ties among all members of the "horde"? And second, how did enhanced sociality eventually lead to the formation of nuclear families that could avoid incestuous inbreeding? In our view, increased sociality was sorely needed once hominids left the forest fringe for an open country habitat where predators abounded; yet increasing attachments to the group and thereby keeping male and female offspring in the group past puberty raised the problem of inbreeding. To strengthen ties and then to create nuclear families lit the "red lamp of incest," as Robin Fox (1980) phrased the matter.

Increasing the Strength of Ties and Social Solidarity

Ingredients of Strong Ties and Solidarity

One way to reconstruct the route that natural selection took in making relatively low sociality hominids more socially inclined is to perform a thought experiment that addresses the question, What is necessary among contemporary humans to produce stronger social ties and bonds of solidarity? Since we know the outcome of what natural selection did, we can use this understanding of outcomes to help reconstruct just how the human brain was rewired to increase the strength of social ties among our hominid ancestors.

The first ingredient of stronger social bonds is the ability to mobilize and channel positive emotions. Without the flow of positive emotions, it is difficult to create and sustain social relationships among humans. Thus natural selection had to work on centers of the brain that could increase hominids' capacity for positive emotional arousal, while reducing the disruptive effects of negative emotions.

A second ingredient of solidarity is interpersonal attunement or, in George Herbert Mead's (1934) terms, "role taking" whereby the gestures emitted by individuals are mutually read so that each person derives a sense of how the other is likely to act. Natural selection would therefore need to enhance the ability of hominids to read body language so that the dispositions and likely courses of action of others could be anticipated. Such "role taking" would be particularly effective if the level and direction of emotional arousal of others could be read visually during role taking. A related transformation arising from the ability to read the emotional dispositions of others would be the capacity for empathy, whereby one person understands and, in high levels of empathy, actually feels the emotional dispositions of another. So, along with enhancing the ability to role take, natural selection also worked to increase the capacity for empathy during hominid evolution (Singer et al. 2004).[7] Since contemporary apes appear to evidence the capacity for empathy, there was already in place a structure on which natural selection could work to enhance empathy.

---

7. As reported by Singer et al. 2004, apparently the anterior cingulate cortex is one area responsible for people's ability to experience empathy. This area "lights up" when individuals begin to feel the pain and sadness of others; thus there appears to be a clear, hardwired basis for this emotional state.

A third feature of solidarity-producing interactions among humans is emotional entrainment whereby interactions develop a rhythmic synchronization of mutual give and take of positive emotions (Collins 2004). As interactions become synchronized, the flow of positive emotions increases and, thereby, raises the level of solidarity. Hence, natural selection would work on the hominid brain to enhance mutual responsiveness in ways that increased the rhythm of interactions and the flow of emotions.

A fourth characteristic of high solidarity interactions is the exchange of valued resources, one of the most important of these resources being positive affect. Exchanges that generate positive emotions and solidarity always involve reciprocity whereby the giving of resources by one actor is returned by the other actors; and even in relatively sterile experimental situations where the actors do not know each other personally, reciprocal exchanges generate commitments to the relationship (Lawler and Yoon (1996). Indeed, as Durkheim (1912) and Marcel Mauss (1924) emphasized long ago, commitments among individuals emerge from the reciprocal exchanges of gifts, which is just a special case of reciprocity. More recent theorizing in sociobiology makes much the same point with the concept of "reciprocal altruism." Natural selection worked on the hominid brain to increase responsiveness to reciprocity, while also increasing the cognitive capacity to remember who had, and had not, reciprocated offerings of resources in the past (Cosmides 1989). Given that "friends" in chimpanzee communities already engage in "sharing" and "cooperative exchange," directed selection on this trait could easily augment this existing tendency (Mitani et al. 2000). Moreover, a recent study of chimpanzees by Sarah Bronson reveals that when they are in close relationships, they tend to ignore unfair exchanges. In contrast, those in less close relationships refuse to exchange when shortchanged. If this willingness to "forgive" was evident in humans' distant ancestor, this behavioral propensity could be subject to further selection (preliminary report from *Science* online).

A fifth ingredient of solidarity among humans is sanctioning, in which conformity to expectations is rewarded with positive sanctions and lack of conformity is punished with negative sanctions. The key to solidarity, however, is a high ratio of positive to negative sanctioning because too many negative sanctions generate negative emotional arousal and resentments. Thus natural selection began to increase the capacity of hominids to monitor behaviors for conformity and to increase the likelihood that such conformity would be rewarded with positive sanctions, while at the same time, making individuals reluctant to use too many negative sanctions.

A final feature of solidarity is moral coding in which individuals in the group are able to symbolize with objects their social relationships and to regulate the flow of interaction with norms, beliefs, and values. This capacity for moral coding in which symbols take on a moral character, whose violation arouses righteous anger, would greatly increase commitment to the group. Although moral coding may not have been a force in early hominid evolution, it would greatly enhance the ability to regulate group activity and to increase commitments to the group. Hence, as natural selection increased brain size, while enhancing hominids' capacities for emotions, role taking, empathy, exchanging, sanctioning, and moral coding increasingly became a feature of later hominid groupings.

If this list of ingredients for stronger social bonds and increased solidarity is accurate, we should see signs on the neurology of humans. The brain was rewired among hominids to increase the capacities for those behaviors listed above; and although it is not possible yet to pinpoint areas of the brain responsible for each item in the list, there are data that point to certain areas of the brain as is discussed below that are known to be responsible for many of the solidarity-enhancing behaviors necessary for more tightly knit group structures. Thus, although nothing like a complete portrait of the neurological basis for stronger social ties can be drawn, elements of the picture can still be seen. There are footprints in the neurology of the human brain that provide a sense for how natural selection was working on the hominid brain of our ancestors to increase the strength of ties among those who became better organized.

The Neurology of Strong Ties and Solidarity

Figure 5.2 delineates some of the key structures in the human brain. For our purposes, the brain can be roughly separated into the neocortical and subcortical areas. The subcortical areas evolved earlier than the neocortex; and it is in these subcortical regions that emotions are ultimately generated. These emotional modules are what is sometimes termed the limbic system (MacLean 1990), although it might be better to see the limbic system as a series of modules in the brain that produce varying types of emotional responses that generate emotions.[8] The neocortex gets much of the press in sociological discussions of humans because it is so much larger compared to the neocortex of other animals (controlling for body size which is correlated with brain size); and because of the size of the neocortex, humans can create and use culture to a degree beyond any other animal. But long before the hominid neocortex became very large, the emotion systems or modules in subcortical areas of the brain had evolved, and since stronger social ties and enhanced solidarity depend on emotional arousal, these subcortical areas are just as interesting as the larger neocortex that enables humans to possess culture. Hominid brains did not become very large until late in hominid evolution around 2.5 millions years ago; up to *Homo habilis* (1.8 to 2.5 million years ago) and later *Homo erectus* at 1.5 to 1.8 million years ago, the overall size of the brain was about the same as contemporary chimpanzees at around 400 cc. With *Homo erectus,* the brain had evolved to a range of 700 cc to 1100 cc but was still smaller than the average human brain.[9]

Thus increased sociality and social organization, we believe, did not initially come with an enlarged neocortex that enabled hominids to produce culture but, rather, with alterations in older areas of the hominoid brain, most of which are subcortical. One way to get a gross sense for what natural selection was doing can be seen in table 5.1, which reports the relative size of ape and human brains, relative to a base of "1" for a primitive mammal *(Tenrecinae)* that is very much like the one that originally climbed into the arboreal habitat and initiated the primate line some 60 million years ago. The numbers in the table report how much greater than *Tenrecinae* various brain structures are for apes and humans

---

8. Emotions are generated by four basic body systems (Le Doux 1996; Turner 2000): the neurotransmitter and neuroactive peptide system, the general hormonal system, the autonomic nervous system, and the musculoskeletal system. The complex emotions that humans use are generated by interactions among these four systems.

9. It is now possible to assess the action of genes known to influence brain size in humans. One study examining the ASPM gene (affect abnormal spindle-like microcephaly) demonstrated that selection on this gene was significantly accelerated (examining the pace of protein evolution scaled to mutation rate) in the great apes, but even more so in the lineage leading to humans. Thus genes affecting brain size were subject to selection, leading to the larger brains of the great apes and especially humans (see Evans et al. 2004). For a more general view of how gene and chromosomal structure caused specialization of primates, especially humans, see Navarro and Barton 2003.

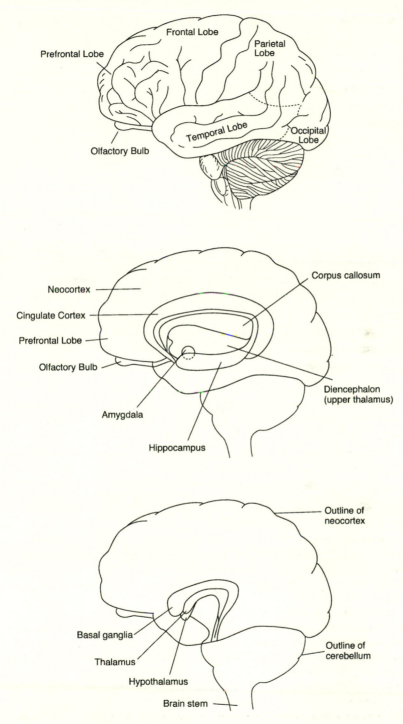

Figure 5.2 The Human Brain and Emotions

Table 5.1 Relative Size of Brain Structures in Apes and Humans, Compared to *Tenrecinae**

	Apes	Humans
Neocortex	61.88	196.41
Subcortical		
Thalamus/		
hypothalamus	8.57	14.76
Amygdala	1.85	4.48
Centromedial	1.06	2.52
Basolateral	2.45	6.02
Septum	2.16	5.45
Hippocampus	2.99	4.87
Transition cortices	2.38	4.43

Sources: Stephan 1983; Stephan and Andy 1969, 1977; Eccles 1989.
*Numbers in the table denote how many times larger than *Tenrecinae* each structure of the brain is, with the structure in *Tenrecinae* representing a base of 1.

(Stephan 1983; Stephan and Andy 1969, 1977). Thus the neocortex of apes is, on average, almost sixty-two times as large as that for *Tenrecinae,* whereas the neocortex of humans is 196 times as large; and a disproportionate amount of this increase in size is in the prefrontal cortex.[10] By using *Tenrecinae* as a base of 1, then, it is possible to compare the relative size of ape and human brains. Another feature of the figures in table 5.1 is that they control for

---

10. Another way to measure and compare the brain structures of apes and humans is to assess the relative size among various regions of the brain. In essence, this procedure involves increasing the overall size of an ape brain to the same size as the human brain and, then, determining the relative size of different areas of the brain. For example, Semendeferi et al. 2002 have compared the size and structure of areas such as the prefrontal cortex, finding that this area is slightly larger in humans relative to overall brain size than it is in apes, although other data by Semendeferi and Damasio 2000 report that the prefrontal cortex in humans and apes is about the same. Holloway 2002 has argued that the prefrontal cortex is only moderately larger, perhaps 4–6 percent, concluding that the *relative* size of those portions of the brain devoted to cognition has not grown much since the split with the common ancestor to humans and the great apes. Yet in our view, *absolute* size matters. Natural selection is a conservative process, and if there were selection pressures for higher cognitive functioning, it would be unlikely to select and increase one structure like the prefrontal cortex to the exclusion of other neuro structures. It would be far easier to grow the entire neocortex rather than increase one area and leave another area as it was. The brain of higher primates represented an integrated system, and it would be far less disruptive to fitness to increase the overall size of the brain, leaving the relative size of structures in the brain largely intact.

body size that, as noted above, is correlated with brain size. Hence the numbers report the relative size of various regions of the brain, controlling for the relative body size of different species of apes and humans. As is evident, the neocortex of humans is dramatically larger than that of apes, but equally intriguing is the increase in size of subcortical areas. The diencephalon (composed of the thalamus and hypothalamus which route stimuli to emotion centers *and* the neocortex) is almost twice as large in humans as that evident in the brains of apes; the amygdala (the center for anger and fear) is over twice as large; the septum (the area for sexual drives and pleasure in mammals) is over twice as large; the hippocampus (the region for intermediate-term memory and associations between cognitions and emotions) is 50 percent larger than in apes; and the transition cortices connected to the hippocampus (that store working and short-term memory) are over 50 percent larger.

The differences in size of these modules do not, of course, offer fine-grained details about function, but they do suggest that many of the differences between apes and humans revolve around subcortical neuroanatomy. Indeed, data now indicate that, even though humans share 98.7 percent of their genes with chimpanzees, much larger differences can be found in how base pairs on specific genes are sequenced, in deletions and insertions of genetic material on genes, and in how genes are expressed in phenotypes (Pennisi 2003, 2002b; Kasserman et al. 1999). Of particular note are changes in the genes regulating brain structures that, apparently, have been far more active in humans and, no doubt, their hominid ancestors than in all other primates over the past few million years, giving genes new expressions in humans not evident among other primates.[11] Thus, while the genes are similar or the same, their expression has varied over the course of hominid evolution and, as a consequence, produced a brain that is significantly different from humans' closest relatives, the apes. Moreover, much of this rewiring of the brain did not revolve around speech functions. There are now techniques for measuring genes for how much selection pressure they have been under; and one recent study of the first gene known to be associated with speech structures reveals that this gene has been under intense selection pressures for less than 200,000 years and, more likely, only about 120,000 years or roughly

---

11. This finding also lends support to our use of chimpanzees as a model for speculating on the nature of the last common ancestors to humans and their closest relative. Chimpanzees have evolved, but much less than the hominid line leading to humans.

the time that modern humans have existed (as summarized by Balter and Gibbons 2002, 1105; see also Enard et al. 2002a). Thus full-blown speech as we know it was probably a very recent evolutionary event, coming perhaps only with the emergence of humans as a species. Other evidence suggests that the brain expanded during hominid evolution for more than language and speech. For example, new techniques using MRIs and then creating casts of the relative size for areas of the brain allow for the comparison among the brains of chimpanzees, humans, and fossilized hominid skulls. One of the surprising findings of this technique (Falk 2002; also reported by Gibbons 2002e) is that the right side of the brain in hominids and then human hominids grew as much or even more than the left side where the major language and speech centers are located (Broca's area for speech production and Wernicke's area for speech comprehension, and related tissues on the left temporal lobe). Since it is generally assumed that as the language-bearing side of the brain, more asymmetry should be evident on the left temporal lobe. But, the right side was also larger, and this growth is evident in older hominid casts. The author (Falk 2002) of the study suggests that the enlargement along the right side is important for understanding the "prosodic features of speech" such as rhythm, tone, and emotional content. This conclusion still reveals a speech bias because it assumes that the right side supports speech, but given the early emergence of this asymmetry among hominids, the opposite could be concluded: rhythm, tones, and emotion came first; speech was piggy-backed onto a system for rhythmic communication revolving around emotions, as expressed in body language and perhaps intonations of vocal sounds (but not fully articulated speech).

The significance of these data is that stronger social ties and solidarity were not the result of spoken language and culture. Rather, as Jonathan Turner (2000) has hypothesized, the first languages revolved around emotional phonemes and syntax expressed through body language: facial expressions, body movements, body countenance, and maybe auditory intonations. Long before humans used verbal language and symbols to build more complex cultures, hominids were communicating, via their bodies, emotions that were used to forge stronger bonds and increase social solidarity. The footprints of how selection was working are all over subcortical portions of the brain involved in emotions.

Let us briefly summarize some of the activities of key subcortical areas. The thalamus receives sensory inputs (sound, vision, smell, and touch) from the relevant sense modality and then sends signals to the key limbic systems that activate emotions. The thalamus also sends a signal to the appropriate lobe in the neocortex: occipital lobe for vision; parietal for touch or, more generally, haptic senses; temporal for auditory; and the olfactory bulb (which is still subcortical) for smell. The circuits to the neocortex are, however, longer than those to subcortical areas of the brain, and hence the emotions are aroused before individuals become cognitively aware of what has stimulated the emotions (Le Doux 1996). The amygdala is responsible for fear and anger responses (on different portions of this structure), while serving as an important conduit between subcortical limbic systems and the prefrontal cortex where rational thought occurs and where many longer-term memories are stored. In humans, the amygdala has areas for pleasure attached to its basolateral segments, and in fact, it is these additional areas for pleasure that account for much of the increase in the overall size of the human amygdala relative to that of apes (Eccles 1989, 102). It is indeed curious that centers for positive emotions would be attached to the most primal center of emotions in mammals, especially negative emotions. The septum generates the pleasure associated with the sex drive, and it is also interesting that an area which is already a source of pleasure in mammals would have additional areas for pleasure in humans, a fact that will have relevance for understanding the emergence of the nuclear family. The hippocampus and adjacent transition cortices store intermediate-term memories (around two years) by attaching emotions to cognitions. After two years, if the memory has been recalled and the emotions associated with it relived, the memory is shipped to the prefrontal cortex for longer-term memory. The hippocampus also appears to be the repository of unconscious emotional memories that activate the body systems that generate emotions (Le Doux 1996). Reduced hippocampal activity, coupled with activity in the dorsolateral prefrontal cortex, are both involved in the repression of unwanted memories (thus giving repression a neurological mechanism; see Anderson et al. 2004). The cingulate cortex, a distinctive band of neocortical tissue sitting atop and around the subcortical limbic systems, has many important effects on emotions, cognitions, and memories.

What these footprints signal is that hominids' emotional capacities were being expanded, perhaps even before the increases in the neocortex that began with early *Homo* and then continued through *Homo erectus* to *Homo sapiens*. The rather modest growth in the size of the brain for 5 million years after the separation from the last common ancestor to humans and chimpanzees may have been mostly subcortical and, if the neocortex was subject to selection for increased size, it seems reasonable to hypothesize that the cingulate cortex was the first neocortical structure subject to selection because it is older than those distinctly different neocortical tissues on top and surrounding the cingulate ring. The cingulate cortex is the center for ancient mammalian responses such as mother–infant bonding, the infant separation cry, and playfulness, as well as a growing list of other involvements in mediating between subcortical and cortical functions in the human brain.[12]

Let us now see how these areas of the brain could have been involved in generating stronger social ties and increased solidarity among hominids. The first ingredient for stronger social bonds and solidarity is positive emotions, and control of negative emotions. Apes do not have high levels of cognitive control over their emotions as they increase in intensity, whereas humans do. The prefrontal cortex is one area where this control is gained, as is the anterior cingulate cortex (Kerns et al. 2004; Matsumoto et al. 2003); and it is likely that the amygdala, as a routing station for limbic stimuli on their way to the prefrontal cortex is also involved. Certainly one of the earliest adaptations that hominids on the open country savanna had to achieve was control over emotions and noise that comes from emotional outbursts. With neocortical control over limbic processes—at least until the emotions become too intense—the breadth and complexity of hominid emotions could expand. More variations on the primary emotions could now occur, as is summarized in table 5.2 for the four emotions that all scholars agree are primary.[13] Other candidates for primary emotions include surprise, disgust, anticipation, and interest; and while some researchers add additional primary emotions to their lists, these appear to be variations of the four summarized in table 5.2. The growth of all these subcortical areas for emotional arousal indicates that selection was working on emotion centers to expand hominids' emotional repertoire; and this expansion is best explained by assuming that emotions were the backbone of stronger social ties and increased group solidarity—just as they are

---

12. For details of this argument and the underlying neurological systems involved, see Turner 2000.

13. For examples of research and theory on primary emotions, see Emde 1980; Panskepp 1982; Turner 1996c; Trevarthen 1984; Arnold 1960; Izard 1992; Ekman 1984; Plutchik 1980; Kemper 1987.

Table 5.2 Variants of Primary Emotions

Satisfaction–Happiness

Low intensity	Moderate intensity	High intensity
contentment	cheerfulness	joy
sanguineness	buoyance	bliss
serenity	friendliness	rapture
gratification	amiability	jubilance
enjoyment	gaiety	

Aversion–Fear

Low intensity	Moderate intensity	High intensity
concern	misgivings	terror
hesitance	trepidation	horror
reluctance	anxiety	high anxiety

Assertion–Anger

Low intensity	Moderate intensity	High intensity
annoyance	displeasure	dislike
agitation	frustration	loathing
irritation	belligerence	disgust
vexation	contention	hatred
perturbance	hostility	despisement
	ire	detestation
	animosity	wrath

Disappointment–Sadness

Low intensity	Moderate intensity	High intensity
discouragement	dismay	sorrow
dispiritedness	disheartenment	heartsickness
	glumness	despondence
	resignation	anguish
	gloom	
	woe	
	pain	

for contemporary humans (for another evolutionary analysis of emotions and social organization, see Hammond 2003).

One of the real evolutionary obstacles to building social relations with positive emotions is that three out of the four primary emotions in mammals are negative. Anger, fear, and sadness are not emotions that, by themselves, lead to strong social relations; and so natural selection needed to find a way around this fact, perhaps by grafting areas for pleasure and positive affect onto the amygdala, which as noted earlier, is the center for fear and anger. By essentially "mixing" positive with negative emotions, more associative emotions are produced, as is outlined in table 5.3, which lists what are termed first-order emotions that come from

Table 5.3 First-Order Elaborations of Primary Emotions

Satisfaction–Happiness

Satisfaction–happiness +   *produces*
    aversion–fear   →   wonder, hope, relief, gratitude, pride
Satisfaction–happiness +   *produces*
    assertion–anger   →   vengeance, appeasement, calm, relish,
                                               triumph, bemusement
Satisfaction–happiness +   *produces*
    disappointment–sadness   →   nostalgia, yearning, hopefulness pride

Aversion–Fear

Aversion–fear +   *produces*
    satisfaction–happiness   →   awe, reverence, veneration
Aversion–fear +   *produces*
    assertion–anger   →   revulsion, repulsion, antagonism,
                                               dislike, envy
Aversion–fear +   *produces*
    disappointment–sadness   →   dread, wariness

Assertion–Anger

Assertion–anger +   *produces*
    satisfaction–happiness   →   snubbing, mollification, rudeness,
                                               placation, righteousness
Assertion–anger +   *produces*
    aversion–fear   →   abhorrence, jealousy, suspiciousness
Assertion–anger +   *produces*
    disappointment–sadness   →   bitterness, depression, feeling betrayed

Disappointment–Sadness

Disappointment–sadness +   *produces*
    satisfaction–happiness   →   acceptance, moroseness, solace,
                                               melancholy
Disappointment–sadness +   *produces*
    aversion–fear   →   regret, forlornness, remorse, misery
Disappointment–sadness +   *produces*
    assertion–anger   →   aggrievement, discontent, dissatis-
                                               faction, lack of fulfillment,
                                               boredom, envy, sullenness

combinations among the four primary emotions.[14] Moreover, more complex second-order emotions emerge from combinations of the

---

14. See Plutchik 1980 for another conceptualization along these lines. The metaphor is mixing primary colors on a color wheel, but obviously this is not what actually occurs. The interactions among the body systems responsible for emotions, coupled with larger size of key limbic structures, are involved in generating this larger array of emotions. But no one currently understands how these emotions are actually generated.

Table 5.4 The Structure of Shame and Guilt

Rank order of primary emotions	Second-order emotions
	Shame
1	disappointment–sadness (at self)
2	assertion–anger (at self)
3	aversion–fear (about consequences to self)
	Guilt
1	disappointment–sadness (at self)
2	aversion–fear (about consequences to self)
3	assertion–anger (at self)

three negative emotions. As table 5.4 shows, emotions like guilt and shame are the outcome of different rank orderings of negative emotions. Such emotions are essential to a moral order because if people did not feel guilty when violating moral codes or ashamed of their incompetent actions in social contexts, social order by rules and morality would be impossible. Evolution probably worked over a long period of time, first generating cortical control over emotions, then elaborating variants of the primary emotions, next building up combinations of positive emotions to dilute the power of the three negative emotions, and finally combining the three negative emotions to produce shame and guilt. The end result is that emotions became the basis for increasing the strength of social ties and promoting solidarity among low-sociality hominids who have no bioprogrammers for behaviors that create herds, packs, pods, or prides, flocks, and other hardwired propensities for group cohesion evident among most other mammals.

Emotions provide a means for assessing the internal dispositions of others and their likely courses of action. Role taking is thus a process of reading body cues and voice inflections; and since humans are, like all primates, visually dominant, the brain is wired to look at others when seeking information. Vision is also a very fast process because it allows for larger gestalts of information to be taken in rapidly, thus increasing both the speed and range of inputs from role taking (compare, for example, vision with touch or speech which are sequential modalities; it is necessary to wait for a sequence of touches or words to gain a full sensory input, whereas vision operates as a gestalt modality by taking in a great deal of information simultaneously). Since apes also communicate through visual signals, primarily through the face (Menzel 1971) but also by touching, body positioning, and vocal cries, natural selection had existing structures on which to select (Whiten 2002; Ladygina-Kohts 2002). The visual dominance of all higher primates is already wired to orient individuals to the face, where information about emotions is easily read, thereby increasing the capacity for interpersonal attunement and bonding. In fact primates reveal areas of the brain—the fusiform face area (or FFA)—that biases visual attention to the faces of others; furthermore, this area of the brain allows for the "seeing of face" even when only contextual cues are available, with the brain filling in the missing details of the face (Cox, Meyers, and Sinha 2004). When human beings engage in face-to-face speech or talking, they always direct their attention to the faces of others and simultaneously read their emotional cues. To engage someone in conversation and look elsewhere while speaking to them usually brings an exchange to an abrupt end. Moreover, humans are particularly sensitive to fear and anger in the face. In one study, for example, reading the direction of another's gaze determined whether the activation of the amygdala generated a sense of fear or anger in the observer (Adams et al. 2003). In other studies on humans, the hippocampus is actively involved in associations of faces with names and in learning new associations (Wirth et al. 2003); and it is likely that in the past the hippocampus was active in associating emotional states of others with various lines of potential behavior. All of these abilities are possible *without* an elaborate neocortex, thus taking the burden off natural selection during early hominid evolution to produce a big-brained animal who could use culture to forge social bonds. Instead, emotional attunement could be achieved primarily through coupling visual dominance with subcortical limbic systems.

At some point in hominid evolution, Turner (2000) hypothesizes, a "body language" of phonemes and syntax emerged to denote and communicate specific emotional states; and indeed, emotions through face and body countenance were likely the first language in hominids, probably appearing relatively early in hominid evolution and providing the primary basis for stronger social ties and enhanced solidarity. In fact, humans still rely on this body- and visually based emotional language system to "really know" what someone is thinking and feeling. Later, auditory language could be grafted onto the body language of emotions. Since contemporary apes can learn the vocabulary and syntax of spoken language, there was a hardwired capacity for natural selection to work on (see Savage-Rumbaugh et al. 1993); and using emotions and the visual sense modality would be the easiest route for natural selection to take, especially since reworking of the muscles and tissues of the lips, tongue, and vocal track involved much more genetic material. Early *Homo* on the savanna had to get organized rapidly, or die, and natural selection found a route for increasing interpersonal attunement, using the existing wiring for visual dominance and cortical control of emotions that first emerged in the hominid line.

Indeed, the initial movement to visual dominance among higher primates in the arboreal habitat created the brain structures—association cortices such as the inferior parietal lobe—that integrate the sense modalities and make vision dominant. These association areas of the brain, located where occipital, parietal, and temporal lobes meet, constituted a preadaptation for language which natural selection usurped for the language of emotions, with this area only later being adapted for auditory language (Geschwind 1970, 1965a,b; Geschwind and Damasio 1984).[15]

A third feature of interaction that produces solidarity is emotional entrainment through rhythmic synchronization of gestures signaling positive emotions (Collins 2004). The asymmetries on the right side of the brain represent one footprint of how natural selection was working. By expanding the capacity to use emotional language and to get interaction in rhythm, the emotional "effervescence," as Émile Durkheim (1912) termed it, that comes from the give-and-take of emotions would strengthen social bonds and cause increased group solidarity. Later, as spoken language was grafted onto the innate language abilities, the rhythmic flow of talk and conversation could achieve the same end; and when both body and spoken language are in sync, the flow of positive emotions increases and thereby enhances group solidarity.

A fourth element of stronger social bonds and solidarity is reciprocal exchange of valued resources. Reciprocal altruism has long been a centerpiece of biological theories of cooperation, with the

---

15. A preadaptation is a structure that emerged for reasons other than what it eventually becomes with further natural selection. Thus the association areas that make language possible originally arose as the mechanism that shifted the brain of primates from olfactory to visual dominance; these association cortices were not created for language but simply made language possible, given a later fitness-enhancing value of language. Without a random mutation, language could not emerge unless there was an existing structure on which natural selection could select. It likely emerged only because there was a preadaptation for this behavioral capacity in the great apes (see Rumbaugh and Washburn 2003).

argument being that when unrelated individuals help each other, there is an implicit expectation that any help given now will later be reciprocated (Trivers 1971). With mutual assistance, fitness of all kin is increased, and thus natural selection programmed into the neuroanatomy of many animals' behavioral propensities for reciprocity (Cosmides 1989). Selection pressures for reciprocity would be particularly intense on animals such as apes, who do not have other bioprogrammers for strong social bonds and group cohesion among adults. There is mounting evidence that among primates, especially monkeys, individuals have a sense of fairness. Sarah Bronson and Frans de Waal (2003), for example, have found that Capuchin monkeys (New World monkeys) will exchange resources with investigators, but when they see another individual getting an even more valuable reward, they will refuse to exchange until given the better payoff—thus suggesting that reciprocity is a very old behavioral propensity in primates and, probably, for most higher mammals. Not surprisingly, chimpanzees, the authors note, reveal similar tendencies. Thus it is likely that natural selection had neurological structures to work on, if exchange reciprocity would increase group cohesion and, thereby, promote fitness. In humans, certain areas of the brain—the bilateral anterior insula and the dorsolateral prefrontal cortex—are activated during gaming exercises involving calculations of payoffs (Sanfey et al. 2003). Thus natural selection clearly did some rewiring of the hominid brain to increase the capacity to calculate costs, rewards, and reciprocity in exchange payoffs. Such calculations would, of course, become more elaborate as cultural "rules of the game" and conceptions of "justice" emerged with expansion of the neocortex, but the fact that monkeys and apes make implicit calculations of fairness indicates that exchange reciprocity does not depend on culture; it is hardwired into the primate line. Also of interest is the finding that humans in games are willing to punish those who do not reciprocate, even if pursuit of punishment reduces the overall rewards that a person will get (Vogel 2004). Revenge is thus an emotion than overrides rationality (and, as table 5.3 summarizes, is a combination of anger and happiness).

The final ingredient that we suggested as promoting solidarity is sanctioning. Normally, we think of sanctioning only in relation to the moral codes of culture. We punish those who violate expectations, while offering rewards to those who conform to norms, beliefs, and values. Yet it is also likely that sanctioning was a mechanism of social control long before culture emerged to provide the moral yardstick by which conformity could be measured. The fact that monkeys and apes have a sense of fairness hardwired into their neuroanatomy indicates that noncultural standards can exist and that, in all likelihood, punishments will be given to those who are not fair. Natural selection would, therefore, have an existing capacity to select on, pushing hominids toward propensities to sanction negatively those who did not cooperate. However, negative sanctions do not build solidarity; in fact, if used too frequently, they do just the opposite and arouse negative emotions like anger, fear, and sadness that do not promote strong bonds or social solidarity. Thus, as hominids' emotional capacities expanded, selection worked on increasing the use of positive sanctions or rewards for individuals who cooperated and reciprocated. Much of this positive sanctioning would occur as a byproduct of rhythmic synchronization of gesturing, with being in rhythm synchronization, per se, marking reciprocity for the emotions exchanged as well as mutual giving of positive sanctioning. For relatively low sociality hominids to begin cooperating, subordinating their individualism and mobility to group goals, would require a delicate balance between a predominance of positive sanctions (perhaps built into the very process of rhythmic synchronization) and strategic use of negative sanctions when severe transgressions of expected cooperation occurred.

In sum, then, our argument is simple, even though we have left out many of the important neurological details (see Turner 2000 for more of these details): natural selection began early in *Homo* evolution of hominids to work on subcortical limbic systems, increasing the range of emotions that individuals could use to forge social bonds. Thus in the early horde, mothers and their sons, adult males, and brothers could become more emotionally attuned to each other, giving and receiving affect that would promote solidarity. We can assume that incoming females to the "horde" could also have become more emotionally attuned to each other, although chimpanzee females do not evidence high solidarity; and, as a consequence, there may have been very little for natural selection alone to work on in creating stronger bonds among unrelated females[16]

---

16. Joan Silk et al. (2003) found that highly social baboon females have a much better chance than less social females of seeing their infants survive. Staying in touch, literally through reciprocal grooming activities, gives these social females a reproductive advantage. Of course, baboons are monkeys and, thus, have natural tendencies to form matrilines and cohesive groups. Female apes who have migrated into the group from another community and hence are not related, and

who would be strangers to each other. For most species of hominids, selection may not have taken the route of enhancing the emotional bonds among the horde, perhaps condemning them to death because they could not become sufficiently organized to survive in open country savanna conditions. When animals do not have bioprogrammers for forming stable groups, as is the case for chimpanzees and as was certainly true for the ancestors of humans, an alternative mechanism for bonding had to be "found" by natural selection, especially if selection pressures for group cohesion were strong.[17] For hominids, the route to cohesion depended on expanding the use of emotions as is so evident in the emotional complexity of modern humans, and the more complex the emotional repertoire of hominids, the more subtle emotional communication could become, enabling them to form flexible bonds of social cohesion.

New Dilemmas Arising from Emotionally Based Solidarity

Using emotions as the basis for forging stronger bonds, however, creates a new problem. Emotional attachments began, at some point, to disrupt the transfer patterns that had prevented inbreed-

---

(note 16 continued) in fact are strangers to each other, experience less of this kind of sociality. Yet if selection could have made female hominids more social, the cooperation that would have arisen from grooming and other social activities would have increased the fitness of not only individuals but also the group as a whole.

17. One such alternative mechanism for increased sociality is the heightened sexuality and rather bizarre sexual rituals of adult female bonobos (Pan paniscus). Bonobos, who branched away from common chimpanzees about 2–3 million years ago, comprise a small isolated population living along the Zaire River basin. In this habitat, with food resources concentrated in large patches, individuals are forced to cluster together much more than common chimpanzees (Pan troglodytes). For a successful adaptation to this specialized environment, selection worked on the sexuality of female bonobos (compared to common chimpanzees) by (1) prolonging their receptivity to males in order to strengthen male–female ties and (2) obliging female dyads when in close proximity to ritually perform a "genito-genital rubbing," or GG rubbing, whereby they rub their genitals together rapidly as they ventrally hold each other (to strengthen female–female ties). Craig Stanford (1999, 77) notes that they do this "apparently as a means of reducing what would otherwise be an unacceptable level of social tension between them." Thus, while common chimpanzee females (Pan troglodytes) typically feed and move about alone with their offspring, bonobo females utilize what is a seemingly hardwired, sexually based maneuver to foster nonkinship-based affiliations. In contrast to humans, selection seemingly concentrated on females in bonobo society to facilitate a more cohesive social structure.

ing. Females may have delayed moving from their natal groups as their emotions were aroused and their attachments to the group increased. Moreover, given the life history of hominids for longer periods of maturation through infancy and juvenile periods, there were phylogenetic forces working to keep offspring in their natal groups, thus increasing long-term emotional attachments. As a result, females could potentially become targets of their father's and brothers' sexual interest, although for brothers the Westermarck effect, which appears to run through the primates and most mammals as well, could have operated to reduce brother–sister matings.

With more intense emotional bonds among members of hominid bands, sexual arousal would be more intense. Indeed, as is revealed in table 5.1, the septum as the source of sexual drives is much larger in humans, controlling for body size, than in apes. This increase in size is the result of new areas for pleasure having been added by natural selection to the septum (Eccles 1989), thereby increasing the attractiveness of sexual partners. Even mother–son avoidance that is hardwired into the neuroanatomy of chimpanzees and presumably the ancestor of present-day chimpanzees and humans could potentially be breached if sexual drives and more generalized emotional attachments intensified; and the same could be said for the Westermarck effect if this effect was not fully activated. Perhaps selection pressures were put on the Westermarck effect found among chimpanzees to heighten its effect and, thereby, stave off sexual relations among related members of the hominid band. And maybe the potential for incest represented one source of selection pressure for the expansion of the neocortex capable of developing a culturally based incest taboo that could suppress incestuous sexual relations. Yet it is likely that the incest taboo emerged rather late in hominid evolution since the size of the hominid brain did not undergo a dramatic increase in size until *Homo erectus* around 2 million years ago. Thus, as long as emotions, coupled with life history forces, subverted female transfer from the natal group and community, incest remained a distinct possibility in the now more cohesive bands of hominids. And since inbreeding is so dramatically harmful to the offspring of humans, such was no doubt the case for hominids, with the result that incest would reduce not only the fitness of individuals but the hard-won viability of group structures held together by emotions.

There can be no doubt that the incest taboo was created to prevent incest, but just when in hominid evolution did the brain become large enough for such a taboo to emerge and regulate sexual conduct? There is a gap of several million years between the time that hominids' emotional capacities were developing (and producing cohesive group structures built around emotional dynamics) and the moment in hominid history where the brain was large enough to create a culturally based incest taboo. It may be that older transfer patterns persisted right up to the emergence of the incest taboo, late in hominid evolution. It is also possible that inbreeding did occur, thereby decreasing the fitness of some hominid bands. Perhaps hominids recognized the consequences of inbreeding and its source, and somehow developed ways to limit inbreeding. And maybe the Westermarck effect was sufficient to control inbreeding. We will never know for sure just what occurred as emotions were used to forge new bonds, while potentially increasing the possibility for incestuous sexual relations.

We can know that the mother–son avoidance pattern was probably sufficient to ward off high rates of mother–son incest, just as it now does for present-day chimpanzees and humans. But what of brother–sister and father–daughter incest? The Westermarck effect might help lower incest for these dyads; and maybe groups became sufficiently large so that the probability of a "father" having sexual relations with his daughter before she transferred from the group was low. And if brothers had other females whom they could approach, the combination of the Westermarck effect and ready availability to incoming females could have been sufficient to reduce rates of incest.

But at some point, natural selection pushed for the emergence of the nuclear family, the emergence of which would intensify all of the pressures enumerated above for incest. Daughters might stay even longer after puberty; fathers would "know" their daughters because the father–mother pair bond would reduce what had previously been promiscuous sexual relations between males and females. The family unit emerged, no doubt, as a way to increase social solidarity and ensure fitness of offspring, The family also represented a way to create a stable unit for big-bodied primates who could not form large bands, without the "fission–fusion" capacity to break the band apart when resources were scarce (as is frequently the case for large animals during periods when food was widely dispersed on the savanna). By attaching males to females who invested in their offspring, the family represented a stable unit that could break away from a band and form a new, smaller band. Offspring would be protected in these fission–fusion patterns, thus increasing fitness. Yet this new family solidarity was built on even more powerful emotions that could disrupt sexual avoidance mechanisms evident among apes. Moreover, the increase in the size of the septum, making sexual attraction even greater and perhaps producing emotions like love, added additional pressure on the nuclear family. Thus the evolution of the nuclear family, while promoting greater group cohesion as the band organized nuclear family units into hunting and gathering activities, also increased the possibilities for incest (Diggs 1997).

In sum, then, given the problems of potential inbreeding that an emotionally charged nuclear family poses for the brother–sister and father–daughter dyads, it seems likely that hominids first elaborated the basic horde structure described earlier. This horde was populated by mothers, sons, brothers, friendships among males, and incoming females. This horde could form a viable group structure for survival in bush land or savanna habitats if enhanced emotional capacities could generate stronger bonds than those evident among chimpanzees. These members of the horde would develop emotional attachments and increased attunement to each other's emotional needs, and they could use emotions to develop flexible social relations. This level of social organization may have been sufficient, right up to the emergence of *Homo sapiens*, and so the early speculations by scholars about the horde may not have been as far off base as is easy to assume. With the larger brain, an incest taboo could be created that, coupled with the Westermarck effect, could control inbreeding, just as it does today. Perhaps this transition occurred earlier, with *Homo erectus* or even *Homo habilis*. But hordes composed of nuclear families would be more cohesive and structured if they could limit incestuous relationships, and as a result, they would have displaced other hominids. It probably would not take a brain much larger than that among chimpanzees to create a rudimentary culture with a taboo, since more intelligent primates today can all develop some cultural-like traditions. But the taboo would become increasingly necessary as males and females formed more permanent pair bonds (that eventually became enshrined in marriage rules) and their offspring stayed for a time or, indeed for their lifetime, in the natal group. As the horde was transformed into the hunting and gathering band, the nuclear family became its structural centerpiece, forcing the evolution of cultural rules prohibiting incest.

CONCLUSION

The primordial horde composed of mothers and her sons, brothers, friendships among adult males, and immigrant females was the structure that allowed hominids to survive in the predator-ridden African savanna. This structure is evident, in its rudimentary form, among contemporary chimpanzees, our best mirror in which to see our distant hominid ancestors reflected. For this protohuman society to be viable, however, stronger ties among its members were necessary; and so, natural selection began to alter the neurology of hominids in ways that increased the range and intensity of emotions, eventually producing an emotional language that enabled hominids to develop stronger social ties and enhanced group solidarity. Other behavioral options, such as selecting on dominance hierarchies, would prove unviable without the matrilines so essential to monkey societies. This behavioral propensity to form matrilines may have been selected out of apes during their evolution in marginal niches of the arboreal habitat. Most apes forced to live under open country conditions perished; and indeed, apes represent one of the great evolutionary failures, especially compared to monkeys. The only hominoid to survive to the present day under these environmental conditions is *Homo sapiens*; and of course, we pose a threat to the survival of all our primate cousins.

The footprints of natural selection are all over the brain of humans, especially its subcortical regions but also in the neuro nets that connect the neocortex to the limbic systems generating human emotions. As much as culture has enabled humans to construct complex societies, it is our emotional capacities that allowed our ancestors to survive before the neocortex became sufficiently large to create culture. Even today, we can see the operation of the emotional languages that our distant ancestors used to forge stronger bonds; solidarity among humans is ultimately an emotional process. And, when we want to really understand what others are thinking, how they feel, and how they are prepared to act, we rely less on what they say than on the emotions that they signal through body language. So it was for millions of years, as emotions were used to generate the strong bonds and group solidarity that allowed our hominid ancestors to survive where, at some unknown point, selection began to grow the neocortex that ushered in a culturally driven way of life.

Emotions are, of course, a double-edged sword. They can bring animals together in more tightly knit bonds, but they can arouse passions in ways that tear societies apart. The emotions surrounding acts of suicide bombers in the contemporary world are sufficient notice of the dark side of negative emotions. This dark side revolving around emotionally charged acts of violence was probably less visible in the primordial horde during most of hominid evolution, but another dark side was more problematic: potential inbreeding among more sexually aroused and passionate hominid primates who did not have powerful bioprogrammers for sexual avoidance, save for the mother–son dyad and activation of a Westermarck effect for siblings. Transfer patterns of all females from their natal group and community home range had ensured that incest between fathers and daughters was unlikely to occur, at least at a rate that threatened the survival of the horde. But, if emotions began to act as a centripetal force to keep daughters in the horde, then the probability for incestuous relations increased. And, as selection began work on emotions in general and the emotions surrounding sexual unions in particular (as evidenced by the larger septum in humans compared to apes) to forge conjugal bonds between males and females who would share in the raising of their offspring, the potential for inbreeding depression would increase, unless new mechanisms for sexual avoidance emerged. The Westermarck effect may have been one of these mechanisms, but at some point, the incest taboo was created. Thus, as hominids moved toward bands of nuclear families, it became increasingly necessary for evolved apes to create cultural prohibitions to incestuous relations. The nuclear family and the incest taboo are, as all the early theorists on the matter recognized, interwoven. The family, held together by love associated with sex and by strong emotional attachments, is made viable with an incest taboo. Yet, except for mother–son incest, where there is an ancient hardwired propensity for sexual avoidance, the taboo must overcome enhanced sexuality and emotionality to keep brothers and sisters as well as fathers and daughters, to say nothing of other closely related kin, apart. It should not be surprising that, without strong bioprogrammers save for the Westermarck effect, that the taboo proves inadequate to the task, especially in highly stressed and often dysfunctional families of the modern world.

6
FAMILY AND TABOO

֎

> What could be more interesting than to see the life of the modern family, so simple in appearance, resolved into a multitude of tightly intertwined elements and relationships and to follow through history the slow development in the course in which they were successively formed and combined?
>
> —Émile Durkheim (1888)

At some point during hominid evolution, the horde became the hunting and gathering band populated by families. The earliest this transition could have been made, we believe, is with *Homo erectus*, whose brain was much larger than *Homo habilis* and who had a much greater capacity to create and use culture. The family is not viable without the incest taboo because otherwise it would have to rely solely on the mother–son avoidance pattern and activation of the Westermarck effect. Once the family as a kinship unit emerged, selection became cultural as much as biological, although natural selection would favor animals who had larger brains and could store cultural prescriptions and proscriptions in their memories and who would feel shame and guilt for violating these norms. Family and taboo evolved together and made hunting and gathering bands more cohesive, but around a new nexus composed of bonded males and females who stayed together for longer periods of time than is evident among chimpanzees and who would, together, raise their sons and daughters.

Of course, the creation of stable heterosexual bonds surely included both monogamous and polygynous unions (or one male and several females) because 83 percent of recent human societies in the *Ethnographic Atlas* (Murdock 1967) either permitted or preferred this mating arrangement (in fact societies that allow only monogamous arrangements are quite rare). Yet polygyny in hunting and gathering societies is very limited, and even in horticultural societies where it is common, families composed of single bonded pairs and offspring are still the most frequent marital pattern because of the near equal sex ratio (see van den Berghe 1990; Pasternak 1976). In either case, our concern here is with explaining the origin of bonded pairs and shared parental investment that led to the establishment of the family as a stable kinship unit and not whether the bonded pairs are monogamously attached for life (since many humans obviously do not mate for life).

We also need to emphasize that the pronounced sexual division of labor in hunting and gathering societies, where males hunt game and females gather plant foods, also played a crucial role in the evolution of family life by creating productive and stable economic units through the establishment of mutual dependencies. Such a strict division of tasks is highly unusual in the animal world (even among monogamous birds), although according to Galdikas and Teleki (1981, 241) "chimpanzees, more than any other non-human primate in existence today, practice an incipient form of labor division" where the sexes often exploit different foods and where adult males, in particular, occasionally share their freshly killed prey with both males and females. If we assume that chimpanzees have a primitive proclivity for "sharing" along with a rudimentary "principle of reciprocity," the cognitive footings for a full-blown hominid division of labor were probably already in place and ready for modification by natural selection over time. However, before an economic division of labor was feasible for selection to act on, some initial emotional and cognitive steps had to be taken to stabilize relations between males and females. Without enhanced bonds through emotions, hominids could not make the critical transition from horde to band.

We are about to address the forces of selection pushing for increased emotionality in hominids, but we should at least mention the effects of the sexual division of labor in enhancing emotions in the emerging family. It is not unreasonable to view males and females in hunting and gathering bands as engaged in an exchange of plant food for meat. Men generally hunt and provide meat in exchange for the fruits, berries, and tubers gathered by women; and as the horde shifted to the hunting and gathering band, this exchange became ever more explicit. Like all exchanges, the act of exchange per se enhances social bonds, as Marcel Mauss (1924) argued a long time ago. And there is now considerable research to document that any exchange relation that is iterated increases the flow of positive emotions, commitments, and social solidarity. Thus, the sexual division of labor, through the exchange relationship that it establishes, furthered the emotional bonds between males and females.

SELECTION PRESSURES CREATING THE NUCLEAR FAMILY

The Emergence of "Love" and the Nuclear Family

Chimpanzee females are promiscuous, often allowing males to line up and have a turn when they are sexually receptive. Promiscuity would pose a real barrier to the nuclear family because if males and females pursued a wide array of sexual partners without any enduring sexual bonds, the structure of the nuclear family would be so fluid that whatever selective advantages it had would be destroyed by constantly shifting sexual partners. Natural selection probably worked over a long period of time to reduce levels of promiscuity in the horde, but not so much by taking the promiscuity out of hominids but by placing into hominid neurology new cognitive and emotional capacities, such as the ability to experience "love," that would work to counter promiscuity. Moreover, if expanding cognitive capacities of hominids allowed for the development of cultural proscriptions and prescriptions, then another counterforce to rampant promiscuity was available. Still, people are not monogamous in the vast majority of preliterate societies, to say nothing of extramarital alliances in contemporary societies. Clearly, at their ape core, many men and women are still willing to line up for each other for short-term sexual pleasure.

Hominids' expanding emotional and cognitive capacities increasingly led to stronger attachments among all horde members, and over time selection could have produced emotions that resemble what we call love between males and females, thus setting the stage for the more permanent conjugal pair. Since all mammals are already programmed for at least maternal care of offspring and, in rare cases, paternal care of offspring as well, there was something for natural selection to work on. Wiring for generating mother–

infant bonds is located in the anterior cingulate gyrus (as it acti-
vates the body systems producing the emotions driving care of
offspring), and thus selection could begin to work on this area of
the brain to increase a mother's attachment not just to her young
but also to a male sexual partner who could help care for the
couple's offspring. Selection may have found neuro nets in males
to increase male attachments to females and children but probably
to a lesser degree than for females, since chimpanzee males are not
particularly "maternal" (although gibbons are; gorilla silverbacks
will baby-sit youngsters, suggesting hominid neurobiology could
be subject to selection).[1] As more intense positive emotions revolving around emotional attachments evolved, these same attachments probably increased the chances that sons and daughters
would stay longer in the emerging band after puberty, thus increasing the selection pressures for new mechanisms of sexual avoidance.

The comparatively large size of the human septum—the area
where sexual drives are located in mammals—may represent another footprint left by natural selection as it generated new emotional states like love. It is curious that an area of the brain already
devoted to pleasure would need additional tissues for pleasure, but
if a more enduring sense of emotional attachments could be associated with sex, the septum is an obvious place for selection to go
to work. If we think about the matter for a moment, what is
conjugal love but additional pleasure and positive emotions surrounding sexual acts. If sex brought additional feelings, above and

---

1. A recent study on voles, a mouse-like rodent, by a team headed by Larry
Young suggests a much shorter and simpler mechanism reducing promiscuity
and increasing monogamy (Lim et al. 2004). Monogamy among voles and many
mammals revolves more around partnerships than sexual fidelity, but, nonetheless, prairie voles (*Microtis ochrogaster*) pair up, whereas meadow voles (*Microtis
pennsylvanicus*) are more promiscuous. Using common gene therapy techniques,
researchers were able to make promiscuous voles more monogamous. By inject-
ing a virus carrying the single gene responsible for production of vasopressin into
the forebrain of *Microtis pennsylvanicus*, these meadow voles began to behave like
prairie voles. The genes controlling vasopressin in men (oxytocin to the key
hormone in women) vary widely, perhaps influencing the wide variation in the
sexual behaviors of men. The key point is that a mutation on the genes responsible for the production of vasopressin could have increased fitness for pair-
bonded males and females, thus ushering in the nuclear "family." Because the
biological basis of monogamy is controlled by a single gene or, at most, a few
genes in voles, perhaps this was true for hominids, with promiscuity being
"switched" to fidelity, if the latter would have fitness-enhancing value.

beyond the immediate pleasure of the sexual act, males and females would feel more for each other; and over time, these feelings would begin to resemble "love" and to make more permanent the conjugal pair. Since the horde was likely a viable form of adaptation, perhaps for as long as 3 million years, selection could take its time in rewiring the septum, cingulate gryus, and other limbic systems to produce emotions that would make males and females stay together for longer periods of time. At first, the conjugal pair may have remained together for only a few weeks or months as orangutans occasionally do, but if pair bonding between adult males and adult females enhanced reproductive fitness and the viability of the group, selection would continue to rewire the brain for increasingly intense emotional commitments between males and females.

Yet if more intense emotions revolving around sexual acts were necessary to create the bonded pair, these same emotions could make both adult males and females attracted, respectively, to their daughters and sons because natural selection is not a finely tuned working machine that pinpoints the ideal adaptation.[2] Love then becomes a double-edged sword. It pulls adults together and leads to a more stable and permanent relationship between adult males and females; but love also intensifies sexual attraction per se, and there is no reason to assume that this attraction would not be directed at sons, daughters, sisters, and brothers. And the longer the young stayed attached to their parents after puberty, the greater the chances for incest.

Perhaps the Westermarck effect was heightened during the transition from horde to band composed of nuclear families. Other primates reveal this effect, and so selection may have had an extant behavior propensity on which to select. And, if daughters stayed only a short time after puberty, the Westermarck effect might have been adequate to limit inbreeding. But, as females stayed longer

---

2. The dynamics of evolution (or change and adaptation over time) proceed through four interactional processes; natural selection, mutation, gene flow, and genetic drift (flow and drift refer to the movement of genes into or out of a population). Selection can act only on the hereditary gene pool of what is available and requires mutation for a potential source of new variability. Directive selection acts only until pressures are relaxed on a trait, even if the final product is a mixed review. In point is human upright walking. The hominid shift to bipedalism left behind plenty of evolutionary scars, as can be heard often in the cry of "oh, my aching back" as we age. Monkeys and apes have few such problems (for a comprehensive discussion of evolution, probably more than you ever wanted to know, see Gould 2002).

because they "loved" the members of their family, sexual attraction to offspring and to siblings may have increased. Such is particularly likely to have been the case because male and female promiscuity had not been wiped out by natural selection; instead, it had been counterbalanced by connecting feelings of love attached to the pleasure of sex. Sleeping around was, therefore, a constant threat to the viability of the family; and as emotions increased the intensity of love attachments among members of the emerging nuclear family in order to reduce libertinism, it also heightened sexual attraction among the family's members and, thereby, raised the specter of incest and inbreeding depression—events that dramatically lower fitness.

The longer life course of apes may also have contributed to increased potential for inbreeding. As we noted in the previous chapters, apes take longer to develop and mature—a phylogenetic trait that seemingly dates from the early Miocene some 17 million years ago. As the hominid brain grew, offspring would have to be born before neurological maturity if the larger skull was to pass from the female's womb. But, as natural selection worked for an early birth, it also had to select on the longer life course of all descendants of early Miocene apes, prolonging each period of maturation (infant, juvenile, and adolescent) so that the brain could develop in a protected environment. Thus the life history traits of apes provided a preadaptation on which to select so that infants could be born early and remain dependent on their mothers (and eventually fathers), but this pattern of selection was also a double-edged sword because it may have kept offspring in the emerging family beyond puberty and early sexual responsiveness, especially if the larger brain was also enhancing emotions associated with sex. And so, the specter of incest and inbreeding depression came with selection on the life history patterns of all apes, including later hominids like *Homo erectus*.

For mothers, the potential for incest with sons would be less than it was for fathers and daughters or brothers and sisters. As we emphasized in chapter 4, chimpanzee sons distance themselves from mothers who are sexually receptive. This hardwired propensity for sexual avoidance may well have been enough to limit incest for this pair—just as it does today. The real stumbling block is fathers and brothers who do not evidence bioprogrammers for sexual avoidance with daughters and sisters—save for the Westermarck effect. Transfer patterns among early Austropiths, just like their contemporary ape descendants, likely pushed females from their natal group and community at puberty, thus removing the temptations among male members for sex with daughters and sisters. But, with the arrival of *Homo erectus*, the longer females lingered in their natal group, the greater potential for incest—just as is the case today in nuclear families where female offspring (and males as well) remain part of the nuclear family for several years after reaching puberty. Indeed, given ape bioprogrammers for promiscuity, which are masked and mitigated by "love" in humans, incest should be more common when male and female offspring remain in the nuclear unit after puberty. We could hypothesize, therefore, that incest was more common in patriarchal families in agrarian times and in families of today because offspring would remain in the family unit for a longer period and, in some agrarian societies, for a lifetime. Even without the pathologies and dysfunctions of many modern families, keeping the generations together after puberty can be a formula for incest. In traditional societies before industrialization, incest was probably most common in families where generations remained together, although the ability to monitor activities of family members in crowded households may have worked against incest because it was too easy to see and sanction illicit sex. In modern households, however, where the family is more isolated from other kin and from the community, the ability of others to monitor what occurs behind closed front doors is significantly reduced. Thus the social pressures against incest provided by the ability of kin and community members to monitor and sanction sexual activities are reduced as families become more isolated.

Clearly people in preliterate communities were aware of the dangers of incest in families. In many horticultural societies, for example, fathers often live in community compounds for males only, and sons join them as soon as they reach puberty. While these communal compounds also preserve male privilege and power, they may have originally evolved as a mechanism to reduce the potential of fathers and sons having sexual relations, respectively, with daughters and sisters in settled communities. The fact that these same societies almost always have a residence rule that pushes females (in the vast majority of preliterate societies) out of a village and into another village and frequently into another kinship unit (e.g., lineage or clan) is one way to institutionalize with cultural traditions older innate propensities of all chimpanzees (and their common ancestor with humans) for female transfer to another community at puberty. Thus patrilocal residence and patrilineal descent achieve the same ends as does female transfer among apes, although these culturally based transfer patterns also lead to the formation of political and economic alliances among communities that exchange women, thereby creating bridges and networks that mitigate against conflict and war (as alliance theories reviewed in chapter 2 argue). And, in societies with matrilocal or avunculocal (i.e., maternal uncle) residence rules and matrilineal descent rules, the same objective is achieved by pushing sons away from communities where their sisters and mothers reside.

Thus the evolution of love to create bonds of intimacy pulls the members of the nuclear family together and often keeps them together beyond the age when sons and daughters are sexually responsive. This power of love may have been supplemented by phylogenetic tendencies for prolonged life histories of hominids. Hunting and gathering bands have a bias toward patrilocal residence, but this is loose (Murdock 1949), and in fact neolocal residence is the most common pattern among studied hunter-gatherers. As the hunting and gathering horde moved to the hunting and gathering band, then, females probably had more choice about when and where they moved after reaching puberty, although life history traits coupled with love and more intense bonds may have kept females in the natal band past puberty. Moreover, kinship rules for descent and residency among hunter-gatherers probably did not carry the same power as they later would among horticulturalists, thereby increasing the likelihood that daughters could stay in their natal unit well past puberty. Hence an alternative mechanism was needed, if the nuclear family was to remain viable. This alternative mechanism was the incest taboo.

Selection and the Incest Taboo

At the earliest, coevolution began some 2.5 million years ago with *Homo habilis.* Its brain was certainly large enough for culture—shared meanings and understandings that could be transmitted across generations—but a culture still built around emotional syntax. With *Homo erectus,* we can be certain that this species had cultural capital (their sophisticated tool kits alone tell us that) but probably not culture revolving around spoken language, although we cannot be certain. But sometime during the past 2 million years, biological and cultural selection began to interact. Since chimpanzees can make and use tools, one path of coevolution was the interplay among tool technologies that enhanced fitness, leading to further selection for smart animals who could make better tools; and eventually as hominids became smarter, the threshold was passed on the road to auditory languages. Another path of coevolution may have revolved around hominids expanding emotional capacities, and as these promoted fitness, both subcortical and neocortical regions of the brain expanded; and at some point, hominids could use moral codes that could arouse guilt and shame, thereby increasing conformity to norms and promoting group fitness. And still another path was the intense selection pressure surrounding the gradual formation of nuclear families and the beginning of cultural selection for moral codes prohibiting incest; and as the first codes proved effective and promoted the fitness of the band, selection would push for a larger brain capable of holding cultural codes and feeling guilt and shame when they were violated. All of these paths of coevolution may have been operative at the same time; but the key point is that, over the past 2 million years, such cultural innovations as tool making, fire use, and the sanctions attached to moral codes began to solve problems that had once been left to natural selection alone.

In addition, during most of hominid history, an emotion-based language system must have easily met the elementary needs of most food foraging hordes, given their small size. However, the fitness-enhancing value of culture led selection to make increasingly intelligent hominids by enlarging the size of the neocortex, and maybe some subcortical regions like the hippocampus and transition cortices that are so important in tagging cognition with emotions and in ordering stored memories. Eventually this cortical expansion led to a modal shift from nonverbal communication to a greater reliance on communication by spoken sounds. While the time-honored tradition of viewing language as speech makes it unique to humans, it is nonetheless also an evolving cognitive capacity with roots in our hominoid legacy. In fact, chimpanzees possess the neurological equipment to learn complex visual symbols or gestural signs for symbolic communication with human caretakers. Although chimps cannot speak, when they are raised in a linguistic environment they can *spontaneously* learn a phonological code and use it to understand (and respond to) English words and sentences at the same level as a two-and-a-half or three-year-old human child (Gardner et al. 1989; Savage-Rumbaugh et al. 1993; Rumbaugh and Washburn 2003). However, these hidden talents are not utilized under natural conditions in their adaptation to a forest living habitat. In the same fashion, early hominids probably shared with chimpanzees these same cognitive capacities but they also remained dormant until they had greater adaptive value. Alterations in vocal tract anatomy (e.g., in the larynx and pharynx to make sounds) and alterations in the brain (e.g., Broca's area for the serial programming of speech sounds) apparently came late in hominid evolution and under intense selection pressures because such changes in the vocal tract greatly increased human vulnerability for blockage and choking when swallowing (Hamilton 1974). Why a need, then, for spoken language? One reason, we think, was to upgrade emotionally based or affect ties by adding on to this system the evolutionary novelty of expressing ideas guided by the intellect to create rational or cortically based ties. Such a vocally based system could also be utilized to strengthen ties among resident males and incoming females by enhancing social skills and thereby increasing sociality. Although speech is an individual act, it rests on a linguistic community of speakers for agreement on the meanings of symbols and for intergenerational continuity through time (see Maryanski et al. 1997; Maryanski 1997).

Arising out of the coevolution of cultural and biological forces came the incest taboo. As noted above, mother–son avoidance has a hardwired basis, as is evident for chimpanzees and hence our common ancestor. Selection could have enhanced the Westermarck effect, although we do not know where in human neurology this effect is generated; but it is a widespread phenomenon in both humans and other animals. But a Westermarck effect alone was probably insufficient to fully dampen emotionally bonded individuals in whom love and sex had become intertwined via the enlargement of the septum and, no doubt, other areas of the brain as well. The first taboo, if it came before *Homo sapiens,* was probably installed via the emotional syntax of body language as the effects of inbreeding depression became immediately evident in the offspring of incestuous liaisons, as we reported in chapter 2. Early observers of preliterate peoples sometimes assumed that they were unaware of the relationship between sex and birth, but with just a moment of thought, this is an ethnocentric notion that is obviously absurd. Long before science and medicine emerged to specify the mechanisms by which sex leads to birth, humans had easily made the connection, especially since food foraging requires an intimate knowledge of birth and death cycles in the animal and plant world. Indeed, late hominids like humans today could watch, with horror, the consequences of hominid inbreeding—birth defects, infant mortality, retardation, cleft palate, and other biological problems. Earlier hominids likely saw the connection and consequently recognized that certain acts had to be prohibited.

It is not necessary to have spoken language for a norm to emerge, and especially for an emotionally charged norm like an incest taboo. By simply communicating negative emotions, prohibitions can be created and sustained. In fact, if we think about how the incest taboo operates in modern culture, we can see some of what may have transpired in the distant past. Rarely does a parent take a child and instruct him about the dangers of incest and of the importance of not violating the taboo. There are no pictures of deformed children who are the victims of inbreeding depression. There are no public alert announcements. There is no instruction manual about incest in sex education, and in fact, it is probably rarely mentioned. Yet just about everyone in modern societies comes to sense that certain actions are taboo, without ever talking about them. In many societies, the taboo is not even part of the legal system because everyone "knows" (but how?) that incest is not done. There is an emotional intensity surrounding taboos that any person can pick up, via the emotional language of the body. The taboo could have emerged in this manner during hominid evolution, long before spoken language was part of the cultural tool kit of hominids. For example, mothers might have sanctioned inappropriate touching between their offspring, without ever speaking a word, through their communication of negative emotions. A conjugal mate to a man could also sanction any acts involving her mate's sexual orientation to a daughter, again without the use of speech. The frown, shake of the head, the expression of anger and fear in the eyes, facial muscles, and body countenance, and many other more subtle gestures from body systems communicating emotions, would create a taboo that was never spoken or written down. Indeed, this is how the taboo works today; and in fact, sometimes acts are so tabooed that no one speaks of them, but somehow everyone knows about the prohibition. The incest taboo and cannibalism are probably the deepest held universal taboos, but rarely is anyone given formal instruction on avoiding incest and nobody (to our knowledge) is given instruction on avoiding human body parts as food. Yet both elicit the same emotional reaction of sheer horror when an act of either is committed.

Thus a taboo could have emerged before spoken language developed; it could have been formulated by the language of emotions, being communicated and sanctioned purely by body language. Normative "agreements" and "understandings" are possible without spoken language; and these understandings would have promoted fitness by making hominids better organized and better able to coordinate their efforts.

It is conceivable, but not likely, that *Homo habilis* could have developed the beginnings of the incest taboo, but we suspect that the taboo emerged during the time of *Homo erectus.* Whenever hominids began to bond in conjugal pairs and to develop commitments for the joint care of their offspring, the incest taboo would emerge, or the nuclear family would collapse, as all of the sociological theories summarized in chapter 2 have emphasized. Moreover, the horrors of deformed or dead babies would immediately show what happens when incest occurs, arousing emotions of fear and anger that would be codified into understandings that such acts in the future would be prohibited.

Not only would there be harmful physical effects from incest, there would also be pathological and psychological outcomes for the victims of incest, just as there are today. We need to remember that the emotion systems of hominids had been developing much more rapidly after the split from the last common ancestor of humans and chimpanzees than had the cognitive capacities made possible by a larger neocortex, especially the prefrontal cortex (although early hominids reveal a very clear pattern in their skull casts for prefrontal lobe development). Thus all of the emotions that victims of incest among humans now experience were likely felt by hominids with a much smaller neocortex. In fact, the emotions—betrayal, fear, anger, guilt, shame, sadness, surprise, and other emotions—could be experienced even more directly without the fully developed neocortex to mediate and even repress negative emotions. The psychological effects of incest on victims would have been recognized relatively early in hominid evolution and would have led hominids to "formulate" implicit prohibitions through the emotional language of the body.

All of these considerations make pinpointing the time frame for when the incest taboo merged difficult. If the taboo were purely a verbal construction, we could say with more confidence that it emerged with *Homo sapiens,* some 150,000 years ago. But, given the capacity of hominids to use emotional languages, the taboo could have emerged a million years earlier. Norms do not require spoken language because so many of the normative arrangements that we follow in today's societies have never been articulated. If we are asked to articulate them, we usually have difficulty because they are part of our stocks of knowledge at hand, to use Alfred Schutz's (1932) phrase, that remain unarticulated. For example, individuals in modern societies would have difficulty explaining the norms that they use in public places, whereby they avoid running into people and otherwise maintain the public order. Or, to take another example, spacing between bodies during interaction is rarely discussed openly, but people in different cultures learn the appropriate spacing between self and others, without ever saying what the norms are (two feet, three feet, etc.) for various categories of others (friends, lovers, strangers, etc.). Sociology has a spoken-language bias, often assuming that anything in culture is the product of speech. But long before spoken language emerged, hominids were using a primal language to create norms and sanction nonconformity. Humans still use this language for many normative agreements today, despite our verbal abilities. Thus we cannot say for sure just when the nuclear family and the incest taboo emerged, but the two came together as a means for limiting father–daughter and brother–sister sexual contact, and perhaps even mother–son relationships, although for this latter dyad there were hardwired bioprogrammers for sexual avoidance.

Cultural Elaboration of the Incest Taboo

Some early explanations of the incest taboo, summarized in chapters 1 and 2, emphasized that the incest taboo was, at its core, a rule of exogamy because it specified who could *not have* sexual relations with whom and thereby pushed individuals out from the nuclear family to find sexual mates elsewhere. These arguments are, we believe, fundamentally correct. For hunter-gatherers, incest prohibited sexual relations among different age and sex categories in the family and consequently forced either or both females and males to look elsewhere for mates. It is not difficult to see how this taboo, as it pushed individuals away from the nuclear family, could be elaborated into more explicit rules of exogamy when humans began to settle down and live in more permanent settlements.[3] Most kinship systems among horticulturalists have

---

3. Just as ancient hardwired propensities for transfer from the natal group had done for the first hominids (and as chimpanzees still do).

explicit rules of exogamy; and indeed, children learn very early who is not available and who is available as a potential mate. Thus the rule of exogamy will specify the unit in which an individual cannot seek a marriage partner (certainly the nuclear family, usually the most immediate lineage, and even the clan or moiety). This rule is but a small extension of the incest taboo within the nuclear family. And as alliance theories argue, it had the added consequence of generating bonds of reciprocity as marriage partners were exchanged among kin units and villages. Thus the incest rule became, as some kinship theorists have argued, a cultural preadaptation for the foundation for more complex kinship systems revolving around unilineal descent. The marriage rule would become the basis for residence and descent rules because once you have been informed who is prohibited to you for marriage, it is a short step to specifying the groups into which you must marry (rule of endogamy) and where you must live (rule of residence in relation to rule of endogamy). And from this base, it is easy to see how a rule of descent specifying whose side of the family—the male's or female's—is to be the most important could emerge.

The incest taboo came first and, once in place, it could set into motion these more complex patterns of kinship among horticulturalists. Thus the taboo not only made the nuclear family viable but provided a basis for organizing the first settled societies of horticulturalists at a later stage of human evolution. Here cultural selection is operating without natural selection. By the time fully modern humans emerged in bands composed of nuclear families, the taboo could potentially provide a basis for elaborating kinship systems that could organize larger, settled populations. This elaboration of kinship systems increased the power of the incest taboo in several senses. First, kinship rules increasingly specified rules of exogamy and endogamy, residence, and descent, all of which limited the options of individuals growing up in the nuclear family. By the time males or females reached puberty, they knew whom they could marry, where they must live, and whose side of the family was most important with respect to power and authority as well as inheritance of material wealth. This kind of control would limit incest. In essence, older hardwired transfer patterns among hominids were recreated by a more complex set of kinship rules. Second, as mentioned earlier, fathers and sons were often relegated to male-only huts and compounds, which limited their access to incestuous relations with mothers, daughters, and sisters. Third, even though a certain amount of privacy is possible in simple "huts" and other housing arrangements, monitoring of activities by other kin and community members is still likely to occur as part of the daily routine; thus, enforcing rules of incest was relatively easy. Fourth, as religion became an increasingly prominent institutional system among horticulturalists, all rules but particularly powerful taboos were enforced by supernatural forces, thus making the taboo and related kinship rules that much more powerful. Although a rule of exogamy is not the same as the incest taboo, once a taboo is in place, it can operate to encourage rules of exogamy and endogamy, *when* they become fitness enhancing at a later stage of societal evolution.

The Contemporary Nuclear Family and the Incest Taboo

We emphasized above the elaboration of kinship rules and their power not so much as a digression but as background for the subsequent evolution of human societies. As long as kinship was the organizing principle of society, the rules of kinship, including the incest taboo, were highly salient. They were the backbone of social organization, and consequently everyone knew the rules and enforced them, just as early hunter-gatherers had. But as alternative forms of organizing larger numbers of individuals began to displace unilineal descent systems of horticulturalists—alternatives such as markets and bureaucracies—kinship began a long odyssey back to the basic structure of hunter-gatherers. As noted earlier, this movement back created a much more isolated family unit that was no longer the central organizing principle of society. Alternative modes of organization had emerged, pushing the family to predominately reproductive functions. As such, what went on inside the family was less subject to monitoring and sanctioning by outsiders, at the very time when marriage rules became less precise and children stayed inside the family for prolonged periods of time after puberty. The incest taboo was forced to carry the full load of maintaining sexual avoidance among mothers and sons, fathers and daughters, and brothers and sisters, although the Westermarck effect added weight to the taboo and ancient mother–son avoidance patterns made this dyad less problematic than the brother–sister and father–daughter dyads.

This isolation from older forms of community control was often intensified by beliefs and ideologies about the right of the family to be immune to governmental and other forms of institutional monitoring. The phrase "a man's home is his castle" captures not only the patriarchy of the isolated nuclear family but also a fortress imagery that reduced the ability of "outsiders" to monitor and sanction what transpired within the family. And, as reviewed in chapter 3, especially in table 3.2, other normative systems often worked at cross-purposes with the incest taboo, particularly for brother–sister and father–daughter sexual relations. Only for mother–son sexual relations were the normative systems all lined up against sexual liaisons between members of this dyad. Rates of incest should therefore have increased for father–daughter and brother–sister incest under these structural and cultural conditions.

Not only was the modern nuclear family becoming more isolated from community control, but its members became more isolated from each other. If male and female children had separate bedrooms and lived in distinctive youth subcultures, they would interact less with each other and their parents. As a result, the imprinting for sexual avoidance or the Westermarck effect that comes from high rates of interaction among family members, particularly brothers and sisters and, perhaps, fathers and daughters would not be activated (see Erickson 2005).

At the same time that the nuclear family was becoming more isolated, it was also becoming more unstable. Personal pathologies of individual family members—drug use, drinking, stress, and domestic violence—all increased with late industrialization. The causes of these pathologies often reduced inhibitions and promoted sexually aggressive behavior that would inevitably increase physical abuse, sexual abuse, and incest. More families became dysfunctional, a fact that is reflected in rising divorce rates in all industrial societies after World War II, and such instability further eroded the power of kinship norms, including the incest taboo, to control prohibited sexual relations. The Westermarck effect could still operate, but as dissolved families became reconstituted with stepfathers and stepchildren, the power of this effect was reduced. Moreover, the conditions under which the Westermarck effect evolved had dramatically changed; hominids did not have drug and alcohol problems, nor were hunter-gatherers patriarchal, with the consequence that within hunting and gathering bands the incest taboo had not been undermined by personal pathologies that reduced sexual inhibitions or by norms that, especially when coupled with personal pathologies, implicitly sanctioned men's aggressive sexual behavior.

Thus the odyssey in contemporary societies back to the small family that had been the backbone of hunter-gatherer bands occurred under very different conditions, all of which weakened the power of the taboo for males who, like their ape ancestors, were still disposed to promiscuity. Of course, the same personal pathologies and family dysfunctions that increased male sexual abuse also escalated female sexual abuse, but not to the same extent as for fathers and sons, and particularly so for actual incest when the Westermarck effect does not get activated in dysfunctional families.

The outcome is that rates for all kinds of abuse in the nuclear family, including sexual abuse and incest, have increased (although they appear to have declined somewhat in the United States). We should not be surprised by this fact, since the modern nuclear family occupies a very different place in the organization of large and complex societies. Our concern, as emphasized in chapter 3, is on the *relative rates* of incest and the *varying* psychological effects of incest on victims, whatever its overall rate in the modern nuclear family. Why are brother–sister and father–daughter incest more frequent than mother–son incest, and why are the psychological effects on sons of mother–son sexual relations so much more severe than those for sisters and daughters? Let us now return to the questions that have guided our inquiry into the origins of the incest taboo.

INCEST AND HARM IN THE NUCLEAR FAMILY

Relative Rates of Incest

Our analysis thus far leads us to the conclusion that we should expect higher rates of incest between members of the brother–sister and father–daughter dyads compared to the mother–son dyad. There is an ancient deep-seated proclivity against mother–son incest that we can still see among our closest ape relatives, the chimpanzees. This sexual aversion is millions of years old, and there is no reason to assume that it would be selected out. Rather, it is essential for apes today and was crucial for the formation of the hominid horde built from a core of mothers and sons. This pattern of sexual aversion has been elaborated into a powerful taboo, probably the most powerful of all, for several reasons. First, as Edmund Westermarck (1891) noted long ago, hardwired biological propensities are capable of arousing emotions; and emotions tend to become codified into cultural prescriptions and proscriptions. Since hominids relied on the body language of emotions to forge social bonds, it is likely that all biological propensities, especially those concerned with sex and attachment, evidenced a capacity to arouse emotions that eventually were codified into powerful norms such as the incest taboo. Second, as Freud and all sociological theories emphasize, sexual relations between a mother and son would set up intense conflict with the father, particularly in patriarchal families but even in more egalitarian ones, with the result that the incest taboo evolved to reduce this potential source of conflict. For when father and son are in conflict, other social relations in the family between brothers and sisters as well as between fathers and daughters are disrupted. For example, the data from the child abuse literature clearly document that sons who abuse their sisters have often been in conflict with their fathers. If a mother's sexual interest is transferred to her son, then fathers and daughters become more likely to have sexual relations. Thus, once one dyad becomes incestuous, tensions reverberate around to the other dyads in the family.

Father–daughter incest should be the most common form of incest because there are no bioprogrammers in apes working against sexual relations between fathers and daughters save for the Westermarck effect, assuming it operates for individuals in such divergent age categories. Indeed, it is unlikely that the Westermarck effect is powerful for fathers since they are long past the critical early years of imprinting that seem to be necessary for this effect to be activated. Hence the sexual avoidance between fathers and daughters is regulated more by cultural norms than biology, and in patriarchal families where father–daughter incest is most common, norms of patriarchy coupled with other pathologies such as alcohol and drug use can work against the incest taboo.

Brother–sister incest should be less common than father–daughter incest because of the Westermarck effect, if it gets activated. Many now argue that sibling incest is the most common, even surpassing in some analysts' mind rates of incest between stepfathers and their stepdaughters. If sibling incest is indeed this frequent, then we need to enumerate the forces dampening the Westermarck effect. Again, paternal abuse of sons, alcohol and drug use, and other pathologies that are often evident in incestuous families may be sufficient to override the Westermarck effect. Moreover, as Robin Fox (1980) emphasized, if brothers and sisters live in different youth cultures and are separated physically when young, then the close physical contact necessary for the activation of the Westermarck effect may not have occurred, thus weakening the power of the effect and opening the door to brother-initiated sexual relations with his sister, especially when other pathologies exist in the nuclear family.

All forms of incest become much easier to conceal in the modern, isolated nuclear family. The family is no longer monitored, as a natural course of daily routines, like its counterpart in more communal societies. Doors are closed to the outside world, and coupled with powerful ideologies about the sanctity of the household from supervision by the state, incestuous relations are more difficult to discover. The communal monitoring that would occur in households and communities of the past is simply not present in the modern family in most societies. Yet the social movement that has built up around child abuse has alerted those who have contact with children—teachers and leaders of organizations in which children participate—to look for abuse, which may partly explain the leveling off of child abuse rates in countries like the United States. In essence, looking for physical and psychological "markers" of abuse restores some degree of monitoring of activities in the nuclear family, but not to the level of hunter-gatherers and horticulturalists.

When dysfunctional family structures also exist outside the purview of the community, then abuse of all kinds becomes more likely. Thus drug use, alcohol abuse, spouse battering, and other pathologies all increase tension and aggression in households, some of which manifests itself in parental sexual abuse of children and in brother-initiated incest with sisters. Coupled with norms of patriarchy and household privacy from agents of social control, all rates of incest should be higher than would be the case in families without dysfunctional relations and behavioral pathologies. Moreover, relatively high divorce rates, at least by historical standards, also increase the presence of males in households, whether as stepfathers or lovers, who are not biologically related to the children of the household. The result is increased opportunities for sexual abuse of children, and particularly so when their presence is accompanied by family tensions and personal pathologies. Under these conditions, the power of the incest taboo is dramatically weakened since males are not biologically related to their victims.

The data reviewed in chapter 3 generally support these conclusions. The only real sticking point is the rate of sibling incest, compared to father–daughter and stepfather–stepdaughter sexual relations. It may be that sibling incest is as frequent as father–daughter incest. We are doubtful, however, that the rates of sibling incest are equal to, or greater than, stepfather–stepdaughter sexual relations, although there are no definitive data on the matter. What is clear is that sibling incest, even by our narrow definition of incest, is far greater than once believed. And the rates of incest for brother–sister and father–daughter dyads are dramatically higher than for the mother–son dyad. There is, to be sure, some under-reporting of mother–son incest, but even with this consideration factored into our rough calculations on relative rates, mother–son incest is rare, probably more rare that mother–daughter sexual relations. The reason for this fact, we believe, resides in our neurology as an evolved ape.

Psychological Harm from Incest

As noted in chapter 3, when mother–son incest occurs, it has more severe psychological effects on sons than other forms of incest have on sisters and daughters. A higher percentage of males evidence severe anxiety disorders and a significant percentage re-veal borderline or full-blown psychosis. Virtually no daughters and sisters reveal psychotic symptoms, and while they all reveal anxiety disorders, these disorders are not, on average, as severe as victims of mother–son incest. The reason, we believe, for this difference is that mother–son incest crosses neurological wiring in the brain of a child, activating more intense and destructive emotions as well as defense mechanisms to control the emotional turmoil.

The hominid horde was viable as long as mothers and sons con-tinued the sexual avoidance still evident among contemporary chim-panzees. Thus, the neurological wiring for sexual avoidance is not only ancient but powerful. In contrast, the Westermarck effect ap-pears to be comparatively weaker and probably applies primarily to siblings. Thus incest in the other two dyads of the nuclear family does not go against the same neurology as mother–son incest does, especially in the case of fathers and daughters. Moreover, the social taboo against mother–son incest is, as we argued in chapter 3, much more powerful than for either brother–sister or father–daughter in-cest. As a result, mother–son incest not only violates the neurology of males but also powerful cultural codes, thus setting into motion the activation of defense mechanisms against the arousal of painful emotions that in turn lead to severe anxiety disorders and, in some cases, psychosis. Brother–sister incest may go against the Wester-marck effect, if it has been activated, but this effect has probably not been activated between brothers and sisters who commit incest, with the result that the incest does not cross the same powerful neurological wiring as does mother–son incest. Father–daughter incest does not go against any discernible bioprogrammers pushing for sexual avoidance; rather, incest is mostly a violation of a cultural taboo whose power is often subverted by norms of patriarchy and by family dysfunctions and personal pathologies. Victims of sibling and father–daughter incest often experience posttraumatic stress syndrome and other anxiety disorders, but rarely are cases of full-blown psychosis reported in the literature. In contrast, while still a relatively small fraction of cases reported, a significant percentage—perhaps 10–15 percent—of the victims of mother–son incest reveal borderline dissociative behaviors or full-blown psychosis. To go against what is built into the male neuroanatomy as an evolved ape, while violating powerful cultural prohibitions, is a formula for severe emotional problems.

CONCLUSION

We are near the end of our argument on the origins of the incest taboo. The basic evolutionary dilemma facing apes trying to become better organized was posed by Robin Fox (1980) several decades ago: the hunting and gathering band was more fit if built around the nuclear family rather than the hominid horde. Fox was not, of course, the first to make this observation. Many thinkers of the nineteenth and early twentieth centuries who pondered the reasons for the incest taboo recognized that the taboo was at the core of human society. What we have added to these earlier insights is this observation: the nuclear family is not a "natural" social form for a great ape. Apes are individualistic, mobile, and not prone to form families in the human sense. Powerful selection pressures had to be in play for hominids to adopt nuclear families as the core structure of the band. For as we argued in chapter 5, the horde came first, long before the nuclear family.

The nuclear family was made possible by the heightening of emotions, especially emotions revolving around sex and perhaps also around the sexual division of labor and the exchange relation that ensues. Males and females began to bond together for longer periods of time, exchange meat for plant food, and share in the raising of their offspring. This is not a natural activity for an ape, but it became a way to increase the fitness of hunting and gathering societies. With both parents attending to the welfare of their offspring and coordinating through a sexual division of labor the exchange of food, the band became more fit because offspring were more likely to survive and reproduce. But, as we emphasized, the emotions needed to forge the nuclear family represent a double-edged sword: emotions, especially emotions revolving around sexual interest, potentially generate sexual interest among incestuous dyads, and particularly so if these emotions override female transfer patterns from the natal group and community (thereby making females potential objects of sexual interest by brothers and fathers).

All early theorists recognized that the family was not possible without the incest taboo, and they were essentially correct. True, the taboo often does not have to be explicit, as Fox (1980) and van den Berghe (1980) have emphasized, when (1) the Westermarck effect can be activated by physical play at a young age between brothers and sisters, (2) the community is able to monitor the behavior of fathers, and (3) the neurologically based wiring for mother–son sexual avoidance can also be allowed to exert its full effect. Under these conditions, the taboo need not be explicitly stated; sexual avoidance among the potentially incestuous dyads occurs as a matter of course. But why, then, would a taboo ever be necessary?

The taboo became necessary because these ideal conditions often could not be met, for historical or ecological reasons. The existence of strong emotional bonds among members generates enormous potential for something to go wrong, with the obvious outcomes being the horrors of inbreeding that make themselves evident immediately in the human genome. And, if phylogenetic inertia for long life histories was extended for bigger-brained offspring, the potential for incest increased as sons and daughters stayed in their natal unit past puberty. There can be little doubt that things did go wrong in perhaps hominid and certainly in human history. Inbreeding depression was exposed and conflict between mothers and fathers over sexual relations became intense. As these conflicts spread from family members to other band members, the fitness-enhancing effects of the nuclear family on the band could easily be undone, if not reversed. Thus, by trial and error over many generations, more and more societies instituted incest prohibitions. For some, these were implicit understandings; for others they were codified into law-like edits; and for all, they decreased the likelihood of inbreeding depression and disruptive conflict in the family and band. The near universality of the prohibition signals that the incest taboo is an outcome of intense biological and sociocultural selection pressures.

UNRAVELING THE MYSTERY OF THE INCEST TABOO

The common notion is that history begins with monuments and literary records—that is, when civilization is already far advanced. . . . Properly speaking, however, no time should be called prehistoric, if, by any means, we can ascertain the general character of the events that took place in it.

—John Ferguson McLennan (1896)

THE EXPLANATION REVIEWED

Our explanation on the origins of the incest taboo can now be stated more succinctly. Hominids, as evolved apes, inherited the mother–son avoidance pattern of the last common ancestor to present-day chimpanzees and the hominid line culminating in humans. From the beginning, then, there was a hardwired avoidance of sexual relations between a mother and her son. Female transfer at puberty from both the natal group and community represented another behavioral propensity in apes and hominids. Together, these innate behavioral programmers, along with a Westermarck effect, reduced the likelihood that closely related kin would have sex and produce less-fit offspring in hominids, just as they do today for those species of apes closest to humans. As long as the hominid line maintained these patterns of incest avoidance, no other mechanisms were required. The first prekinship "horde," as we and so many others in the past have called it, could function without a high probability for incestuous relations and the resulting inbreeding depression. As long as a mother and her sons, brothers, other males, and incoming females constituted the core of the foraging community horde, selection pressures were muted because the old mechanisms could continue to operate as they had for hominoids over thousands of millennia.

Yet, when fitness could be enhanced by more tightly knit social ties among hominids seeking to survive on the African savanna, selection began to work at cross purposes. Natural selection increased the use of emotions to strengthen social bonds and bind individuals to the group; and by taking this path, natural selection created a new kind of "horde" in which the propensity for females to transfer from the natal group and community may have been delayed or partly inactivated. At the same time, selection pushed emotions to the point where mating couples increasingly formed longer-term bonds, thus creating the conjugal pair that is the backbone of the nuclear family. As offspring stayed for longer periods with their "parents" in the emerging hunting and gathering "band," older transfer patterns were subverted, with the result that enhanced emotions revolving around sex and love raised the specter of incest between fathers and daughters as well as between brothers and sisters. The Westermarck effect was probably strengthened during this transition, building upon innate behavioral propensities in primates. While the Westermarck effect may have been sufficient to stave off incest between brothers and sisters raised together, there is little evidence that this effect also operates in the same way for parents and their children. The mother–son avoidance pattern was probably sufficient to hold off incest for this dyad, but the father–daughter dyad would prove problematic because selection as a directive agent of evolution can only operate to modify existing genetic characteristics. It cannot bring new traits into existence. Only mutation—the creative force in evolution—could actualize an avoidance propensity in fathers. But mutation is purely a random agent—with a "wild card" probability of generating an entirely new behavioral propensity in fathers.

Thus, in making the band more fit by fostering the nuclear family, a remarkable structure for great apes who tend to be individualistic and mobile, the potential for incest and inbreeding depression was increased. Selection may have first worked to bolster the Westermarck effect, but this did not solve the problem of attached fathers becoming sexually attracted to their daughters.

To reduce the potential for incest between fathers and daughters, novel cultural coding was created. At first, this coding may have been in the language of emotions that is primarily communicated through the body, especially the face. Cultural codes can emerge without spoken language as long as body language is indeed a true language with phonemes and syntax. Sanctions could be meted out for violation of the emerging taboo expressed through the body language of emotions—a language revolving around sequences of gestures in the face and body that carried emotional meanings. Eventually spoken language refined the taboo, and perhaps extended it to all dyads, save for the conjugal couple, of the nuclear family. Of course, in many hunting and gathering bands, the taboo was not explicit since the mother–son avoidance pattern and the Westermarck effect were sufficient to inhibit inbreeding, although the problem of "what to do with fathers" remained. But, communal monitoring of fathers' behaviors may have been a sufficient deterrent against incest in many or even most early hunting and gathering bands.

Since the effects of inbreeding are immediate and obvious, the taboo probably emerged very early in human evolution when the first incestuous relationships produced deformed children. As people looked in horror at the results of inbreeding depression, they gave explicit voice to a taboo. And once in place this taboo could be passed down across generations and, perhaps, be picked up by other bands in a process of cultural diffusion.

This scenario, we feel, accounts for the emergence of the taboo and helps answer the questions that have guided our inquiry: Why is the taboo stronger for the mother–son dyad and weaker for the brother–sister and father–daughter dyads? Why are rates of incest so much greater for the father–daughter and brother–sister dyads than the mother–son dyad? And why are the psychopathologies for violating the taboo so much more severe for victims of mother–son than the other two incestuous dyads in the nuclear family? Our answer to these questions is straightforward, and it incorporates elements of sociological theories. The taboo is stronger for the mother–son dyad because it rests on phylogeny; and while it can be argued that it does not need to be as strong when there is a firm biological basis, the potential horror of violating such propensities leads people to create a powerful taboo to express this horror— much as Edward Westermarck argued over a century ago.

The intense taboo plus the biology of mother–son sexual avoidance explain why rates of incest between mothers and sons are so much lower than for members of the other two incestuous dyads. Since the Westermarck effect is also an ancestral proclivity, brother–sister incest should be much lower than father–daughter incest. And this may have indeed been the case in evolutionary history, as long as the nuclear family was structured in ways that allowed for the activation of this effect through play and physical contact between brothers and sisters. It is only the modern nuclear family, we feel, with its attendant pathologies and with increased sex role segregation between brothers and sisters, that operates in ways that either overwhelm the Westermarck effect or prevent its activation. Thus, by Westermarck's logic, the taboo against brother–sister incest in the hunting and gathering bands of the past should also be strong because it reflects people's shock at violating a biologically based avoidance pattern.

The taboo should be least effective for father–daughter incest in societies of the past because it is mostly cultural. It has no known ancestral, biological basis in fathers, although the Westermarck effect may be activated in daughters. People are disturbed when the taboo is violated but not to the degree as when the violation is also crossing biological roadblocks. For to violate what is deeply rooted in human nature will always seem "unnatural" and hence more upsetting.

The rates of incest follow from these lines of argument. Mother–son incest is rare because sexual avoidance rests on phylogenetic bedrock, and as a result is the most tabooed. In traditional societies, brother–sister incest should be more common than mother–son and less frequent than father–daughter because it has a weaker biological basis than mother–son incest, but still, unlike father–daughter sexual avoidance, it has some basis in biology. Father–daughter incest should be most frequent because avoidance is regulated mostly by cultural prohibitions. The fact that, in modern societies, sibling incest is as common or more common than father–daughter incest is the result, we believe, of the problems inherent in the modern nuclear family where the Westermarck effect is arrested in some households. In the historical past in the earliest hunting and gathering societies, we think that our generalizations would probably hold true.

The psychological effects of incest on the younger victim should be greatest for mother–son incest because sexual relations in this dyad violate not only a strong taboo but ancient wiring in the brain. Father–daughter incest should be the least harmful because it does not violate any discernible hardwiring, although it is still taboo. The psychological harm of sibling incest should fall between that evident for father–daughter and mother–son incest because there is some hardwiring through the Westermarck effect. There are some additional factors, however, that may help explain why the level of harm for sisters and daughters in incestuous relationships is about the same, at least in the modern nuclear family. Because a daughter is in a dependent relationship with her father, episodes of father–daughter incest violate not only the taboo but also bonds of trust. Moreover, this incestuous dyad places daughters in sexual competition with their mothers, thus forcing even more strain on the daughter. In contrast, while sibling incest violates a taboo and the Westermarck effect, it does not undo accumulated parental trust or put a sister in competition with the opposite-sex parent. Thus the sociological problems facing daughters in incest are perhaps as great or greater than going against the hardwired Westermarck effect. These sociological difficulties for daughters also operate on sons in incestuous relationships with their mothers and help explain the severity of a son's psychopathologies arising from mother–son incest. Not only has a son crossed both biological and cultural barriers, but the trust given to mother has been violated. Moreover, the son is now in competition with his more powerful father. And so, in addition to the injury resulting from crossing powerful biological programmers, sons must deal with violating cultural taboos, loss of trust, and potential confrontations with father. This combination of forces puts the son under enormous anxiety; and given these pressures, it should not be surprising that sons reveal more severe symptoms than daughters and sisters in incestuous relationships.

ALTERNATIVE EXPLANATIONS

Let us see how our explanation stacks up against the main alternatives that were summarized in chapters 1 and 2. We should emphasize again that our explanation incorporates elements of these alternatives and, thereby, supplements rather than supplants other theories. Still, none of the alternatives can, we believe, answer all of the questions that have guided our inquiry into the origins of the incest taboo.

The Westermarck Effect

It could be argued that the Westermarck effect creates sexual avoidance between parents and offspring. On the child's side, the effect would be much the same as it is with siblings; physical contact and play with parents at an early age create biological imprinting for sexual avoidance. On the parent's side, it is possible that asexual imprinting could occur but there is little evidence that such is the case; and since parents are long past the formative early years where most imprinting of this nature emerges in mammals, it does not seem likely that a full-blown Westermarck effect would emerge in parents. Still, in a scenario revolving around an expanded Westermarck effect, children would have imprinting for asexual relations with their parents, and if the effect could be implanted in parents, they would have the same asexual orientations to their sexually maturing offspring.

Some variations in rates of incest could potentially be explained by this extension of Westermarck's argument. It might be assumed, for example, that imprinting would be less on parents and offspring, and so, rates of incest should be greater between parents and their children than between siblings. Moreover, since it is the mother who is most likely to have extensive physical contact with her children when they are young, she would be less likely than fathers to be sexually attracted to her children because of the greater imprinting for avoidance, whereas fathers and especially fathers who do not play and cuddle their children when they are young would evidence less asexual imprinting with their offspring. As a result, father-initiated incest would be more frequent than other forms of incest.

This explanation is plausible, but it relies upon imprinting in human adults for which there is no solid evidence. Moreover, this explanation cannot explain the varying effects of incest on children. Why are sons more damaged psychologically than daughters and sisters in incestuous relationships? Can imprinting, per se, explain variations in the psychological harm? We think not; for, while the Westermarck effect is real, it cannot answer all three questions guiding our inquiry.

Sociobiological Theories

Sociobiological theories all argue that the incest taboo is a cultural expression of deeper biological mechanisms for sexual avoidance that have evolved from natural selection. Inbreeding depression selected out those individuals who did not reveal a propensity for avoidance among closely related kin, while favoring and selecting on existing propensities for avoidance. Thus the Westermarck effect and other mechanisms for sexual avoidance evolved to ensure that those who share a high proportion of their genes would not mate.

Yet, since all members of the nuclear family share one half of their genes, sociobiological theories cannot explain why some forms of incest are more common than others, nor can they explain why the taboo is stronger for the mother–son dyad or why the psychological effects on some are greater than those for sisters and daughters. Yet, we could construct a plausible scenario like the following: Males seek to pass on their genes through impregnating as many female eggs as is possible (in order to "maximize" their fitness), while females attempt to make sure their eggs are supported by fit males who can help protect their children; therefore, females are more selective than males choosing sexual partners, and especially so for relations that increase the chances for inbreeding depression which would burden women and decrease female fitness. Yet, this kind of scenario does not explain greater psychological harm to sons than daughters and sisters in incestuous dyads.

Sociobiology is correct in its basic argument. Natural selection has operated to limit inbreeding depression; and there are two clear biological propensities that have emerged from selection: the mother–son avoidance pattern and the Westermarck effect. Beyond these two biologically based behavioral propensities, no other biological mechanisms are evident in humans, save for, perhaps, the persistence of female transfer patterns (as codified in rules of exogamy and endogamy) from the last common ancestors to apes and hominids. But even if female transfer remained a biological propensity, the nuclear family began to undermine or overwhelm this behavioral tendency inherited from our ape ancestors, and at this point humans or perhaps late hominids began to rely upon culture to achieve the necessary sexual avoidance. Cultural selection thus began to supplement natural selection operating on the genome.

As long as sociobiological explanations are willing to admit to coevolution, they can explain the questions that we have raised. Indeed, our analysis is coevolutionary, but it does not assume for every universal trait there is a biological underpinning. Natural selection took hominids so far, but with the emergence of the nuclear family, the heightening of emotions revolving around love and sex, and the weakening of the propensities for female transfer, cultural selection supplanted biological selection, thereby producing the incest taboo. Thus the taboo is more than a cultural expression of innate biological propensities; it exists because it was needed (i.e., selected) during the evolution of the nuclear family which, in turn, transformed the horde to the hunting and gathering band.

Evolutionary Psychology

From the perspective of evolutionary psychology, natural selection wired into the hominid and human brain modules influencing cognitions that direct behaviors. The problem here is that, aside from the Westermarck effect, there is no clear evidence that father–daughter incest avoidance has a neurological basis. At some point during hominid and, then, human evolution in hunting and gathering bands, cultural selection began to operate and, for most behaviors, supplanted selection of neurostructures. As we emphasized in chapter 2 and outlined in chapter 5, much of our argument contains elements of an evolutionary psychology. The emotional capacities that enabled low sociality descendants of apes to become better organized clearly have a neurological basis; and the footprints of natural selection's effects on the emotion centers of the brain can be readily seen, once one looks for them. But what made for higher degrees of emotionality and sociality also increased the potential for incest, as older avoidance mechanisms—particularly, the Westermarck effect and female transfer at puberty—were potentially subverted as nuclear families in bands emerged. By the time emotions were keeping offspring in the family and band past puberty, however, later hominids like *Homo erectus* and, of course, humans were developing culture which would be a much more rapid and easier route to preventing incest. Cultural codes could now supplement the ancient mother–son avoidance pattern evident in virtually all primates, reinforce the Westermarck effect, and make taboo father–daughter incest (where no clear biologically based mechanisms for sexual avoidance, especially on the father's side, appear to exist).

The alternative explanation from evolutionary psychology would need to specify just which structures in the brain were subject to selection such that cognitions among all members of the emerging nuclear family would direct behaviors of sexual avoidance. True, one can just assert that there are modules of the brain generating cognitive and behavioral propensities for incest avoidance for all three heterosexual dyads in the nuclear family, but without some details about which parts of the brain under what selection pressures generated these propensities, the argument lacks the necessary details. One could make the argument, perhaps, that natural selection rewired the brain so that humans possessed a cognitive structure that, in turn, predisposed them to create an incest taboo, but such an explanation would simply involve translating the sociological argument into the vocabulary of evolutionary psychology. Moreover, beyond the mother–son avoidance pattern and the Westermarck effect, there is no evidence that there is a hardwired basis for father–daughter incest avoidance, save for some potential Westermarck effect on young daughters who play with and are socialized by their fathers.

Sociological Theories

Sociological theories all emphasize that incest disrupts role relationships, increases conflict, and erodes trust in the nuclear family. From a sociological perspective, then, the incest taboo was created to reduce role confusion, interpersonal conflict, and erosion of trust. More Freudian variants add the caveat that the repressed desire of children for their opposite-sex parent provides the emotional energy to conform to the taboo and to impart it to subsequent generations. Furthermore, repressed desires to violate what is taboo also become a motivational force behind commitments to the general cultural values of a society as well as its status role structure.

While sociological theories are probably correct in their essentials, they cannot explain variations in the strength of the taboo, varying rates of incest, and different degrees of psychological harm to younger members of incestuous dyads. For most sociologists, the taboo and sexual avoidance are only based in culture, but, if such is the case, the taboo should be of equal strength on all dyads in the family. It should lead to equal amounts of conformity for each family member; and it should cause the same amount of harm to sons, sisters, and daughters.

Feminist versions of sociological theories can go a bit further by emphasizing patriarchy, which privileges the actions of males— fathers and brothers—in ways that encourage them to make sexual advances on daughters and sisters. Moreover, it reduces the power of the wife so that she is forced into an "enabling role," while being too terrified of male violence to make advances toward her son. Patriarchy can also explain the power of the taboo since it is in the male's interest to have a strong taboo against mother–son incest, and a weaker one for male-initiated sexual acts. Further-more, given the power of males to control acts in the family and the normative structure of the family, feminist theories can ac-count for why rates of male-initiated incest are higher than female incest. Yet patriarchy did not exist in the first hunting and gather-ing bands, if we can use the few hunting and gathering popula-tions that survived into the modern era as our guide to what occurred in the distant past. Thus conceptions of patriarchy can-not explain the origins of the taboo in a more egalitarian family structure, as was probably the case for early hunter-gatherers, but feminist theories can help explain the dynamics of incest in the family once patriarchy emerged during horticulture. Moreover, it is difficult to see how feminist theories can explain the more harmful psychological outcomes for sons compared to sisters and daugh-ters in incestuous relationships.

Anthropological Alliance Theories

All alliance theories in anthropology argue that exogamy, endog-amy, and incest are part of a larger kinship system that operates to reduce conflict by alliances formed through intermarriage across kin units. When members of one kin unit, such as a lineage or clan, must marry out of their own nuclear family (incest rule) and lineage or clan (rule of exogamy) and into another, specified lin-eage or clan (rule of endogamy), not only is inbreeding depression reduced but alliances are formed between the kin units, thereby integrating the society and reducing conflict.

These kinds of unilineal descent systems are, however, most typical of horticultural (gardening with human power) and pasto-ral (herding) societies that evolved long after hunting and gather-ing. Thus they cannot help in explaining the origins of the incest taboo and the questions that we have addressed. It is true that, with an incest taboo in place, adolescent and adult children are pushed out of the nuclear family when seeking sexual and mar-riage partners; and from this initial base, it is relatively easy to expand the number of kin who fall under the taboo and, thereby, foster a rule of exogamy that, in turn, can lead to rules of endog-amy.

This line of argument does not explain the incest taboo itself, but instead, documents that once present, the taboo can be the early basis for a more complex kinship system that reduces in-breeding and creates alliances. However, unilineal descent systems do not always reduce inbreeding because they often allow individuals who share one-eighth of their genes to marry, thus increasing the chances of inbreeding depression. In fact, once kinship rules are used to integrate a society, there is a bias for marrying close kin because they can be trusted and relied upon. And it may be that rules of exogamy were designed to lower the chances that individuals will marry the equivalent of first cousins and thus decrease the potential for inbreeding depression.

And so, unilineal descent systems must also develop rules to ensure that marriage does not occur among too closely related kin and that individuals marry kin who, at most, share only one-eighth of their genes and preferably only one-sixteenth of their genes. But none of this speculation about the operation of unilineal kinship systems helps us explain the origins of the incest taboo, or the questions that have guided our analysis.

Fox's Synthetic Theory

As we emphasized in chapter 2, our approach comes closest to Robin Fox's (1980) analysis that combines insights from diverse sources: the Freudian tradition, the sociological tradition that Freud's ideas help found, the diverse strands of sociobiology, the arguments of Westermarck, the rapidly advancing science of neurology, the alliance theories of anthropology, and the data from primatology. Fox emphasized that once selection favored the evolution of the nuclear family, older transfer patterns that had reduced the chances of incest were weakened. The Westermarck effect would perhaps be sufficient for the avoidance of sibling incest, but as emotional and the cognitive capacities of the brain increased (with big game hunting that could provide the necessary protein for brain growth), alternative mechanisms for incest avoidance would be necessary. As primates, Fox argued, there is a tendency for males to horde access to females, thus setting up the classic Oedipal situation, but as the brain expanded and as new patterns of thought, emotion, and decision making ensued, rules were created whose violation activated guilt and shame. Thus it became possible to supplement the Westermarck effect by instituting an incest taboo that would force males to seek sexual partners outside the nuclear family.

In broad strokes, our argument is similar to Fox's analysis. Fox's approach can explain why the taboo emerged: to prevent incest in the emerging nuclear family that was eroding older primate

transfer patterns and pushing the entire burden for incest avoidance onto the Westermarck effect. For us, this is Fox's key insight.
The emergence of the nuclear family changed older patterns of
sexual avoidance among primates and, hence, required new, culturally based mechanisms to prevent incest. And, as Fox notes,
people would be well aware of the harmful effects on children of
incestuous relationships, thereby motivating them to prevent incest from occurring.

While we have updated Fox's brilliant synthesis with new data not
available to him at the time, we differ from Fox on several key points.
First, as Fox implies, the entire burden for incest aversion was not
placed upon the imprinting described by the Westermarck effect as
the nuclear family began to emerge during hominid and human
evolution. Mother–son avoidance in chimpanzees tells us that there
was an even more powerful biological mechanism for preventing
incest between members of this one key dyad in the nuclear family.
Moreover, we argue that the horde was built around this innate
avoidance pattern, leading to a protohuman grouping consisting of
mothers and their sons, a fellowship of males, and immigrant females.

Second, apes are not as quite hierarchical as portrayed by Fox,
particularly chimpanzees. In addition, while male chimpanzees,
lead gorilla males, and Old World monkey males may attempt to
monopolize females when given an opportunity, they do not actually horde them, with the rare exception of the *Papio hamadryas*
baboon. In light of these more recent data on primates, Fox's
speculation about a Freudian dynamic is, we think, overdrawn.
Even though a father may try to horde his wife from other males
and his son, the son and mother already have a powerful bioprogrammer working against sexual interest. And so, despite the fact
that the story of Oedipus is found throughout history in both
literate and preliterate societies, it is a moral tale about inadvertent
incest between unknowing partners who, in the natural course of
living together in the nuclear family, would not have sexual interest for each other. The son would not have to repress either his
sexual desire for his mother or hate for his father. More interesting, though less frequent, are tales of fathers seducing their daughters which is a real possibility because there are no clear
bioprogrammers against this sexual relationship. For us, then, the
emotional fuel for the incest taboo does not reside in a son's
repressed emotions but, instead, in the lack of a strong bioprogrammer against father–daughter incest and in the possibility that,
as Fox emphasized, the Westermarck effect will not be activated

when siblings are kept separated, coupled with equally justifiable fears about the consequences on the health of children born from incestuous sexual relations. Instead, despite the ubiquity of the Oedipal tale, it is a cultural "red herring." The real threat comes from the father–daughter and brother–sister dyads becoming incestuous and producing deformed children. Thus the supposed emotional turmoil surrounding the mother–son and father–son dyads did not drive the formation of the incest taboo, despite the ubiquity of the Oedipal tale in human societies.

Third, we would draw more than Fox does on the sociological extensions of Freud's basic insight that competition in the family would be ruinous. People were not just fearful that incest would occur and cause inbreeding depression, but also we see concerns in early written records about the disruptive effects of incest on the nuclear family. Roles become confused, tension mounts, trust is broken, and conflict erupts. And, to the degree that society increasingly hinged on a viable nuclear family, people were very aware of the disruptive effects of sexual relations between parents and offspring, and to a lesser extent, between siblings. This awareness, born of experience, no doubt, also motivated people to create the incest taboo.

While Fox's analysis explains a great deal, it does not fully answer the questions that have been guiding our analysis. He would explain, we imagine, the relative strength of the taboo in terms of Freudian processes. The greater taboo on mother–son incest reflects the ancient conflict between fathers and sons over access to females and the consequence of repressing sexual interest in mothers and hatred of fathers, with such repression providing the extra power behind the mother–son incest taboo. Differential rates of incest can also be explained by Fox's scheme. Mother–son incest is less likely because of the power of the taboo and the guilt that a son feels in repressed sexual desires for his mother and anger toward his father, all of which combine to reduce conscious sexual interest in mothers. In contrast, the Westermarck effect is comparatively weak, and father–daughter sexual relations are regulated solely by the incest taboo. We think that our explanation for lower rates of mother–son incest is more parsimonious: it is hardwired because it exists in our closest primate relatives. The rest of the explanation for sibling and father–daughter incest is close to our reasoning.

As to the differential psychological effects on the younger person in the incestuous dyad, Fox's scheme can offer a Freudian interpretation that might go something like the following: Because sons have repressed and conflicted emotions revolving around sexual interest in, and repulsion from, their mothers as well as a complex of emotions—fear, anger, and love—revolving around their fathers, these conflicting emotions coupled with violation of the most powerful taboo leads to more severe psychological symptoms when incest does occur. In contrast, the taboo for father–daughter and sibling incest is not as powerful, nor is it fueled by the same complex of repressed emotions. This explanation is plausible, but one has to accept the Freudian argument to make it work. Without Freud, there would be no reason for sons, daughters, and sisters to have varying psychological pathologies from incest, although one could make the case that sons and daughters have more severe emotional reactions because the trust toward the parent has been violated and because the son or daughter is now in a confused role relationship with a parent, while in a conflict relationship with the parent of the opposite sex. This would be our argument, coupled with the recognition that mother–son incest crosses both cultural and biological barriers and, hence, has a much greater effect on sons than either daughters or sisters.

CONCLUSION

We are at the end of our evolutionary journey into why the incest taboo emerged and why the strength of the taboo, rates of incest, and relative psychological harm to victims of incest vary. We have pursued Fox's strategy of trying to integrate very diverse approaches to the problem of understanding the incest taboo; and like virtually all other approaches, our analysis is speculative. We have added certain refinements to Fox's argument and avoided the deep detour into Freudian psychology, while offering an alternative explanation for how the neurology of emotions was important in generating the nuclear family and exacerbating the potential for incest among more emotionally bonded individuals.

At the very least, we hope that we have added some new ideas to the long-standing literature on the taboo. The taboo is the outcome of both biological and sociocultural selection pressures. Sexual avoidance in an emerging nuclear family inhabited by more emotionally charged members could no longer be managed by biological mechanisms alone, especially as patterns of female transfer typical of all apes were subverted by new kinds of family attachments. As transfer was reduced and as individuals stayed in or near the family for longer periods of time, and in many cases for a lifetime, the taboo had to be created, first in the language of emotions and later in spoken language. This taboo reinforced the biology of sexual avoidance, while at the same time giving voice to fears of incest between members of the family not regulated by a biologically based mechanism for sexual avoidance.

We have also sought to understand the relative strength of the taboo, varying rates of incest, and differing psychological outcomes of incest. Even though the family has evolved back to a nuclear form in industrial and postindustrial societies, the modern nuclear family is not the same as it was for the first hunting and gathering bands. It is likely that mother–son incest virtually never occurred in these bands and that sexual relations between the other two incestuous dyads were rare. The Westermarck effect was probably more powerful in the nuclear family of hunter-gatherers than in contemporary families, and coupled with the informal monitoring of sexual activity in the natural course of daily routines among hunter-gatherers, the likelihood of sibling and father–daughter incest was also very low. Moreover, over one-third of studied hunter-gatherers have a patrilocal residence rule which, in sanctioning marriage outside the band, acts very much like ancient ape propensities for female transfer. Today, compared to hunter-gatherers, the nuclear family is more isolated from the community, more likely to house sexually mature offspring well past puberty, more unstable with high rates of dissolution, more likely to bring nonparental males into the household, more governed by rules of patriarchy, more violent and abusive, and more occupied by individuals with drug and alcohol problems. It should not be surprising, then, that the rate of incest is much greater in the modern nuclear family than in the families of hunter-gatherers.

Still, with all of its tensions and pathologies, mother–son incest in the modern family is still rather rare, which tells us that it is a hardwired avoidance pattern; and when it does occur, it has very severe psychological effects on sons. The modern nuclear family structure may also disrupt the activation of the Westermarck effect, thereby increasing rates of sibling incest to levels that would be unheard of in families of hunter-gatherers. And, without any known biological mechanisms for sexual avoidance between fathers and daughters, without easy community monitoring, and with patriarchy, it should not be surprising that incest and, of course, stepfather–stepdaughter incest go well beyond what we would have observed in the first hunting and gathering bands.

The movement of human societies to horticulture and agrarian forms, where the nuclear family became part of larger kin units, probably led to increased incest over what occurred in hunting and gathering societies, but not to the level seen today in postindustrial societies. But it is clear that incest was an issue that people thought and wrote about during the agrarian era, and so it must have been a problem as larger, more tension-filled kinship units were created.

Unfortunately we cannot know today just how common incest in the nuclear family is. The conflation of incest with child sexual abuse and child abuse in general makes data on rates of incest virtually impossible to gather and assess. And, given the expansion of what constitutes incest, we cannot be sure that reports of incest involve actual sexual intercourse. Despite these problems with the data, it is useful to speculate on why the incest taboo emerged because, as early scholars recognized, it is the key to human survival. The nuclear family is not a "natural" unit for an evolved ape, and thus, when it was created to make hominids and humans more fit, it was necessary to supplement biological with sociocultural -evolution. We trust that our speculations, even with the problematic data, can add something to the long-standing interest in the incest taboo. We close with the words of John McLennan who, as one of the first scholars to propose the horde arrangement and to trace the origin of society, wrote, "Whether we have hit the truth or not, we trust we have at least been preparing the way for those who in the fulness of time will reach it" (McLennan, 1869, 408).

BIBLIOGRAPHY

Aberle, D., et al. 1963. "The Incest Taboo and the Mating of Animals." *American Anthropologist* 65:253–65.

Abraham, S. 1993. "Speaking the Truth." *Survivors of Female Incest Emerge* 3:4–6.

Adams, K. M. 1991. *Silently Seduced: When Parents Make Their Children Partners.* Deerfield Beach, FL: Health Communications.

Adams, M. S., and J. V. Neel. 1967. "Children of Incest." *Pediatrics* 40:55–62.

Adams, R. B., Jr., H. L. Gordon, A. A. Baird, N. Ambady, and R. E. Kleck. 2003. "Effects of Gaze on Amygdala Sensitivity to Anger and Fear Faces." *Science* 300:1536.

Adams-Tucker, C. 1982. "Proximate Effects of Sexual Abuse in Childhood: A Report on Twenty-eight Children." *American Journal of Psychiatry* 139:1252–56.

———. 1981. "A Sociological Overview of 28 Abused Children." *Child Abuse and Neglect* 5:361–67.

Adler, N. A., and J. Schutz. 1995. "Sibling Incest Offenders." *Child Abuse and Neglect* 19:811–19.

Agusti, J. P. A., M. Fortelius, and L. Rook. 1998. "Hominoid Evolution and Environmental Change in the Neogene of Europe: A European Science Foundation Network." *Journal of Human Evolution* 34:103–7.

Alexander, P. C., C. L. Anderson, B. Brand, C. M. Schaeffer, B. Z. Grolling, and L. Kretz. 1998. "Adult Attachment and Long-term Effects in Survivors of Incest." *Child Abuse and Neglect* 22:45–61.

Ali, A., A. H. Feroze, Z. H. Rizvi, and T. V. Rehman. 2003. "Consanguineous Marriage Resulting in Homozygous Occurrence of X-linked Retinoschisis in Girls." *American Journal of Ophthalmology* 136:767–69.

Allen, C. M. 1991. *Women and Men Who Sexually Abuse Children: A Comparative Analysis*. Brandon, VT: Safer Society Press.

————. 1990. "Women as Perpetrators of Child Sexual Abuse: Recognition Barriers." In *The Incest Perpetrator: A Family Member No One Wants to Treat*. Edited by A. L. Horton, B. L. Johnson, L. M. Roundy, and D. Williams. Newbury Park, CA: Sage.

Andelman, S. 1986. "Ecological and Social Determinants of Cercopithecine Mating Patterns." In *Ecological Aspects of Social Evolution*. Edited by D. Rubenstein and R. Wrangham. Princeton: Princeton University Press.

Anderson, L. M., and G. Shafer. 1979. "The Character-Disordered Family: A Community Treatment Model for Family Sexual Abuse." *American Journal of Orthopsychiatry* 49:436–45.

Anderson, M. C., K. N. Ochsner, B. Kuhl, J. Cooper, E. Robertson, S. W. Gabrieli, G. H. Glover, and J. D. E. Cabrieli. 2004. "Neural Systems Underlying the Suppression of Unwanted Memories." *Science* 303:232–35.

Andrews, P. 1996. "Palaeoecology and Hominoid Palaeoenvironments." *Biological Review* 71:257–300.

————. 1995. "Ecological Apes and Ancestors." *Nature* 376:555–56.

————. 1992. "Evolution and Environment in the Hominoidea." *Nature* 360:641–46.

————. 1989. "Palaeoecology of Laetoli." *Journal of Human Evolution* 18:173–81.

————. 1981. "Species Diversity and Diet in Monkeys and Apes During the Miocene." In *Aspects of Human Evolution*. Edited by C. B. Stringer. London: Taylor & Francis.

Andrews, P., and L. Martin. 1987. "Cladistic Relationships of Extant and Fossil Hominoids." *Journal of Human Evolution* 16:101–18.

Anton, S. 2003. "Natural History of Homo Erectus." *Yearbook of Physical Anthropology* 46:126–79.

Archibald, E. 2001. *Incest and the Medieval Imagination*. Oxford: Clarendon Press.

Arens, W. 1986. *The Original Sin: Incest and Its Meaning*. New York: Oxford University Press.

Arkin, A. M. 1984. "A Hypothesis Concerning the Incest Taboo." *Psychoanalytic Review* 71:375–81.

Armstrong, L. 1978. *Kiss Daddy Goodnight: A Speak Out on Incest*. New York: Pocket Books.

Arnold, M. 1960. *Emotion and Personality: Psychological Aspects*. Oxford: Columbia University Press.

Arroyo, W., S. Eth, and R. Pynoos. 1984. "Sexual Assault of a Mother by Her Preadolescent Son." *American Journal of Psychiatry* 141:1107–8.

Baba, H., F. Aziz, Y. Kaifu, G. Suwa, R. T. Kono, and T. Jacob. 2003.

"*Homo Erectus* Calvarium from the Pleistocene of Java." *Science* 299:1384–86.

Bachmann, K. M., and J. Bossi. 1993. "Mother–Son Incest as a Defense against Psychosis." *British Journal of Medical Psychology* 66:289–48.

Bachmann, K. M., F. Moggi, and F. Stirnemann-Lewis. 1994. "Mother–Son Incest and Its Long-Term Consequences: A Neglected Phenomenon in Psychiatric Practice." *Journal of Nervous Mental Disease* 182:723–25.

Bachofen, J. J. 1967. *Myth, Religion, and Mother-Right: Selected Writings of J. J. Bachofen.* Translated by Ralph Manheim. New Jersey: Princeton University Press.

———. [1861] 1931. "Das Mutterrecht." In *The Making of Man: An Outline of Anthropology.* Edited by V. F. Calverton. New York: Modern Library.

Bagley, C. 1969. "Incest Behavior and Incest Taboo." *Social Problems* 16:505–79.

Bailey, R., and R. Aunger. 1989. "Humans as Primates: The Social Relationships of Efe Pygmy Men in Comparative Perspective." *International Journal of Primatology* 11:127–46.

Baker, A. W., and S. P. Duncan. 1985. "Child Sexual Abuse: A Study of Prevalence in Great Britain." *Child Abuse and Neglect* 9:457–67.

Balter, M., and A. Gibbons. 2002. "Were 'Little People' the First to Venture Out of Africa?" *Science* 297:26–27.

Banning, A. 1989. "Mother–Son Incest: Confronting a Prejudice." *Child Abuse and Neglect* 13:563–70.

Barnard, C. P., ed. 1984. *Families, Incest, and Therapy.* New York: Human Sciences Press.

Barry, M. J., Jr., and A. M. Johnson. 1958. "The Incest Barrier." *Psychoanalytic Quarterly* 27:485–500.

Bass, A. 1991. "A Touch for Evil." *Boston Globe Magazine,* 12–25.

Bateson, Patrick. 2005. "Inbreeding Avoidance and Incest Taboos." In *Inbreeding, Incest, and the Incest Taboo.* Edited by A. P. Wolf and W. H. Durham. Stanford, CA: Stanford University Press.

Beard, M. 1980. "The Sexual Status of Vestal Virgins." *Journal of Roman Studies* 7:12–27.

Beauvilain, A., and Y. Beauvilain. 2004. "Further Details Concerning Fossils Attributed to Sahelanthropus Tchadenses (Tourmai)." *South African Journal of Science* 100, no. 3–4:142–44.

Beek, J. C., and B. van der Kolk. 1987. "Reports of Childhood Incest and Current Behavior of Chronically Hospitalized Psychotic Women." *American Journal of Psychiatry* 144:1474–76.

Begun. D. 2004. "The Earliest Hominins: Is Less More?" *Science* 303:1478–80.

Bender, L. 1954. *A Dynamic Psychopathology of Childhood.* Springfield, IL: Thomas.

Bender, L., and A. Blau. 1937. "The Reactions of Children to Sexual Relations with Adults." *American Journal of Orthopsychiatry* 7:500–518.

Bender, L., and A. E. Grugett Jr. 1962. "A Follow-up Report on Children Who Had Atypical Sexual Experience." *American Journal of Orthopsychiatry* 22:825–37.

Benefit, B. R. 1999. "Victoriapithecus: The Key to Old World Monkey and Catarrhine Origins." *Evolutionary Anthropology* 7:155–74.

Berendzen, R. 1994. "'Come Here': The Male Victim." Presentation at the Cycle of Sexual Trauma: Treating the Victim and Treating the Offender seminar, Baltimore.

Berendzen, R., and L. Palmer. 1993. *Come Here: A Man Overcomes the Tragic Aftermath of Childhood Sexual Abuse.* New York: Villard.

Berlin, S. F. 1994. "Differential Diagnosis and Treatment of Offenders." Presentation at the Cycle of Sexual Trauma: Treating the Victim and Treating the Offender seminar, Baltimore.

Bermejo, M. 2004. "Home-Range Use and Intergroup Encounters in Western Gorillas (Gorilla g. gorilla) at Lossi Forest, North Congo." *American Journal of Primatology* 64:223–32.

Berry, G. W. 1975. "Incest: Some Clinical Variations on a Classical Theme." *Journal of the American Academy of Psychoanalysis* 3:151–61.

Beve, I., and I. Silverman. 1993. "Early Proximity and Intimacy between Siblings and Incestuous Behavior: A Test of the Westermarck Theory." *Ethology and Sociobiology* 14:171–81.

Bicchieri, M. G., ed. 1972. *Hunters and Gatherers Today.* New York: Holt, Rinehart & Winston.

Bigras, J. 1966. "On Disappointment and the Consequences of Incest in the Adolescent Girl." *Canadian Psychiatric Association Journal* 11:189–204.

Bischof, N. 1972. "The Biological Foundations of the Incest Taboo." *Social Science Information* 11:7–36.

Bittles, A. H. 2005. "Genetic Aspects of Inbreeding and Incest." In *Inbreeding, Incest, and the Incest Taboo.* Edited by A. P. Wolf and W. H. Durham. Stanford, CA: Stanford University Press.

Bittles, A. H., and J. V. Neel. 1994. "The Costs of Human Inbreeding and Their Implications for Variations at the DNA Level." *Nature Genetics* 8:117–21.

Bixler, R. H. 1981. "The Incest Controversy." *Psychological Reports* 49:267–83.

Blanchard, G. 1986. "Male Victims of Child Sexual Abuse: A Portent of Things to Come." *Journal of Independent Social Work* 1:19–27.

Bloch, J. I., and D. Boyer. 2002. "Grasping Primate Origins." *Science* 298:1606–10.

Bobe, René, and A. Behrensmeyer. 2004. "The Expansion of Grassland Ecosystems in Africa in Relation to Mammalian Evolution and the

Origin of Genus *Homo.*" *Palaeogeography, Palaeoclimatology Palaeo-ecology* 207:399–420.

Bock, K. 1956. *The Acceptance of Histories.* Los Angeles: University of California Press.

Boehm, C. 2004. "Variance Reduction and The Evolution of Social Control." Working paper.

———. 1999. *Hierarchy in The Forest: The Evolution of Egalitarian Behavior.* Cambridge: Harvard University Press.

———. 1993. "Egalitarian Society and Reverse Dominance Hierarchy." *Current Anthropology* 34:227–54.

Boesch C., and H. Boesch-Achermann. 2000. "The Chimpanzees of the Tai Forest." In *Behavioural Ecology and Evolution.* Oxford: Oxford University.

Bogorad, B. E. 1998. "Sexual Abuse: Surviving the Pain." American Academy of Experts in Traumatic Stress, www.aaets.org/arts/art31.htm.

———. 1991. "Sexual Abuse: Surviving the Pain." *Clinical Update: The South Oaks Journal* 3:1–5.

Bolton, F. G., Jr., L. A. Morris, and A. E. MacEachron. 1989. *Males at Risk: The Other Side of Child Sexual Abuse.* Newbury Park, CA: Sage.

Bowlby, J. 1969. *Attachment and Loss.* New York: Basic.

Brant, R. S. T., and V. B. Tisza. 1977. "The Sexually Misused Child." *American Journal of Orthopsychiatry* 47:80–90.

Brayton, R. M., G. Dietrich-MacLean, M. S. Dietrich, K. B. Sherrod, and W. A. Altemeier. 1995. *Child Abuse and Neglect* 19:1255–61.

Breines, W., and L. Gordon. 1983. "The New Scholarship of Family Violence." *Signs* 8:490–553.

Briggs, S. L., and P. R. Joyce. 1997. "What Determines Post-traumatic Stress Disorder: Symptomatology for Survivors of Childhood Sexual Abuse." *Child Abuse and Neglect* 21:575–82.

Bronson, S. F., and F. B. M. de Waal. 2003. "Fair Refusal by Capuchin Monkeys." *Nature* 128–40.

Brook, B. W., D. W. Tonkyn, J. J. O'Grady, and R. Frankham. 2002. "Contribution of Inbreeding to Extinction in Threatened Species." *Conservation Ecology* 6, no. 16.

Brooks, B. 1983. "Preoedipal Issues in a Postincest Daughter." *American Journal of Psychotherapy* 37:129–36.

Brown, A., and D. Finkelhor. 1986. "Impact of Child Sexual Abuse: A Review of the Research." *Psychological Bulletin* 99:66–77.

Brown, D. 1991. *Human Universals.* New York: McGraw-Hill.

Brown, J. 1952. "A Comparative Study of Deviance from Social Mores." *American Sociological Review* 17:135–46.

Brown, W. 1963. "Murder Rooted in Incest." In *Patterns of Incest.* Edited by R. E. L. Masters. New York: Julian.

Browning, D. H., and B. Boatman. 1977. "Incest: Children at Risk." *American Journal of Psychiatry* 134:69–72.

Brownmiller, S. 1975. *Against Our Will.* New York: Simon & Schuster.

Bruckner, D. F., and P. E. Johnson. 1987. "Treatment for Adult Male Victims of Childhood Sexual Abuse." *Social Casework* 68:81–87.

Brunet, M. 2002. Reply. *Nature* 582.

Brunet, M., F. Guy, D. Pilbeam, H. T. Mackaye, A. Likius, D. Ahounta, A. Beauvilain, C. Blondel, H. Bocherens, J-R. Boisserie, L. De Bonis, Y. Coppens, J. Dejax, C. Denys, P. Duringer, V. Eisenmann, G. Fanone, P. Fronty, D. Geraads, T. Lehmann, F. Lihoreau, A. Louchart, A. Mahamat, G. Merceron, G. Mouchelin, O. Otero, P. P. Campomanes, M. Ponce De Leon, J-C. Rage, M. Sapanet, M. Schuster, J. Sudre, P. Tassy, X. Valentin, P. Vignaud, L. Viriot, A. Zazzo, and C. Zollikofer. 2002. "A New Hominid from the Upper Miocene of Chad, Central Africa." *Nature* 18:145–51.

Burda, H. 1995. "Individual Recognition and Incest Avoidance in Eusocial Common Mole-rats Rather Than Reproductive Suppression by Parents." *Experientia* 51:411–13.

Burgess, A. W., A. N. Groth, L. L. Holmstrom, and S. M. Sgroi. 1978. *Sexual Assault of Children and Adolescents.* Lexington, MA: Lexington.

Burgess, A. W., A. N. Groth, and M. P. McCausland. 1981. "Child Sex Initiation Rings." *American Journal of Orthopsychiatry* 51:110–18.

Burton, R. 1973. "Folk Theory and the Incest Taboo." *Ethos* 1:504–16.

Butler, S. 1978. *Conspiracy of Silence: The Trauma of Incest.* San Francisco: Volcano.

Calam, R., L. Horne, D. Glasgow, and A. Cox. 1998. "Psychological Disturbance and Child Sexual Abuse: A Follow-up Study." *Child Abuse and Neglect* 22: 901–13.

Campbell, B. 1985a. *Human Evolution.* 3d ed. Chicago: Aldine de Gruyter.

———. 1985b. *Humankind Emerging.* Boston: Little, Brown.

Campbell, B., and J. Loy. 2000. *Humankind Emerging.* Boston: Allyn & Bacon.

Canavan, M. M., and W. J. Meyer. 1992. "The Female Experience of Sibling Incest." *Journal of Marital and Family Therapy* 18:129–42.

Carnes, P. 1991. *Don't Call It Love: Recovery from Sexual Addiction.* New York: Bantam Books.

Carter, C. O. 1967. "Risk to Offspring of Incest." *The Lancet* 289:436.

Catanzarite, V. A., and S. E. Combs. 1980. "Mother–Son Incest." *Journal of the American Medical Association* 243:1807–8.

Catton, W., Jr. 1969. "What's in a Name: A Study of Role Inertia." *Journal of Marriage and the Family* 31:15–18.

Cela-Conde, C., and F. Ayala. 2003. "Genera of the Human Lineage." *PWAS* 100:7684–89.

Cepada, M. L. 1978. "Incest Without Harmful Repercussions." *Medical Aspects of Human Sexuality* 12:131.

Cerling, T., J. Harris, B. MacFadden, M. Leakey, J. Quade, V. Eisenmann, and J. Ehleringer. 1997. "Global Vegetation Change through the Miocene/Bliocene Boundary." *Nature* 389:153–58.

Chartier, R. 1989a. *A History of Private Life: Passions of the Renaissance.* Vol. 3. Cambridge: Belknap Press, Harvard University Press.

———. 1989b. "The Practical Impact of Writing." In *A History of Private Life: Passions of the Renaissance.* Vol. 3. Edited by Roger Chartier. Cambridge: Belknap Press, Harvard University Press.

Chasnoff, I. J., W. J. Burns, S. H. Schnoll, K. Burns, G. Chisum, and L. Kyle-Spore. 1986. "Maternal-neonatal Incest." *American Journal of Orthopsychiatry* 56:577–80.

Chelf, C. M., and J. B. Ellis. 2002. "Young Adults Who Were Sexually Abused: Demographics as Predictors of Their Coping Behaviors." *Child Abuse and Neglect* 26:313–16.

Cheney, D., and R. Seyfarth. 1990. *How Monkeys See the World.* Chicago: University of Chicago Press.

Cheney, D., R. Seyfarth, and B. Smuts. 1986. "Social Relationships and Social Cognition in Non-Human Primates." *Science* 234:1361–66.

Chivers, D. 1984. "Feeding and Ranging in Gibbons: A Summary." In *The Lesser Apes.* Edited by H. Prevschoft, D. Chivers, W. Brockelman, and N. Creel. Edinburgh: Edinburgh University Press.

———. 1974. "The Siamang in Malaya." In *Contributions to Primatology.* Vol. 40. New York: Karger.

Chodorow, N. 1978. *The Reproduction of Mothering: Psychoanalysis and the Sociology of Gender.* Berkeley: University of California Press.

Cohen, T. 1983. "The Incestuous Family Revisited." *Social Casework* 64:154–61.

Cohen, Y. A. 1978. *The Transition from Childhood to Adolescence: Cross-cultural Studies of Initiation Ceremonies, Legal Systems, and Incest Taboo.* Chicago: Aldine.

Cole, A. 1990. "Sibling Incest: The Myth of Benign Sibling Incest." *Women and Therapy* 5:79–89.

Collins, R. 2004. *Interaction Ritual.* Princeton: Princeton University Press.

———. 1998. *The Sociology of Philosophies: A Global Theory of Intellectual Change.* Cambridge: Harvard University Press.

Condy, S. R., D. I. Templer, R. Brown, and L. Veaco. 1987. "Parameters of Sexual Contact of Boys with Women." *Archives of Sexual Behavior* 16:379–94.

Conroy, G. 1990. *Primate Evolution.* New York: Norton.

Cook, J. [1777] 1967. *"The Voyage of the Resolution and Discovery."* Edited by J. C. Beaglehole. London: Cambridge University Press.

Cooney, R., and N. C. Bennett. 2000. "Inbreeding Avoidance and Reproductive Skew in a Cooperative Mammal." *Proceedings of the Royal Society of London,* B series, 267:801–6.

Coppens, Y., M. Pickford, B. Senut, D. Gommery, and J. Treil. 2002.

"Bipedalism in *Orrorin Tugenensis* Revealed in Its Femora." *Comptes Rendus Palevol* 1:191–203.

Cormier, B. M., M. Kennedy, and J. Sangowicz. 1962. "Psychodynamics of Father–Daughter Incest." *Canadian Psychiatric Association Journal* 7:203–17.

Corruccini, R. S., and R. L. Ciochon. 1983. "Overview of Ape and Human Ancestry: Phyletic Relationships of Miocene and Later Hominoidea." In *New Interpretations of Ape and Human Ancestry.* Edited by R. L. Ciochon and R. Corruccini. New York: Plenum.

Corruccini, R., R. Ciochon, and H. McHenry. 1975. "Osteometric Shape Relationships in the Wrist Joint of Some Anthropoids." *Folia Primatologica* 24:250–74.

Cosmides, L. 1989. "The Logic of Social Exchange: Has Natural Selection Shaped How Humans Reason?" *Cognition* 31:187–276.

Coult, A. 1963. "Causality and Cross-Sex Prohibitions." *American Anthropologist* 65:266–77.

Courtois, C. A. 1988. *Healing the Incest Wound: Adult Survivors in Therapy.* New York: Norton.

———. 1979. "The Incest Experience and Its Aftermath." *Victimology: An International Journal* 4:337–47.

Cox, D., E. Meyers, and P. Sinha. 2004. "Contextually Evoked Object-Specific Responses in Human Visual Cortex." *Science* 304:115–17.

Crewdson, J. 1988. *By Silence Betrayed: Sexual Abuse of Children in America.* Boston: Little, Brown.

Crippen, T. 1994. "Toward a Neo-Darwinian Sociology." *Sociological Perspectives* 37:391–401.

Cyr, M., J. Wright, P. McDuff, and A. Perron. 2002. "Comment on 'Intrafamilial Sexual Abuse.'" *Child Abuse and Neglect* 26:955–56.

Daie, N., E. Witztum, and M. Eleff. 1989. "Long-term Effects of Sibling Incest." *Journal of Clinical Psychiatry* 50:428–31.

Dalton, R. 2002. "Face to Face with Our Past." *Nature* 420:735–36.

Dankner, A. 1992. *Dan Ben Amots: The Biography.* Israel: Yeushalayim.

Davis, K. 1949. *Human Society.* New York: Macmillan.

Davis, N. 1970. "*Non-Cycle Plays and Fragments.*" London: Oxford University Press.

De Coulanges, F. [1864] 1889. *The Ancient City.* Translated by Willard Small. 7th ed. Boston: Lee & Shepard.

———. [1864] 1889. *A Study of the Religion, Laws, and Institutions of Greece and Rome.* Translated by Willard Small. 7th ed. Boston: Lee & Shepard.

DeJong, A. R. 1989. "Sexual Interactions among Siblings and Cousins: Experimentation or Exploitation?" *Child Abuse and Neglect* 13:271–79.

———. 1985. "Response to the Article 'The Sexually Abused Child: A Comparison of Male and Female Victims.'" *Child Abuse and Neglect* 9:575–76.

Demarest, W. 1977. "Incest Avoidance among Human and Non-Human Primates." In *Primate Bio-Social Development.* Edited by S. Chevalier-Skolnikoff and F. Poirier. New York: Garland.

De Menocal, P. 2004. "African Climate Change and Faunal Evolution during the Pliocene Pleistocene." *Earth and Planetary Science Letters* 30:3–24.

Denic, S. 2003. "Consanguinity as a Risk Factor for Cervical Carcinoma." *Medical Hypotheses* 60:321–24.

De Ste. Croix, G. E. M. 1963. "Why Were the Early Christians Persecuted?" *Past and Present,* 26:6–38.

De Waal, F. B. M. 1996. *Good Natured: The Origins of Right and Wrong in Humans and Other Animals.* Cambridge: Harvard University Press.

———. 1992. "Coalitions as Part of Reciprocal Relations in the Arnhem Colony." In *Coalitions and Alliances in Humans and Other Animals.* Edited by A. H. Harcourt and F. B. M. de Waal. Oxford: Oxford University Press.

———. 1989. *Peacekeeping among Primates.* Cambridge: Harvard University Press.

———. 1982. *Chimpanzee Politics: Power and Sex among Apes.* New York: Harper & Row.

De Young, M. 1985. *Incest: An Annotated Bibliography.* London: McFarland.

———. 1984. "Counterphobic Behavior in Multiply Molested Children." *Child Welfare* 63:333–39.

———. 1982a. *The Sexual Victimization of Children.* London: McFarland.

———. 1982b. "Innocent Seducer or Innocently Seduced: The Role of the Child Incest Victim." *Journal of Clinical Child Psychology* 11:56–60.

———. 1981a. "Incest Victims and Offenders: Myths and Realities." *Journal of Psychosocial Nursing and Mental Health Services* 19:37–39.

———. 1981b. "Promises, Threats, and Lies: Keeping Incest Secret." *Journal of Humanics* 9:61–71.

Dietz, C. A., and J. L. Craft. 1980. "Family Dynamics of Incest: A New Perspective." *Social Casework* 61:602–9.

Diggs, S. 1997. "The Plural Taboo." *Journal of Analytical Psychology* 42:459–79.

Dimmock, P. T. 1988. "Adult Males Sexually Abused as Children: Characteristics and Implications for Treatment." *Journal of Interpersonal Violence* 3:203–21.

Dixson, A. F. 1981. *The Natural History of the Gorilla.* New York: Columbia University Press.

Dobson, F. S., R. K. Chesser, J. L. Hoogland, D. W. Sugg, and D. W. Foltz. 1997. "Do Black-tailed Prairie Dogs Minimize Inbreeding?" *Evolution* 51:970–78.

Dunaif–Hattis, J. 1984. *Doubling the Brain: On the Evolution of Brain Lateralization and Its Implications for Language.* New York: Peter Lang.

Durham, W. H. 2005. "Assessing the Gaps in Westermarck's Theory." In *Inbreeding, Incest, and the Incest Taboo*. Edited by A. P. Wolf and W. H. Durham. Stanford, CA: Stanford University Press.

———. 1991. *Coevolution: Genes, Culture and Human Diversity*. Stanford, CA: Stanford University Press.

Durkheim, É. [1912] 1984. *The Elementary Forms of the Religious Life*. New York: Free Press.

———. [1898] 1963. *Incest: The Nature and Origin of the Taboo*. New York: Lyle Stuart.

———. [1893] 1933. *The Division of Labor in Society*. New York: Free Press.

Eccles, J. C. 1989. *Evolution of the Brain: Creation of Self*. London: Routledge.

Edmunds, L. 1985. *Oedipus: The Ancient Legend and Its Later Analogues*. Baltimore: John Hopkins University Press.

Edwards, A. W. F. 2003. "Human Genetic Diversity: Lewontin's Fallacy." *Bioessays* 25:798–801.

Eist, H. I., and A. U. Mandel. 1968. "Family Treatment of Ongoing Incest Behavior." *Family Process* 7:216–32.

Ekman, P. 1984. "Expression and Nature of Emotions." In *Approaches to Emotions*. Edited by K. Scherer and P. Ekman. Hillsdale, NJ: Erlbaum.

Ellefson, S. O. 1974. "A Natural History of White-Handed Gibbons in the Malaysian Peninsula." In *Gibbon and Siamang*. Vol. 3. Edited by D. Rumbaugh. Basel: Karger.

Elliott, M., ed. 1994. *Female Sexual Abuse of Children*. New York: Guilford.

———. 1993. *Female Sexual Abuse of Children: The Ultimate Taboo*. London: Longman Information and Reference.

Ember, C. 1978. "Myths about Hunter-Gatherers." *Ethnology* 439–48.

Ember, M. 1975. "On the Origin and Extension of the Incest Taboo." *Behavioral Science Research* 27:223–29.

Emde, R. N. 1980. "Levels of Meaning for Infant Emotions: A Biosocial View." In *Development of Cognition, Affect, and Social Relations*. Edited by W. A. Collins. Hillsdale, NJ.: Erlbaum.

Emslie, G. J., and A. A. Rosenfeld. 1983. "Incest Reported by Children and Adolescents Hospitalized for Severe Psychiatric Problems." *American Journal of Psychiatry* 140:708–11.

Enard, W. M., et al. 2002a. "Molecular Evolution of TOXP2, A Gene Involved in Speech and Language." *Nature* 418:869–72.

Enard, W., et al. 2002b. "Intra- and Interspecific Variation in Primate Gene Expression Patterns." *Science* 296:340–42.

Engel, B. 1990. *The Right to Innocence: Healing the Trauma of Childhood Sexual Abuse*. New York: Ballantine.

Engels, F. 1942. *The Origins of the Family and the State.* New York: International.

Erickson, M. 2005. "Evolutionary Thought and Clinical Understanding." In *Inbreeding, Incest, and the Incest Taboo.* Edited by A. P. Wolf and W. H. Durham. Stanford, CA: Stanford University Press.

Evans, P. D., J. R. Anderson, E. J. Vallendar, S. L. Gilbert, C. M. Malcolm, S. Dorus, and B. T. Lahn. 2004. "Adaptive Evolution of ASPM, a Major Determinant of Cerebral Cortical Size in Humans." *Human Molecular Genetics* 13:489–94.

Excoffier, Laurent. 2002. "Human Demographic History: Refining the Recent African Origin Model." *Current Opinion in Genetics and Development* 12:675–682.

Fa, J., and D. Lindburg. 1996. *Evaluation and Ecology of Macaque Societies.* Cambridge: Cambridge University Press.

Falk, D. 2002. Presentation to the American Association of Physical Anthropologists, Buffalo, NY, April 11.

———. 2000. *Primate Diversity.* New York: W. W. Norton.

Faller, K. C. 1991. "Boy Victims of Sexual Abuse: Treatment of Boy Victims of Sexual Abuse." *The Advisor: American Professional Society on the Abuse of Children* 4:7–8.

———. 1989. "Characteristics of a Clinical Sample of Sexually Abused Children: How Boy and Girl Victims Differ." *Child Abuse and Neglect* 13:281–91.

———. 1987. "Women Who Sexually Abuse Children." *Violence and Victims* 2:263–76.

Farber, E. D., et al. 1984. "The Sexual Abuse of Children: A Comparison of Male and Female Victims." *Journal of Clinical Child Psychology* 13:294–97.

Faulkes, C. G., and N. C. Bennett. 2001. "Family Values: Group Dynamics and Social Control of Reproduction." *Trends in Ecology and Evolution* 16:184–90.

Fay, M., M. Agnagna, J. Moore, and R. Oko. 1989. "Gorillas (Gorilla gorilla gorilla) in the Likouala Swamp Forests of North Central Congo: Preliminary Data on Populations and Ecology." *International Journal of Primatology* 10:477–95.

Fedigan, L. M. 1982. *Primate Paradigms: Sex Roles and Social Bonds.* St. Albans, VT.: Eden.

Fessler, D., and D. Navarette. 2004. "Third-Party Attitudes toward Sibling Incest: Evidence for Westermarck's Hypothesis." *Evolution and Human Behavior* 25:277–94.

Finch, S. M. 1973. "Adult Seduction of the Child: Effects on the Child." *Medical Aspects of Human Sexuality* 7:170–87.

Finkelhor, D. 1994. "Current Information on Scope and Nature of Sexual Abuse." *Future of Children* 4:46–48.

————. 1990. "Early and Long-term Effects of Child Sexual Abuse: An Update." *Professional Psychology: Research and Practice* 21:325–30.

————. 1984a. "How Widespread Is Child Sexual Abuse?" *Children Today* 13:18–20.

————. 1984b. *Child Sexual Abuse: New Theory and Research.* New York: Free Press.

————. 1981. "Sex between Siblings: Sex Play, Incest, and Aggression." In *Children and Sex.* Boston: Little, Brown.

————. 1980a. "Risk Factors in the Sexual Victimization of Children." *Child Abuse and Neglect* 4:265–73.

————. 1980b. "Sexual Socialization in America: High Risk for Sexual Abuse." In *Childhood and Sexuality: Proceedings of the International Symposium.* Edited by Jean-Marc Sampon. Montreal: Editions Etudes Vivantes.

————. 1980c. "Sex among Siblings: A Survey Report on Prevalence, Variety, and Effect." *Archives of Sexual Behavior* 9:171–94.

————. 1979a. *Sexually Victimized Children.* New York: Free Press.

————. 1979b. "What's Wrong with Sex between Adults and Children?" *American Journal of Orthopsychiatry* 49:692–97.

————. 1978a. "Psychological, Cultural, and Family Factors in Incest and Family Sexual Abuse." *Journal of Marriage and Family Counseling* 4:41–49.

————. 1978b. "Social Forces in the Formulation of the Problems of Sexual Abuse." Paper V55, Family Violence Research Program. Durham: University of New Hampshire.

Finkelhor, D., and G. T. Hotaling. 1984. "Sexual Abuse in the National Incidence Study of Child Abuse and Neglect: An Appraisal." *Child Abuse and Neglect* 8:23–33.

Finkelhor, D., G. Hotaling, I. A. Lewis, and C. Smith. 1990. "Sexual Abuse in a National Survey of Adult Men and Women: Prevalence, Characteristics, and Risk Factors." *Child Abuse and Neglect* 14:19–28.

Finkelhor, D., and D. Russell. 1984. "Women as Perpetrators: Review of the Evidence." In *Child Sexual Abuse: New Theory and Research.* Edited by D. Finkelhor. New York: Free Press.

Finlayson, C. 2004. *Neanderthals and Modern Humans: An Ecological and Evolutionary Perspective.* Cambridge: Cambridge University Press.

Fischer, G. J. 1991. "Is Lesser Severity of Child Sexual Abuse a Reason More Males Report Having Liked It?" *Annals of Sex Research* 4:131–39.

Fiske, A. P. 1991. *Structures of Social Life: The Four Elementary Forms of Human Relations: Communal Sharing, Authority Ranking, Equality Matching, Market Pricing.* New York: Free Press.

Fleagle, J. 1999. *Primate Adaptation and Evolution.* San Diego: Academic.

———. 1978. "Size Distributions of Living and Fossil Primate Faunas." *Paleobiology* 4:67–76.

Fleagle, J. G., et al. 1981. "Climbing: A Biomechanical Link with Brachiation and with Bipedalism." *Symposium of the Zoological Society of London* 48:359–75.

Fleming, J., P. E. Mullen, B. Sibthorpe, and G. Bammer. 1999. "The Long-term Impact of Childhood Sexual Abuse in Australian Women." *Child Abuse and Neglect* 23:145–59.

Foley, R. 2002. "Adaptive Radiations and Dispersals in Hominid Evolutionary Ecology." *Evolutionary Anthropology,* suppl. 1:32–37.

Foley, R. A., and P. C. Lee. 1989. "Finite Social Space, Evolutionary Pathways, and Reconstructing Hominid Behavior." *Science* 243:901–6.

Forbes, J., and J. King. 1982. "Vision: The Dominant Sense Modality." In *Primate Behavior.* Edited by J. Forbes and J. King. New York: Academic.

Forbey, J. D., Y. S. Ben-Porath, and D. L. Davis. 1999. "A Comparison of Sexually Abused and Non-sexually Abused Adolescents in a Clinical Treatment Facility Using the MMPI-A." *Child Abuse and Neglect* 24:557–68.

Ford, J. [1633] 1995. *The Lover's Melancholy*, 'Tis Pity She's a Whore. Edited by Marian Lomax. Oxford: Oxford University Press.

Forey, P. L., et al. 1994. *Cladistics: A Practical Course in Systematics.* Oxford: Clarendon.

Fortes, M. 1949. *The Web of Kinship among the Tallensi.* Oxford: Oxford University Press.

Forward, S., and C. Buck. 1978. *Betrayal of Innocence: Incest and Its Devastation.* New York: Penguin.

Fossey, D. 1976. "The Behaviour of the Mountain Gorilla." Ph.D. diss., University of Cambridge.

———. 1972. *Living with Mountain Gorillas.* Washington, D.C.: National Geographic Society.

Foucault, M. 1986. *The History of Sexuality* London: Viking.

Fox, J. R. 1962. "Sibling Incest." *British Journal of Sociology* 13:128–50.

Fox, R. 1980. *The Red Lamp of Incest.* London: Hutchinson.

———. 1967. *Kinship and Marriage.* Great Britain: Penguin.

Frances, V., and A. Frances. 1976. "The Incest Taboo and Family Structure." *Family Process* 15:235–44.

Francoeur, R. T. 1991. *Becoming a Sexual Person.* 2nd ed. New York: Macmillan.

Frazer, J. G. [1910] 1968. *Totemism and Exogamy: A Treatise on Certain Early Forms of Superstition and Society.* London: Dawson.

Freeman, L. 2004. *The Development of Social Network Analysis.* Vancouver, B.C.: Empirical.

Freeman-Longo, R. E. 1986. "The Impact of Sexual Victimization on Males." *Child Abuse and Neglect* 10:411–14.

Freshwater, K., C. Leach, and J. Aldridge. 2001. "Personal Constructs, Childhood Sexual Abuse, and Revictimization." *British Journal of Medical Psychology* 74:379–97.

Freud, S. [1913] 1950. *Totem and Taboo*. London: Routledge & Kegan Paul.

———. [1930] 1949. *Civilization and Its Discontents*. Translated by A. A. Brill. New York: Vintage.

Friedrich, W. N., R. L. Beilke, and A. J. Urquiza. 1988. "Behavior Problems in Young Sexually Abused Boys: A Comparison Study." *Journal of Interpersonal Violence* 3:21–28.

Fritz, G. S., K. Stoll, and N. N. Wagner. 1981. "A Comparison of Males and Females Who Were Sexually Molested as Children." *Journal of Sex and Marital Therapy* 7:54–59.

Fromuth, M. E., and B. R. Burkhart. 1989. "Long-term Psychological Correlates of Childhood Sexual Abuse in Two Samples of College Men." *Child Abuse and Neglect* 13:533–42.

———. 1987. "Childhood Sexual Victimization among College Men: Definitional and Methodological Issues." *Violence and Victims* 2:241–53.

Fuentes, A. 2000. "Hylobatid Communities: Changing Views on Pair Bonding and Social Organization in Hominoids." *Yearbook of Physical Anthropology* 43:33–60.

Furuichi, T. 1989. "Social Interactions and the Life History of Female Pan Paniscus in Wamba, Zaire." *International Journal of Primatology* 10:173–97.

Fuster, V., and S. E. Colantonio. 2003. "Inbreeding Coefficients and Degree of Consanguineous Marriages in Spain." *American Journal of Human Biology* 15:709–16.

Gabbard, G. O., and S. W. Twemlow. 1994. "The Role of Mother–Son Incest in the Pathologies of Narcissistic Personality Disorder." *Journal of the American Psychoanalytic Association* 42:171–89.

Gabow, S. 1977. "Population Structure and the Rate of Hominid Evolution." *Journal of Human Evolution* 6:643–65.

Gagneux, Pascal. 2002. "The Genus Pan: Population Genetics of an Endangered Outgroup." *Trends in Genetics* 18, no. 7:327–30.

Gagneux, P., C. Boesch, and D. Woodruff. 1999. "Female Reproduction Strategies, Paternity, and Community Structure in Wild West African Chimpanzees." *Animal Behavior* 57:19–32.

Gagneux, P., and A. Varki. 2001. "Genetic Differences between Humans and Great Apes." *Molecular Phylogenetics and Evolution* 18:2–13.

Gagnon, J. H., and W. Simon. 1967. *Sexual Deviance*. New York: Harper & Row.

Galdikas, B. 1995. *Reflections of Eden: My Years with the Orangutans of Borneo*. New York: Little, Brown.

———. 1988. "Orangutan Diet, Range, and Activity at Tanjung Puting, Central Borneo." *International Journal of Primatology* 9:1–35.

———. 1985. "Orangutan Sociality at Tanjung Putting." *American Journal of Primatology* 9:101–19.

Galdikas, B., and G. Teleki. 1981. "Variations in Subsistence Activities of Male and Female Pongids: New Perspectives on the Origins of Hominid Labor Division." *Current Anthropology* 22:241–56.

Galik, K., et al. 2004. "External and Internal Morphology of the BHR 102'00 *Orrorin Tugenensis* Femur." *Science* 305:1450–53.

Galili, U., and P. Andrews. 1995. "Suppression of A-Galactosyl Epitopes Synthesis and Production of the Natural Anti-Gal Antibody: A Major Evolution Event in Ancestral Old World Primates." *Journal of Human Evolution* 29:433–42.

Galst, L. 1993. "Assumptions of HIV/AIDS Prevention Education: Interviews with Gay Male Incest Survivors." *Sex Information and Education Council of the U. S. (SIECUS) Report* 21:17–20.

Gannon, J. P. 1989. *Soul Survivors: A New Beginning for Adults Abused as Children*. New York: Prentice-Hall.

Gardner, R., B. Gardner, and T. Cantfort. 1989. *Teaching Language to Chimpanzees*. Albany: State University of New York Press.

Gatti, S., F. Leviéro, N. Ménard, and A. Gautier-Hiow. 2004. "Population and Group Structure of Western Lowland Gorillas (Gorilla gorilla gorilla) at Lokoué, Republic of Congo." *American Journal of Primatology* 63:111–23.

Gay, P. 1988. *Freud: A Life for Our Time*. New York: Norton.

Gebhard, P. H., J. H. Gagnon, W. Pomeroy, and C. Christenson. 1965. *Sex Offenders: An Analysis of Types*. New York: Harper & Row.

Gebo, D. L. 1996. "Climbing, Brachiation, and Terrestrial Quadrupedalism: Historical Precursors of Hominid Bipedalism." *American Journal of Physical Anthropology* 101:55–92.

———. 1992. "Plantigrady and Foot Adaptation in African Apes: Implications for Hominid Evolution." *American Journal of Physical Anthropology* 89:29–58.

Geiser, R. L. 1981. "Incest and Psychological Violence." *International Journal of Family Psychiatry* 2:291–300.

Geissmann, T. 2002. "Taxonomy and Evolution of Gibbons." *Evolutionary Anthropology,* suppl. 1:28–31.

Geissmann, T., and M. Orgeldinger. 2000. "The Relationship between Duet Songs and Pair Bonds in Siamangs." *Animal Behaviour* 60:805–9.

Gelinas, D. J. 1983. "The Persisting Negative Effects of Incest." *Psychiatry* 46:312–32.

Gentry, C. E. 1978. "Incestuous Abuse of Children: The Need for an Objective View." *Child Welfare* 57:355–64.

Gerbubterm K, C. Boesch, and H. Rothe. 2001. "Territory Characteristics among Three Neighboring Chimpanzee Communities in the Tai National Park, Côte d'Ivoire." *International Journal of Primatology* 2, no. 2:143–67.

Geschwind, N. 1985. "Implications for Evolution, Genetics, and Clinical Syndromes." In *Cerebral Lateralization in Non-Human Species*. Edited by Stanley Glick. New York: Academic.

———. 1970. "The Organization of Language and the Brain." *Science* 170:940–44.

———. 1965a. "Disconnection Syndromes in Animals and Man, Part I." *Brain* 88:237–94.

———. 1965b. "Disconnection Syndromes in Animals and Man, Part II." *Brain* 88:585–644.

———. 1965c. "Disconnection Syndromes in Animals and Man." *Brain* 88:237–85.

Geschwind, N., and A. Damasio. 1984. "The Neural Basis of Language." *Annual Review of Neuroscience* 7:127–47.

Gibbons, A. 2004. "Oldest Human Femur Wades into Controversy." *Science* 305:835–37.

———. 2002a. "In Search of the First Hominids." *Science* 295:1214–19.

———. 2002b. "One Scientist's Quest for the Origins of Our Species." *Science* 298:1708–11.

———. 2002c. "First Member of Human Family Uncovered." *Science* 297:171–73.

———. 2002d. "African Skull Points to One Human Ancestor." *Science* 295:2192–93.

———. 2002e. "Humans' Head Start: New Views of Brain Evolution." *Science* 296:855–56.

———. 2000. "Genomics: Building a Case for Sequencing the Chimp." *Science* 289:1267.

———. 1997. "The Women's Movement." *Science* 278:805.

Gibbons, A., and E. Culotta. 1997. "Miocene Primates Go Ape." *Science* 276:355–56.

Giddings, F. 1900. *The Elements of Sociology*. London: Macmillan Company.

Gies, F., and J. Gies. 1987. *Marriage and Family in the Middle Ages*. New York: Harper & Row.

Gingerich, P. 1990. "African Dawn for Primates." *Nature* 346:411.

Gingerich, P., and M. Uhen. 1994. "Time of Origin of Primates." *Journal of Human Evolution* 27:443–45.

Gittens, S. P. 1980. "Territorial Behavior in the Agile Gibbon." *International Journal of Primatology* I:381–99.

Glenn, Mary E., and Maroma Cords. 2001. "The Guenons: Diversity and Adaptation in African Monkeys." In *International Primatological Society Congress*. Vol. 18. New York: Kluwer Academic/Plenum, 2002.

Gold, S. N., et al. 1999. "A Comparison of Psychological/Psychiatric Symptomatology of Women and Men Sexually Abused as Children." *Child Abuse and Neglect* 23:683–92.

Goldsmith, M. 1999. "Gorilla Socioecology." In *The Nonhuman Primates*. Edited by P. Dolhinow and A. Fuentes. Mountain View, CA: Mayfield.

Goodall, J. 1996. *The Chimpanzees of Gombe: Patterns of Behavior*. Cambridge: Harvard University Press.

———. 1986. *The Chimpanzees of Gombe: Patterns of Behavior*. Cambridge, MA: Belknap Press.

Goodall-Lawick, J. 1975. "The Behavior of the Chimpanzee." In *Hominisation and Behavior*. Edited by G. Kurth and I. Eibl-Eibesfeldt. Stuttgart: Gustav Fischer Verlag.

Goodman, M., C. A. Porter, J. Czelusniak, S. L. Page, H. Schneider, J. Shashani, G. Gunnell, and C. P. Groves. 1998. "Towards a Phylogenetic Classification of Primates Based on DNA Evidence Complemented by Fossil Evidence." *Molecular Phylogenetics and Evolution* 9:585–98.

Goodman, M., D. A. Tagle, D. H. A. Fitch, W. Bailey, J. Czelusniak, B. F. Koop, P. Benson, and J. L. Slightom. 1990. "Primate Evolution at the DNA Level and a Classification of Hominids." *Journal of Molecular Evolution* 30:260–66.

Goodwin, J. 1982. *Sexual Abuse: Incest Victims and Their Families*. Boston: John Wright/PSG.

Goodwin, J., and P. DiVasto. 1979. "Mother–Daughter Incest." *Child Abuse and Neglect* 3:953–57.

Goody, J. 1983. *The Development of the Family and Marriage in Europe*. New York: Cambridge University Press.

Goosen, C. 1980. *On Grooming in Old World Monkeys*. Rijswijk, Netherlands: Primate Center of the Organization for Health Research TNO, 1980.

Gordon, L. 1955. "Incest as Revenge against the Preoedipal Mother." *Psychoanalytic Review* 42:284–92.

Gordon, L., and P. O'Keefe. 1984. "Incest as a Form of Family Violence: Evidence from Historical Case Records." *Journal of Marriage and the Family* 46:27–34.

Gordon, M. 1990. "Males and Females as Victims of Childhood Sexual Abuse: An Examination of the Gender Effect." *Journal of Family Violence* 5:321–33.

Gould, S. 2002. *The Structure of Evolutionary Theory*. Cambridge: Harvard University Press.

Grant, P. R., B. R. Grant, L. F. Keller, J. A. Markert, and K. Petren. 2003. "Inbreeding and Interbreeding in Darwin's Finches." *Evolution* 57:2911–16.

Greef, J. M., and N. C. Bennett. 2000. "Causes and Consequences of Incest Avoidance in the Cooperatively Breeding Mole-rat." *Ecology Letters* 3:318–28.

Green, A. H. 1988. "Special Issues in Child Sexual Abuse." In *Child Sexual Abuse: A Handbook for Health Care and Legal Professionals.* Edited by D. H. Schetky and A. H. Green. New York: Brunner-Mazel.

———. 1984. "Child Abuse by Siblings." *Child Abuse and Neglect* 8:311–17.

———. 1983. "Child Abuse: Dimensions of Psychological Trauma in Abused Children." *Journal of American Academy of Child Psychiatry* 22:231–37.

Greenwood, P. J. 1980. "Mating Systems, Philopatry, and Dispersal in Birds and Mammals." *Animal Behavior* 28:1140–62.

Groth, A. N. 1982. "The Incest Offender." In *Handbook of Clinical Intervention in Child Sexual Abuse.* Edited by S. M. Sgroi. Lexington, MA: Heath.

———. 1979. *Men Who Rape: The Psychology of the Offender.* New York: Plenum.

Groves, C. 1984. "A New Look at the Taxonomy of the Gibbons." In *The Lesser Apes: Evolutionary and Behavioural Biology.* Edited by H. Prevschoft, D. Chivers, W. Brockelman, and N. Creel. Edinburgh: Edinburgh University Press.

Gustavson, K. H. 2003. "Follow-up Study of Children in Pakistan." *Lakartidningen* 20:867–71. In Swedish.

Gutheil, T. G., and N. C. Avery. 1977. "Multiple Overt Incest as Family Defense against Loss." *Family Process* 16:105–16.

Guttmacher, M. S. 1951. *Sex Offenses: The Problem, Causes, and Prevention.* New York: Norton.

Haile-Selassie, Y. 2001. "Late Miocene Hominids from the Middle Awash, Ethiopia." *Nature* 178–81.

Haile-Selassie, Y., G. Suwa, and T. D. White. 2004. "Late Miocene Teeth from Middle Awash, Ethiopia, and Early Hominid Dental Evolution." *Science* 5663:1503–5.

Haj-Yahia, M. M., and S. Tamish. 2001. "The Rates of Child Sexual Abuse and Its Psychological Consequence as Revealed by a Study among Palestinian University Students." *Child Abuse and Neglect* 25:1303–27.

Halperin, S. O. 1979. "Temporary Association Patterns in Free-Ranging Chimpanzees: An Assessment of Individual Grouping Preferences." In *The Great Apes.* Edited by D. Hamburg and E. McCown. Menlo Park, CA: Benjamin-Cummings.

Hamilton, J. 1974. "Hominid Divergence and Speech Evolution." *Journal of Human Evolution* 3:417–24.

Hammond, M. 2003. "The Enhancement Imperative: The Evolutionary

Neurophysiology of Durkheimian Solidarity." *Sociological Theory* 21:359–74.

Harcourt, A. 1981. "Gorilla Reproduction in the Wild." In *Reproductive Biology of the Great Apes.* Edited by Charles Graham. New York: Academic Press.

———. 1979a. "The Social Relations and Group Structure of Wild Mountain Gorillas." In *Reproductive Biology of the Great Apes.* Edited by Charles Graham. New York: Academic.

———. 1979b. "Social Relationships among Adult Female Mountain Gorillas." *Animal Behavior* 27:251–64.

———. 1979c. "Social Relationships between Adult Male and Female Gorillas in the Wild." *Animal Behavior* 27:325–42.

———. 1978. "Strategies of Emigration and Transfer by Primates, with Particular Reference to Gorillas." *Zeitschrift für Tierpsychologie* 48:401–20.

———. 1977. "Social Relationships of Wild Mountain Gorillas." Ph.D. diss., Cambridge University.

Harcourt, A., K. Stewart, and D. Fossey. 1976. "Male Emigration and Female Transfer in Wild Mountain Gorilla." *Nature* 263:226–27.

Harcourt-Smith, W. E. H., and L. C. Aiello. 2004. "Fossils, Feet, and the Evolution of Human Bipedal Locomotion." *Journal of Anatomy* 204:403–16.

Harel, T., Y. Goldberg, S. A. Shalev, I. Cherviaski, R. Ofir, and O. S. Birk. 2004. "Limb-girdle Muscular Dystrophy 21." *European Journal of Human Genetics* 12:38–43.

Harris, M. 1968. *The Rise of Anthropological Theory.* New York: Columbia University.

Harrison, H. 1993. "Female Abusers: What Children and Young People Have Told ChildLine." In *Female Sexual Abuse of Children: The Ultimate Taboo.* Edited by M. Elliott. London: Longman Information and Reference.

Hayaki, H. 1988. "Association Partners of Young Chimpanzees in the Mahale Mountains National Park, Tanzania." *Primates* 29:147–61.

Haydrock, J., W. D. Koenig, and M. T. Stanback. 2001. "Shared Parentage and Incest Avoidance in the Cooperatively Breeding Acorn Woodpecker." *Molecular Ecology* 10:1515–25.

Heilbroner, P., and R. Holloway. 1989. "Anatomical Brain Asymmetry in Monkeys: Frontal, Temporoparietal, and Limbic Cortex in Macaca." *American Journal of Physical Anthropology* 80:203–11.

Heims, L. W., and I. Kaufman. 1963. "Variations on a Theme of Incest." *American Journal of Orthopsychiatry* 33:311–12.

Henderson, D. J. 1983. "Is Incest Harmful?" *Canadian Journal of Psychiatry* 28:34–40.

———. 1980. "Incest: A Synthesis of Data." In *Traumatic Abuse and Neglect of Children at Home.* Edited by G. J. Williams and J. Money. Baltimore: Johns Hopkins University Press.

————.1972. "Incest: A Synthesis of Data." *Canadian Psychiatric Association Journal* 17:299–313.

Hennig, W. 1966. *Phylogenetic Systematics.* Urbana: University of Illinois Press.

Herbinger, I., C. Boesch, and H. Rothe. 2001. "Territory Characteristics among Three Neighboring Chimpanzee Communities in the Tai National Park, Cote d'Ivoire." *International Journal of Primatology* 22:143–67.

Herbst, M., and N. C. Bennett. 2001. "Recrudescence of Sexual Activity in a Colony of the Mashona Mole-Rat: An Apparent Case of Incest Avoidance." *Journal of Zoology* 254:163–75.

Herman, J. L. 1983. *Father–Daughter Incest.* Cambridge: Harvard University Press.

————. 1981a. "Father–Daughter Incest." *Professional Psychology* 12:76–80.

————. 1981b. *Father–Daughter Incest.* Cambridge: Harvard University Press.

————. 1977. "Father–Daughter Incest." *Journal of Women in Culture and Society* 2:735–56.

Herman, J. L., and L. Hirschman. 1981. "Families a Risk for Father–Daughter Incest." *American Journal of Psychiatry* 138:967–70.

————. 1977. "Incest between Fathers and Daughters." *Sciences,* October 4–7.

Heyer, E., B. Toupance, C. Perri, O. De Vito, J. F. Foncin, and A. Bruni. "Manic Depressive Illness in a Founder Population." *European Journal of Human Genetics* 22:597–602.

Hinde, R. 1983. *Primate Social Relationships.* Oxford: Blackwell.

————. 1976. "Interactions, Relationships, and Social Structure." *Man:*1–17.

Hindman, J. 1989. *Just Before Dawn: From the Shadows of Tradition to New Reflections in Trauma Assessment and Treatment of Sexual Victimization.* Ontario, OR: AlexAndria.

Hoebel, E. A. 1949. *Man in The Primitive World.* New York: McGraw-Hill.

Holloway, R. L. 2002. "Brief Communication: How Much Larger Is the Relative Volume of Area 10 of the Prefrontal Cortex in Humans?" *American Journal of Physical Anthropology* 11:399–401.

Holloway, R. W. 1968. "The Evolution of the Primate Brain: Some Aspects of Quantitative Relations." *Brain Research* 7:121–72.

Honigmann, J. 1976. *The Development of Anthropological Ideas.* Homewood, IL: Dorsey.

Horton, A., B. Johnson, L. Roundy, and D. Williams, eds. 1990. *The Incest Perpetrator: A Family Member No One Wants to Treat.* Newbury Park, CA: Sage.

Howard, G. 1904. *A History of Matrimonial Institutions.* Vol. 1. Chicago: University of Chicago Press.

Hunt, K. 1994. "The Evolution of Human Bipedality: Ecology and Functional Morphology." *Journal of Human Evolution* 26:183–202.

———. 1991. "Positional Behavior in the Hominoidea." *International Journal of Primatology* 12:95–118.

Hunter, M. 1991. *Abused Boys: The Neglected Victims of Sexual Abuse.* New York: Ballantine.

———. 1990. *Abused Boys: The Neglected Victims of Sexual Abuse.* New York: Fawcett.

Isbell, L. A., and T. P. Young. 1996. "The Evolution of Bipedalism in Hominids and Reduced Group Size in Chimpanzees: Alternative Responses to Decreasing Resource Availability." *Journal of Human Evolution* 30:389–97.

Itani, J. 1972. "A Preliminary Essay on the Relationship between Social Organization and Incest Avoidance in Non-Human Primates." In *Primate Socialization.* Edited by F. E. Poirier. New York: Random House.

Izard, C. 1992. "Basic Emotions, Relations among Emotions, and Emotion-Cognition Relations." *Psychological Review* 99:561–65.

James, K. L. 1977. "Incest: The Teenager's Perspective." *Psychotherapy: Theory, Research, and Practice* 14:146–55.

Janas, C. 1983. "Family Violence and Child Sexual Abuse." *Medical Hypoanalysis* 4:68–76.

Janecke, A. R., T. Muller, I. Gassner, A. Kreczy, A. Schmid, F. Kronenberg, B. Utermann, and G. Utermann. 2004. "Joubert-like Syndrome Unlinked to Known Candidate Loci." *Journal of Pediatrics* 144:264–69.

Jeffers, R., and I. Lehiste. 1979. *Principles and Methods for Historical Linguistics.* Cambridge: MIT Press.

Jennings, K. T. 1993. "Female Child Molestation: A Review of the Literature." In *Female Sexual Abuse of Children: The Ultimate Taboo.* Edited by M. Elliott. London: Longman Information and Reference.

Johnson, A. W., and D. R. Price-Williams. 1996. *Oedipus Ubiquitous: The Family Complex in World Folk Literature.* Stanford, CA: Stanford University Press.

Johnson, D. M., J. L. Pike, and K. M. Chard. 2001. "Factors Predicting PTSO, Depression, and Dissociative Severity in Female Treatment-Seeking Childhood Sexual Abuse Survivors." *Child Abuse and Neglect* 25:179–98.

Johnson, M. S. 1983. "Recognizing the Incestuous Family." *Journal of the National Medical Association* 75:757–61.

Johnson, R. L., and D. Shrier. 1987. "Past Sexual Victimization by Females of Male Patients in an Adolescent Medicine Clinic Population." *American Journal of Psychiatry* 144:650–53.

Jolly, A. 1985. *The Evolution of Primate Behavior.* New York: Macmillan.

Jones, C., and J. Sabater Pi. 1971. *Comparative Ecology of Gorilla gorilla*

(Savage and Wyman) and Pan troglodytes (Blumenbach) in Rio Muni, West Africa. New York: Karger.

Jones, E. 1990. "Modulatory Events in the Development of Evolution of Primate Neocortex." In *Cerebral Cortex.* Edited by E. Jones and A. Peters. New York: Plenum.

Jones, K. L., L. W. Shainberg, and C. O. Byer. 1985. *Dimensions of Human Sexuality.* Dubuque, IA: Brown.

Julian, V., and C. Mohr. 1979. "Father–Daughter Incest: Profile of the Offender." *Victimology: An International Journal* 4:348–60.

Jung, K. E. 2001. "Posttraumatic Spectrum Disorder: A Radical Revision." *Psychiatric Times,* www.psychiatrictimes.com/p011158.html.

Justice, B., and R. Justice. 1979. *The Broken Taboo: Sex in the Family.* New York: Human Sciences Press.

Kaessmann, H., and S. Pääbo. 2002. "The Genetical History of Humans and the Great Apes." *Journal of Internal Medicine* 2002:251:1–18.

Kano, T. 1992. *The Last Ape: Pygmy Chimpanzee Behavior and Ecology.* Stanford, CA: Stanford University Press.

Kaplan, S. L., and E. Poznanski. 1974. "Child Psychiatric Patients Who Share a Bed with a Parent." *Journal of the American Academy of Child Psychiatry* 13:344–56.

Kasl, C. D. 1990. "Female Perpetrators of Sexual Abuse: A Feminist View." In *The Sexually Abused Male: Prevalence, Impact, and Treatment.* Vol. 1. Edited by M. Hunter. Lexington, MA: Lexington.

Kasserman, H., V. Wiebe, and S. Pääbo. 1999. "Extensive Nuclear DNA Sequence Diversity among Chimpanzees." *Science* 286:1159–61.

Kaufman, I., A. L. Peck, and C. K. Tagiuri. 1954. "The Family Constellation and Overt Incestuous Relations Between Father and Daughter." *American Journal of Orthopsychiatry* 24:266–77.

Kay, R., and P. Ungar. 1997. "Dental Evidence for Diet in Some Miocene Catarrhines with Comments on the Effects of Phylogeny on the Interpretation of Adaptation." In *Function, Phylogeny, and Fossils: Miocene Hominoid Evolution and Adaptations.* Edited by D. Begun, C. Ward, and M. Rose. New York: Plenum.

Kay, R. F., and E. L. Simons. 1987. "The Ecology of Oligocene African Anthropoidea." In *Primate Evolution and Human Origins.* Edited by R. L. Ciochon and J. Fleagle. New York: Aldine de Gruyter.

Kelley, J. 2002. "Life-History Evolution in Miocene and Extant Apes." In *Human Evolution through Developmental Change.* Edited by N. Minugh-Purvis and K. J. McNamara. Baltimore: Johns Hopkins University Press.

———. 1997. "Paleobiological and Phylogenetic Significance of Life History in Miocene Hominoids." In *Function, Phylogeny, and Fossils: Miocene Hominoid Evolution and Adaptations.* New York: Plenum Press.

Kelley, J., and T. M. Smith. 2003. "Age at First Molar Emergence in

Early Miocene *Afropithecus turkanensis* and Life-History Evolution in the *Hominoidea*." *Journal of Human Evolution* 44:307–29.

Kelly, R. J., J. J. Wood, L. S. Gonzales, V. McDonald, and J. Waterman. 2002. "Effects of Mother–Son Incest and Positive Perceptions of Sexual Abuse Experiences on the Psychosocial Adjustment of Clinic-referred Men." *Child Abuse and Neglect* 26:425–41.

Kempe, C. 1980. "Incest and Other Forms of Sexual Abuse." In *The Battered Child*. 3rd ed. Edited by C. H. Kempe and R. E. Helfer. Chicago: University of Chicago Press.

Kempe, R. S., and C. Henry. 1984. *The Common Secret: Sexual Abuse of Children and Adolescents*. New York: Freeman.

Kemper, T. S. 1987. "How Many Emotions Are There? Wedding the Social and Autonomic Components." *American Journal of Sociology* 93:263–89.

Kenney, K. L. 1987. "Maternal Incest: An Annotated Review of the Literature on Mother–Daughter and Mother–Son Incest." Master's thesis, California State University.

Kerns, J. G., J. D. Cohen, A. W. MacDonald III, R. Y. Cho, V. Andrew Stenger, and C. S. Carter. 2004. "Anterior Cingulate Conflict Monitoring and Adjustment in Control." *Science* 303:1223–26.

Kingston, J. D., B. D. Marino, and A. Hill. 1994. "Isotopic Evidence for Neogene Hominid Paleoenvironments in the Kenya Rift Valley." *Science* 264:955–59.

Kinsey, A. C., W. B. Pomeroy, C. E. Martin, and P. H. Gebhard. 1953. *Sexual Behavior in the Human Female*. Philadelphia: Saunders.

———. 1948. *Sexual Behavior in the Human Male*. Philadelphia: Saunders.

Klein. R. 2003. "Wither the Neanderthals?" *Science* 299:1525–27.

Knittle, B. J., and S. J. Tuana. 1980. "Group Therapy as Primary Treatment for Adolescent Victims of Intrafamilial Sexual Abuse." *Clinical Social Work Journal* 8:236–42.

Knopp, F. F., and L. B. Lackey. 1987. *Female Sexual Abusers: A Summary of Data from 44 Treatment Providers*. Orwell, VT: Safer Society Press.

Knott, C. 1999. "Orangutan Behavior and Ecology." In *The Nonhuman Primates*. Edited by A. Dalhinou and A. Fuentes. Mountain View, CA: Mayfield.

Koch, M. 1980. "Sexual Abuse in Children." *Adolescence* 15:643–48.

Koenig, W. D., M. T. Standack, and J. Haydock. 1999. "Demographic Consequences of Incest Avoidance in Cooperatively Breeding Acorn Woodpecker." *Animal Behavior* 57:1287–93.

Krug, R. S. 1989. "Adult Male Report of Childhood Sexual Abuse by Mothers: Case Descriptions, Motivations, and Long-term Consequences." *Child Abuse and Neglect* 13:111–19.

Kubo, S. 1959. "Researches and Studies on Incest in Japan." *Hiroshima Journal of Medical Sciences* 8:99–159.

Kumar, S., and B. Hedges. 1998. "A Molecular Timescale for Vertebrate Evolution." *Nature* 392:917–20.

Kumaramanickavel, G., B. Joseph, A. Vidhya, T. Arokiasamy, and N. Shetty. 2002. "Consanguinity and Ocular Genetic Diseases in South India." *Community Genetics* 5:182–85.

Laaser, M. R. 1992. *The Secret Sin: Healing the Wounds of Sexual Addiction.* Grand Rapids, MI: Zondervan.

Ladygina-Kohts, N. N. [1935] 2002. *Infant Chimpanzee and Human Child.* Oxford: Oxford University Press.

Latimer, B., and C. O. Lovejoy. 1990. "Metatarsophalangeal Joints of Australopithecus Afarensis." *American Journal of Physical Anthropology* 83:13–23.

Lauc, T., P. Rudan, I. Rudan, and H. Campbell. 2003. "Effects of Inbreeding and Endogamy on Occlusal Traits in Human Isolates." *Journal of Orthodontics* 30:301–8.

Laviola, M. 1992. "Effects of Older Brother–Younger Sister Incest: A Study of the Dynamics of 17 Cases." *Child Abuse and Neglect* 16:409–21.

———. 1989. "Effects of Older Brother–Younger Sister Incest: A Review of Four Cases." *Journal of Family Violence* 4:259–74.

Lawler, E. J., and J. Yoon. 1996. "Commitment in Exchange Relations: A Test of a Theory of Relational Cohesion." *American Sociological Review* 61:89–108.

Lawson, C. 1993. "Mother–Son Sexual Abuse: Rare or Underreported? A Critique of the Research." *Child Abuse and Neglect* 17:261–69.

———. 1991. "Clinical Assessment of Mother–Son Sexual Abuse." *Clinical Social Work Journal* 19:391–403.

Leakey, M. G., C. S. Feibel, I. McDougall, and A. Walker. 1995. "New Four-Million-Year-Old Hominid Species from Kanapoi and Allia Bay, Kenya." *Nature* 376:565–71.

Leakey, M., C. Feibel, I. McDougall, C. Ward, and A. Walker. 1998. New Specimens and Confirmation of an Early Age for Australopithecus Anamensis." *Nature* 393:62–66.

Leavitt, G. C. 1989. "Disappearance of the Incest Taboo: A Cross-Cultural Test of General Evolutionary Hypotheses." *American Anthropologist* 91:116–31.

Le Doux, J. 1996. *The Emotional Brain: The Mysterious Underpinnings of Emotional Life.* New York: Simon & Schuster.

Lee, S. H., and M. Wolpoff. 2003. "The Pattern of Evolution in Pleistocene Human Brain Size." *Paleobiology* 29:186–96.

Lehmann, J., and C. Boesch. 2004. "To Fission or to Fusion: Effects of Community Size on Wild Chimpanzee (Pan troglodytes verus) Social Organization." *Behavioral Ecology and Sociobiology* 56:207–26.

Lehmann, C., and N. Perrin. 2003. "Inbreeding Avoidance through Kin Recognition: Choosy Females Boast Male Dispersal." *American Naturalist* 16:638–52.

Leighton, D. 1987. "Gibbons: Territoriality and Monogamy." In *Primate Societies.* Edited by B. Smuts, D. Cheney, R. Seyfarth, R. Wrangham, and T. Struhsaker. Chicago: University of Chicago Press.

Lester, D. 1972. "Incest." *Journal of Sex Research* 8:268–85.

Lévi-Strauss, C. [1949] 1967. *The Elementary Structures of Kinship.* Boston: Beacon.

Levitt, C. J. 1990. "Sexual Abuse of Boys: A Medical Perspective." In *The Sexually Abused Male: Prevalence, Impact, and Treatment.* Vol. 1. Edited by M. Hunter. Lexington, MA: Lexington.

Lewis, M. 1988. *Victims No Longer: Men Recovering from Incest and Other Sexual Child Abuse.* New York: Nevraumont.

———. 1986. *Victims No Longer: Men Recovering from Incest and Other Sexual Child Abuse.* New York: Harper & Row.

Lieberman, D., J. Tooby, and L. Cosmides. 2003. "Does Morality Have a Biological Basis: An Empirical Test of the Factors Governing Moral Sentiments Relating to Incest." *Proceedings of the Royal Society of London,* B series, 270:819–26.

Lim, M., Z. Wang, D. E. Olazábal, X. Ren, E. F. Terwilliger, and L. J. Young. 2004. "Enhanced Partner Preference in a Promiscuous Species by Manipulating the Expression of a Single Gene." *Nature* 429:754–57.

Lindzey, G. 1967. "Some Remarks Concerning Incest, the Incest Taboo, and Psychoanalytic Theory." *American Psychologist* 22:1051–9.

Lockwood, C., and P. Tobias. 2002. "Morphology and Affinities of New Hominin Cranial Remains from Member 4 of the Sterk Fontein Formation, Gauteng Province, South Africa." *Journal of Human Evolution* 42:389–450.

Lockwood, C. A., W. H. Kimbel, and J. M. Lynch. 2004. "Morphometrics and Hominoid Phylogeny: Support for a Chimpanzee-Human Clade and Differentiation among Great Ape Subspecies." *Proceedings of the National Academy of Sciences of the United States of America* 101, no. 13:4356–60.

Lockwood, C. A., B. G. Richmond, and W. L. Jungers. 1996. "Randomization Procedures and Sexual Dimorphism in *Australopithecus Afarensis.*" *Journal of Human Evolution* 31:537–48.

Long, J. C., and R. A. Kittles. 2003. "Human Genetic Diversity and Nonexistence of Biological Races." *Human Biology* 75:449–71.

Longdon, C. 1993. "A Survivor's and Therapist's Viewpoint." In *Female Sexual Abuse of Children: The Ultimate Taboo.* Edited by M. Elliott. London: Longman Information and Reference.

Lopreato, J. 1984. *Human Nature and Biosocial Evolution.* London: Allen and Unwin.

Love, P., and J. Robinson. 1990. *The Emotional Incest Syndrome: What to Do When a Parent's Love Rules Your Life.* New York: Bantam.

Luis-Martinez, Z. 2002. *In Words and Deeds: The Spectacle of Incest in English Renaissance Tragedy.* Amsterdam: Netherlands: B. V. Rodopi.

Lukianowicz, N. 1972. "Incest: I: Parental Incest; Incest II: Other Types of Incest." *British Journal of Psychiatry* 120:301–13.

Lustig, N., J. W. Dresser, S. W. Spellman, and T. B. Murray. 1966. "Incest: A Family Group Survival Pattern." *Archives of General Psychology* 14:31–40.

Maas, P. 1958. *Textual Criticism.* Oxford: Oxford University Press.

MacFarlane, K., and J. Korbin. 1983. "Confronting the Incest Secret Long After the Fact: A Family Study of Multiple Victimization with Strategies for Intervention." *Child Abuse and Neglect* 7:225–37.

Machalek, R., and M. W. Martin. 2004. "Sociology and the Second Darwinian Revolution: A Metatheoretical Analysis." *Sociological Theory* 22:455–76.

Machota, P., F. S. Pittman, and K. Flomenhaft. 1967. "Incest as a Family Affair." *Family Process* 6:98–116.

MacKinnon, J. 1971. "The Orang-utan in Sabah Today." *Oryx* 2:141–9.

MacKinnon, J. R., and K. S. MacKinnon. 1984. "Territoriality, Monogamy, and Song in Gibbons and Tarsiers." In *The Lesser Apes.* Edited by H. Prevschoft, D. Chivers, W. Brockelman, and N. Creel. Edinburgh: Edinburgh University Press.

Maclatchy, Laura. 2004. "The Oldest Ape." *Evolutionary Anthropology* 13:90–103.

MacLean, P. D. 1990. *The Triune Brain in Evolution: Role of Paleocerebral Functions.* New York: Plenum.

Magal, V., and H. Z. Winnick. 1963. "Role of Incest in Family Structure." *Israel Annals of Psychiatry and Related Disciplines* 6:173–89.

Maine, H. [1861] 1905. *Ancient Law: Its Connection with the Early History of Society and Its Relation to Modern Ideas.* London: John Murray.

Maisch, H. 1972. *Incest.* New York: Stein & Day.

Malinowski, B. 1932. *Sexual Life of Savages.* 3rd ed. London: Routledge & Kegan Paul.

———. 1929. *The Sexual Life of Savages in North-Western Melanesia.* London: Routledge & Kegan Paul.

———. 1927. *Sex and Repression in Savage Society.* London: Routledge & Kegan Paul.

Malone, D. 1987. "Mechanisms of Hominoid Dispersal in Miocene East Africa." *Journal of Human Evolution* 16:469–81.

Maloney, B., and K. Trappe. 1993. "It Never Happens: Mother/Son Incest." In the *Fifth Annual National Conference on Male Survivors: "Advancing National Awareness of Male Victimization."* Bethesda, MD.

Maltz, W., and B. Holman. 1987. *Incest and Sexuality: A Guide to Understanding and Healing.* Lexington, MA: Lexington.

Mapel, D. 1994. "We Shall Be Reborn: A Book for Men Recovering from Mother–Son Sexual Abuse." Unpublished manuscript.

Margolis, M. 1984. "A Case of Mother–Adolescent Son Incest: A Follow-up Study." *Psychoanalytic Quarterly* 53:355–85.

————. 1977. "A Preliminary Report of a Case of Consummated Mother–Son Incest." *Annual Psychoanalytic* 5:267–93.

Mars, D. 1992. "A Case of Mother–Son Incest: Its Consequences for Development and Treatment." *Journal of Clinical Psychoanalysis* 7:401–20.

Martin, R. D. 1990. *Primate Origins and Evolution: A Phylogenetic Reconstruction*. London: Chapman & Hall.

Marvasti, J. 1986. "Incestuous Mothers." *American Journal of Forensic Psychiatry* 7:63–69.

Maryanski, A. 1997. "Primate Communication and the Ecology of a Language Niche." In *Nonverbal Communication: Where Nature Meets Culture*. Edited by U. Segerstrale and Peter Molnar. Hillsdale, NJ: Erlbaum.

————.1996a. "African Ape Social Networks: A. London: Routledge. Blueprint for Reconstructing Early Hominid Social Structure." In *The Archaeology of Human Ancestry*. Edited by J. Steele and S. Shennan. London: Routlege.

————. 1996b. "Was Speech an Evolutionary Afterthought?" In *Communicating Meaning: The Evolution and Development of Language*. Edited by B. Velichikovsky and D. Rumbaugh. Mahwah, NJ: Erlbaum.

————. 1994. "Hunting and Gathering Economic Systems." In *Magill's Survey of Social Science: Sociology*. Pasadena: Salem.

————. 1993. "The Elementary Forms of the First Proto-Human Society: An Ecological/Social Network Approach." *Advances in Human Ecology* 2:215–41.

————. 1992. "The Last Ancestor: An Ecological-Network Model on the Origins of Human Sociality." *Advances in Human Ecology* 2:1–32.

————. 1987. "African Ape Social Structure: Is There Strength in Weak Ties?" *Social Networks* 9:191–215.

————. 1986. "African Ape Social Structure: A Comparative Analysis." Ph.D. diss., University of California.

Maryanski, A., P. Molnar, U. Segerstrale, and B. Velichikovsky. 1997. "The Social and Biological Foundations of Human Communication." In *Human by Nature*. Edited by P. Weingart, S. Mitchell, P. Richerson, and S. Maasen. Mahwah, NJ: Erlbaum.

Maryanski, A., and J. H. Turner. 1992. *The Social Cage: Human Nature and The Evolution of Society*. Stanford, CA: Stanford University Press.

Masters, R. E. L., ed. 1963. *Patterns of Incest*. New York: Julian.

Masters, W. H., and V. E. Johnson. 1976. "Incest: The Ultimate Sexual Taboo." *Redbook Magazine* 146:54–58.

————. 1970. *Human Sexual Inadequacy*. Boston: Little, Brown.

Mathews, F. 1996. *The Invisible Boy: Revisioning the Victimization of Male Children and Teens*. Ottawa, CA: National Clearinghouse on Family Violence.

Mathews, R., L. K. Matthews, and K. Speltz. 1989. *Female Sexual Offenders: An Exploratory Study.* Orwell, VT: Safer Society Press.

Mathias, R. A., C. A. Bickel, A. Shahani, T. H. Beaty, and K. C. Barnes. 1999. "A Net Avoidance of Close Consanguinity on Tangier Island Virginia." *American Journal of Human Genetics* 65:390.

Mathis, J. L. 1972. *Clear Thinking About Sexual Deviations: A New Look At Old Problems.* Chicago: Nelson-Hall Company.

Matsumoto, K., W. Suzuki, and K. Tanaka. 2003. "Neural Correlates of Goal-Based Motor Selection in the Prefrontal Cortex." *Science* 301:229–32.

Mauss, M. 1924 [1967]. *The Gift: Forms and Functions of Exchange in Archaic Societies.* New York: Norton.

Maybury-Lewis, D. 1965. "Durkheim on Relationship Systems." *Journal for the Scientific Study of Religion* 4:253–60.

––––––. [1924] 1954. *The Gift.* Translated by I. Connison. New York: Free Press.

Mayr, E. 1942. *Systematics and the Origin of Species.* New York: Columbia University Press.

McBean, A. 1987. "Another Secret Out in the Open: Female Sex Offenders." *Looking Ahead: Innovation and Inquiry in Family Sexual Abuse Intervention* 1:5–6.

McCabe, J. 1983. "FBD Marriage: Further Support for the Westermarck Hypothesis." *American Anthropologist* 85:50–69.

McCabe, R. 1993. *Incest, Drama and Nature's Law: 1550–1700.* Cambridge: Cambridge University Press.

McCarty, L. M. 1986. "Mother-Child Incest: Characteristics of the Offender." *Child Welfare* 65:447–58.

McCrossin, M. L. 1997. "Bridging the Gap: Connecting the Origin of Bipedalism in Pliocene Hominidae With the Advent of Semi-Terrestrial Adaptations Among African Miocene Hominoidea." *Journal of Human Evolution* 32:A12.

McHenry, H., and K. Coffing. 2000. "Australopithecus to Homo: Transformations in Body and Mind." *Annual Review of Anthropology* 29:125–46.

McIntyre, K. 1981. "Role of Mothers in Father–Daughter Incest: A Feminist Analysis." *Social Work* 26:462–66.

McKee, J. 1996. "Faunal Turnover in the Pliocene and Pleistocene of Southern Africa." *South African Journal of Science* 92:11–12.

McKusick, F. A., ed. 1978. *Medical Genetics of the Amish.* Baltimore: Johns Hopkins University Press.

McLennan, J. 1896. *Studies in Ancient History.* London, England: Macmillan.

––––––. [1865] 1970. *Primitive Marriage.* Chicago: University of Chicago Press.

―――. "The Worship of Plants and Animals." *The Fortnightly Review* 6:562–82 and 7:194–216.

―――. [1869–1870] 1896. "The Worship of Plants and Animals." In *Studies in Ancient History*. London, England: New York: Macmillan.

Mead, G. H. 1880 [1968]. "Penitence." In *A Dictionary of Christian Antiquities*. Edited by William Smith and Samuel Cheetham. New York: Kraus Reprint Co.

―――. 1934. *Mind, Self, and Society.* Chicago: University of Chicago Press.

Mead, M. 1968. "Incest." *International Encyclopedia of the Social Sciences, Volume 7*. New York: Macmillan.

Medlicott, R. W. 1967. "Parent-Child Incest." *Australia and New Zealand Journal of Psychiatry* 1:180–87.

Meiselman, K. C. 1980. "Personality Characteristics of Incest History Psychotherapy Patients: A Research Note." *Archives of Sexual Behavior* 9:195–97.

―――. 1978. *Incest: A Psychological Study of Causes and Effects With Treatment Recommendations.* San Francisco, CA: Jossey-Bass Publishers.

Menzel, E. W. 1971. "Communication About the Environment in a Group of Young Chimpanzees." *Folia Primatologica* 15:220–32.

Messer, A. A. 1969. "The Phaedra Complex." *Archives of General Psychiatry* 21:213–18.

Mesulam, M. M. 1983. "The Functional Anatomy and Hemispheric Specialization for Directed Attention." *Trends in Neurosciences* 6:384–87.

Meyer, V. A. 1993. "Sohne Brechen Ihren Schweigen: Verfuhrt Durch Ihren Mutter" [Sons are breaking their silence: Seduced by their mother]. *Stern.*

Meyrick, F. [1880] 1968. "Marriage." In *A Dictionary of Christian Antiquities*. Edited by William Smith and Samuel Cheetham. New York: Kraus Reprint Co.

―――. [1880] 1968. "Prohibited Degrees." In *A Dictionary of Christian Antiquities*. Edited by William Smith and Samuel Cheetham. New York: Kraus Reprint Co.

Middleton, R. 1962. "Brother–Sister and Father–Daughter Marriage in Ancient Egypt." *American Sociological Review* 27:603–11.

Mikkelsen, G. S. 2004. "What Makes Us Human?" *Genome Biology* 5 (8). Art no. 238.

Miletski, H. 1995. *Mother–Son Incest: The Unthinkable Taboo: An Overview of Findings.* Brandon, VT: Safer Society Press.

Mimmack, F. W. 1993. "Breaking the Silence." *Men's Issues Forum: Dedicated to Healing Male Survivors of Childhood Sexual Abuse* 4:1–2, 6–7.

Mireille, C., J. Wright, P. McDuff, and A. Perron. 2002. "Intrafamilial Sexual Abuse: Brother–Sister Incest Does Not Differ from Father–

Daughter and Stepfather–Stepdaughter Incest." *Child Abuse and Neglect* 26:957–73.

Mitani, J. C., D. A. Merriwether, and C. B. Zhang. 2000. "Male Affiliation, Cooperation and Kinship in Wild Chimpanzees." *Animal Behaviour* 59 (Part 4):885–93.

Mitani, J. C., D. P. Muller, and M. M. Muller. 2002. "Recent Developments in the Study of Wild Chimpanzee Behavior." *Evolutionary Anthropology* 11(1):9–25.

Molnar, G., and P. Cameron. 1975. "Incest Syndromes: Observations in a General Hospital Psychiatric Unit." *Canadian Psychiatric Association Journal* 20:1–24.

Moore, J. 1984. "Female Transfer in Primates." *International Journal of Primatology* 5:537–89.

Morgan, L. [1871] 1997. *Systems of Consanguinity and Affinity of the Human Family.* Lincoln: University of Nebraska Press.

———. [1877] 1985. *Ancient Society.* Tucson: University of Arizona Press.

Morgan, L. H. [1877] 1985. *Ancient Society.* New York: Holt.

Moya-Solà, S., M. Köoher, D. Alba, I. Casanovas-Vilar, and J. Galindo. 2004. "*Pierolapithecus Catalaonicus*: A New Middle Miocene Great Ape From Spain." *Science* 306:1339–44.

Mrazek, P. B., and C. H. Kempe. 1981. *Sexually Abused Children and Their Families.* Oxford: Pergamon.

Mulhern, S. 1990. "Incest: A Laughing Matter." *Child Abuse and Neglect* 14:265–71.

Muller, H. F. 1913. "A Chronological Note on the Physiological Explanation of the Prohibition of Incest." *Journal of Religious Psychology* 6:294–95.

Murdock, G. 1967. *Ethnographical Atlas.* Pittsburgh: University of Pittsburgh Press.

Murdock, G. P. 1949. *Social Structure.* New York: Macmillan.

Napier, J. R., and P. H. Napier. 1985. *The Natural History of the Primates.* Cambridge: MIT Press.

Napier, J. R., and A. C. Walker. 1987. "Vertical Clinging and Leaping: A Newly Recognized Category of Locomotor Behavior of Primates." In *Primate Evolution and Human Origins.* Edited by R. L. Ciochon and J. Fleagle. New York: Aldine de Gruyter.

Nasjleti, M. 1980. "Suffering in Silence: The Male Incest Victim." *Child Welfare* 59:269–75.

Navarro, A., and N. H. Barton. 2003. "Chromosonal Speciation and Molecular Divergence: Accelerated Evolution in Rearranged Chromosomes." *Science* 300:321–24.

Nei, M., and G. V. Glazko. 2002. "Estimation of Divergence Times for a Few Mammalian and Several Primate Species." *Journal of Heredity* 93:157–64.

Nimkoff, M. F. 1947. *Marriage and the Family.* Boston: Houghton Mifflin.

Nishida, T. 1990. "A Quarter Century of Research in the Mahale Mountains." In *The Chimpanzees of the Mahale Mountains.* Edited by T. Nishida. Tokyo: University of Tokyo Press.

———. 1979. "The Social Structure of Chimpanzees of the Mahale Mountains." In *The Great Apes.* Edited by D. Hamburg and E. McCown. Menlo Park, CA: Benjamin-Cummings.

Nishida, T., and M. Hiraiwa-Hasegawa. 1987. "Chimpanzees and Bonobos: Cooperative Relationships among Males." In *Primitive Societies.* Edited by B. Smuts, D. Cheney, R. Seyfarth, R. Wrangham, and I. Struhsaker. Chicago: University of Chicago Press.

Nishida, T., W. Corp, M. Hamai, T. Hasegawa, M. Hiraiwa-Hasegawa, K. Hosaka, K. Hunt, N. Itoch, K. Kawonaka, A. Matsumoto-Oda, J. Mitani, M. Nakamura, K. Noriposhi, T. Sakamaki, L. Turner, S. Vehara, and K. Zamma. 2003. "Demography, Female Life History, and Reproductive Profiles among the Chimpanzees of Mahale." *American Journal of Primatology* 59: 99–121.

Nolan, P., and G. Lenski. 2004. *Human Societies.* Boulder, CO: Paradigm.

O'Connor, A. A. 1987. "Female Sex Offenders." *British Journal of Psychiatry* 150:615–20.

Opler, M. 1941. *An Apache Life Way.* Chicago: University of Chicago Press.

Page, S. L., and M. Goodman. 2001. "Catarrhine Phylogeny: Noncoding DNA Evidence for a Diphyletic Origin of the Mangabeys and for a Human-Chimpanzee Clade." *Molecular Phylogenetics and Evolution* 18, no. 1:14–25.

Panskepp, J. 1982. "Toward a General Psychobiological Theory of Emotions." *Behavioral and Brain Sciences* 5:407–67.

Parker, S. 1976. "The Precultural Basis of the Incest Taboo: Toward a Biosocial Theory." *American Anthropologist* 78:285–305.

Parsons, T. 1964. *Social Structure and Personality.* New York: Free Press.

———. 1954. "The Incest Taboo in Relation to Social Structure and the Socialization of the Child." *British Journal of Sociology* 5:101–17.

Parsons, T., and R. F. Bales. 1955. *Family Socialization and Interaction.* Glencoe, IL: Free Press.

Pasternak, B. 1976. *Introduction to Kinship and Social Organization* Englewood Cliffs, NJ: Prentice-Hall.

Patridge, T. C., D. E. Granger, M. W. Caffee, and R. J. Clark. 2003. "Lower Pliocene Hominid Remains from Sterkfontein." *Science* 300:607–12.

Paz y Minatno, G., and Z. Tang-Martinez. 1999. "Effects of Isolation on Sibling Recognition in Prairie Voles." *Animal Behavior* 57:1091–98.

Peleikis, D. E., A. Mykletun, and A. A. Dahl. 2004. "The Relative

Influence of Childhood Sexual Abuse and Other Family Background Risk Factors on Adult Adversities in Female Outpatients Treated for Anxiety Disorders and Depression." *Child Abuse and Neglect* 28:61–76.

Pennisi, E. 2003. "Genome Comparisons Hold Clues to Human Evolution." *Science* 302:1876–77.

———. 2002a. "Gene Activity Clocks Brain's Fast Evolution." *Science* 296:233–35.

———. 2002b. "Jumbled DNA Separates Chimps and Humans." *Science* 298:719–20.

———. 2001. "Tracking the Sexes by Their Genes." *Science* 291:1733–34.

Peterson, A. L. T. 1992. "Sibling Sexual Abuse: The Emerging Awareness of an Ignored Childhood Trauma." *Moving Forward* 1:12–13.

Petrovich, M., and D. I. Templer. 1984. "Heterosexual Molestation of Children Who Later Became Rapists." *Psychological Reports* 54:810.

Pierce, R., and L. H. Pierce. 1985. "The Sexually Abused Child: A Comparison of Male and Female Victims." *Child Abuse and Neglect* 9:191–99.

Pilbeam, D. 1997. "Research on Miocene Hominoids and Hominid Origins: The Last Three Decades." In *Function, Phylogeny, and Fossils Miocene Hominoid Evolution and Adaptations.* Edited by D. Begun, C. Ward, and M. Rose. New York: Plenum.

Platnick, N., and H. D. Cameron. 1977. "Cladistic Methods in Textual, Linguistic, and Phylogenetic Analysis." *Systematic Zoology* 26:380–85.

Plato. 1980. *The Laws of Plato,* 229. Chicago: University of Chicago Press.

———. 1968. *The Republic of Plato,* 251. New York: Basic.

Plutchik, R. 1980. *Emotion: A Psychoevolutionary Synthesis.* New York: Harper & Row.

Potts, R., A. Behrensmeyer, A. Deino, P. Ditchfield, and J. Clark. 2004. "Acheulean Technology." *Science* 305:75.

Price, E. C. 1998. "Incest in Captive Marmosets and Tamarins." *Journal of Wildlife Preservation Trusts* 34:25–31.

Pusey, A. E. 2005. "Inbreeding Avoidance in Primates." In *Inbreeding, Incest, and the Incest Taboo.* Edited by A. P. Wolf and W. H. Durham. Stanford, CA: Stanford University Press.

———. 1980. "Inbreeding Avoidance in Chimpanzees." *Animal Behavior* 28:543–52.

Pusey, A. E., and C. Packer. 1987. "Dispersal and Philopatry." In *Primate Societies.* Edited by B. Smuts, D. Cheney, R. Seyfarth, R. Wrangham, and T. Struhsaker. Chicago: University of Chicago Press.

Quintano, J. H. 1992. "Case Profiles of Early Childhood Enema Abuse." *Treating Abuse Today: An International Newsjournal of Abuse Survivorship and Therapy* 2:11–22.

Rank, O. [1912] 1992. *The Incest Theme in Literature and Legend.* Baltimore: Johns Hopkins University Press.

Raphling, D. L., B. L. Carpenter, and A. Davis. 1967. "Incest: A Genealogical Study." *Archives of General Psychiatry* 16:505–11.

Rascovsky, A., and M. Rascovsky. 1972. "The Prohibition of Incest, Filicide, and the Sociocultural Process." *International Journal of Psychoanalysis* 53:271–76.

Rascovsky, M. W., and A. Rascovsky. 1950. "On Consummated Incest." *International Journal of Psychoanalysis* 31:42–47.

Read, J. 1998. "Child Abuse and Severity of Disturbance among Adult Psychiatric Inpatients." *Child Abuse and Neglect* 22:359–68.

Reed, K. 1997. "Early Hominid Evolution and Ecological Change through the African Plio-Pleistocene." *Journal of Human Evolution* 32:289–322.

Reinhart, M. A. 1987. "Sexually Abused Boys." *Child Abuse and Neglect* 11:229–35.

Relethford, J. H. 2003. *Reflections of Our Past: How Human History Is Revealed in Our Genes.* Boulder: Westview.

———. 2002. "Apportionment of Global Human Genetic Diversity Bias on Craniometrics and Skin Color." *American Journal of Physical Anthropology* 118:393–98.

Renfrew, C., P. Forster, and M. Hurles. 2000. "The Past within Us." *Nature Genetics* 26:253–54.

Renshaw, D. C. 1982. *Incest: Understanding and Treatment.* Boston: Little, Brown.

Renvoize, J. 1982. *Incest: A Family Pattern.* London: Routledge & Kegan Paul.

Rhine, R. J., P. Boland, and L. Lodwick. 1985. "Progressions of Adult Male Chocma Baboons (Papio Ursinus) in the Moremi Wild Life Reserve." *International Journal of Primatology* 6:116–22.

Rhine, R. J., and A. Maryanski. 1996. "A Twenty-One Year History of a Dominant Stump-tail Matriline." In *Evolution and Ecology of Macaque Societies.* Edited by J. Fa and D. Lindburg. Cambridge: Cambridge University Press.

Rhinehart, J. W. 1961. "Genesis of Overt Incest." *Comprehensive Psychiatry* 2:338–49.

Richardson, A. 1985. "The Dangers of Sympathy: Sibling Incest in English Romantic Poetry." *Studies in English Literature, 1500–1900* 25, no. 4:737–54.

Richter, N. L., E. Snider, and K. M. Gorey. 1997. "Group Work Intervention with Female Survivors of Childhood Sexual Abuse." *Research on Social Work Practice* 7:53–69.

Riemer, S. 1940. "A Research Note on Incest." *American Journal of Sociology* 45:566–75.

Rijksen, H. 1975. "Social Structure in a Wild Orangutan Population in Sumatra." In *Contemporary Primatology.* Edited by S. Kondo, M. Kawai, and A. E. Hara. Basel: Karger.

Rinsley, D. B. 1978. "Borderline Psychopathology: A Review of Aetiology, Dynamics, and Treatment." *International Review of Psycho-Analysis* 5:45–54.

Risin, L. I., and M. P. Koss. 1987. "The Sexual Abuse of Boys: Prevalence and Descriptive Characteristics of Childhood Victimizations." *Journal of Interpersonal Violence* 2:309–23.

Robbins, M. M., M Bermejo, C. Cipelletta, F. Magliocca, R. J. Parnell, and E. Stokes. 2004. *Social Structure and the History Patterns in Western Gorillas (Gorilla gorilla gorilla)*. Published online, pp. 145–59.

Rodieck, R. W. 1988. "The Primate Retina." In *Neurosciences*. Vol. 4. Edited by H. Steklis and J. Erwin. New York: Alan Liss.

Rodman, P. 1973. "Population Composition and Adaptive Organization Among Orang-utans of the Kutai Reserve." In *Comparative Ecology and Behaviour of Primates*. Edited by R. P. Michael and J. H. Crook. London: Academic.

Rodman, P., and J. Mitani. 1987. "Orangutans: Sexual Dimorphism in a Solitary Species." In *Primate Societies*. Edited by B. Smuts , D. Cheney, R. Seyfarth, R. Wrangham, and T. Struhsaker. Chicago: University of Chicago Press.

Rodman, P. S., and H. M. McHenry. 1980. "Bioenergetics and the Origin of Hominid Bipedalism." *American Journal of Physical Anthropology* 52:102–6.

Roos, C., and T. Geissmann. 2001. "Molecular Phylogeny of the Major Hylobatid Divisions." *Molecular Phylogenetics and Evolution* 19:486–94.

Rose, K. D., and J. G. Fleagle. 1987. "The Second Radiation-Prosimians." In *Primate Evolution and Human Origins*. Edited by R. L. Ciochon and J. Fleagle. New York: Aldine de Gruyter.

Rosencrans, B. 1997. *The Last Secret: Daughters Sexually Abused By Mothers*. Brandon, VT: Safer Society Press.

Rosenfeld, A. A. 1977. "Sexual Misuse and the Family." *Victimology: An International Journey* 2:226–35.

Ross, C. 2000. "Into the Light: The Origin of Anthropoidea." *Annual Review of Anthropology* 29:147–94.

Rothstein, A. 1979. "Oedipal Conflicts in Narcissistic Personality Disorders." *International Journal of Psychoanalysis* 60:189–99.

Rouche, M. 1987. "The Early Middle Ages in the West." In *A History of Private Life: From Pagan Rome to Byzantium*. Vol. 1. Edited by Paul Veyne. Cambridge: Belknap Press, Harvard University Press.

Ruch, L. O., and S. M. Chandler. 1982. "The Crisis Impact of Sexual Assault on Three Victim Groups: Adult Rape Victims, Child Rape Victims, and Incest Victims." *Journal of Social Service Research* 5:83–100.

Rudd, J. M., and S. D. Herzberger. 1999. "Brother–Sister Incest—Father–Daughter Incest: A Comparison of Characteristics and Consequences." *Child Abuse and Neglect* 23:915–28.

Rudominer, H. S. 2002. "Consummated Mother–Son Incest in Latency: A Case Report of an Adult Analysis." *Journal of American Psychoanalytic Association* 50:909–35.

Ruggiero, K. J., S. V. McLeer, and J. F. Dixon. 2000. "Sexual Abuse Characteristics Associated with Survivor Psychopathology." *Child Abuse and Neglect* 24:951–64.

Rumbaugh, D., and D. Washburn. 2003. *Intelligence of Apes and Other Rational Beings.* New Haven: Yale University Press.

Rush, F. 1980. *The Best-Kept Secret.* Englewood Cliffs, NJ: Prentice-Hall.

Russell, D. E. H. 1988. "The Incidence and Prevalence of Intrafamilial and Extrafamilial Abuse of Female Children." In *Handbook of Sexual Abuse of Children.* Edited by L. E. A. Walker. Dordrecht: Springer.

———. 1986. *The Secret Trauma: Incest in the Lives of Girls and Women.* New York: Basic.

———. 1984. "The Gender Gap among Perpetrators of Sexual Abuse." In *Sexual Exploitation: Rape, Child Sexual Abuse, and Workplace Harassment.* Edited by D. H. Russell. Beverly Hills, CA: Sage.

Russell, D. O. 1992. *Spanking the Monkey.* Fine Line Features. Film.

Sade, D. E. 1968. "Inhibition of Son–Mother Mating among Free-Ranging Rhesus Monkeys." *Science Psychoanalysis* 12:18–38.

———. 1965. "Some Aspects of Parent–Offspring and Sibling Relations in a Group of Rhesus Monkeys, with a Discussion of Grooming." *American Journal of Physical Anthropology* 23:1–18.

Sagarin, E. 1977. "Incest: Problems of Definition and Frequency." *Journal of Sex Research* 13:126–35.

Sanderson, S. 2001. *The Evolution of Human Sociality.* New York: Rowman & Littlefield.

Sanfey, A. G., J. K. Rilling, J. A. Aronson, L. E. Nystrom, and J. D. Cohen. 2003. "The Neural Basis of Economic Decision-Making in the Ultimatum Game." *Science* 300:1755–58.

Sariola, H., and A. Uutela. 1996. "The Prevalence and Context of Incest Abuse in Finland." *Child Abuse and Neglect* 20:843–50.

Savage-Rumbaugh, S., J. Murphy, J. Seveik, K. Brakke, S. L. Williams, and D. Rumbaugh. 1993. "Language Comprehension in the Ape and Child." *Monographs of the Society for Research in Child Development,* 58. Chicago: University of Chicago Press.

Savage-Rumbaugh, S., R. Sevcik, and W. Hopkins. 1988. "Symbolic Cross-Model Transfer in Two Species." *Child Development* 59:617–25.

Schaik, C. P. van. 1999. "The Socioecology of Fission–Fusion Sociality in Orangutans." *Primates* 40:69–86.

Schaller, G. 1962. "The Ecology and Behavior of the Mountain Gorilla." Ph.D. diss., University of Wisconsin.

Schetky, D. H., and A. H. Green, eds. 1988. *Child Sexual Abuse: A*

Handbook for Health Care and Legal Professionals. New York: Brunner-Mazel.

Scheurell, R. P., and I. P. Rinder. 1973. "Social Networks and Deviance: A Study of Lower Class Incest, Wife Beating, and Non-Support Offenders." *Wisconsin Sociologist* 19:56–73.

Schlesinger, L. B. 1999. "Adolescent Sexual Matricide Following Repetitive Mother–Son Incest." *Journal of Forensic Science* 44:746–49.

Schneider, H. 2000. "Saudi Intermarriages Have Genetic Costs." *Washington Post Foreign Service,* January 16, 2000, A1.

Schull, W. J., and J. V. Neel. 1965. *The Effects of Inbreeding on Japanese Children.* New York: Harper & Row.

Schultz, A. H. 1970. "The Comparative Uniformity of the Cercopithecoidea." In *Old World Monkeys.* Edited by J. R. Napier and P. H. Napier. New York: Academic.

Schultz, L. G., ed. 1980. *The Sexual Victimology of Youth.* Springfield, IL: Thomas.

Schultz, L. G., and P. Jones. 1983. "Sexual Abuse of Children: Issues for Social Service and Health Professionals." *Child Welfare* 62:99–108.

Schutz, A. [1907] 1932. *The Phenomenology of the Social World.* Evanston, IL: Northwestern University Press.

Schwartz, J. 2004. "Getting to Know Homo Erectus." *Science* 305:53–54.

Seemanova, E. 1971. "A Study of Children of Incestuous Matings." *Human Heredity* 21:108–28.

Seligman, B. Z. 1950. "The Problem of Incest and Exogamy: A Restatement." *American Anthropologist* 52:305–16.

———. 1932. "The Incest Barrier: Its Role in Social Organization." *British Journal of Psychology* 22:250–76.

———. 1929. "Incest and Descent: Their Influence on Social Organization." *Royal Anthropological Institute of Great Britain* 59:231–72.

Semaw, S., S. Simpson, J. Quade, P. Renne, R. Butler, W. Mcintosh, N. Levin, M. Dominguez-Rodrigo, and M. Rogers. 2005. "Early Pliocene Hominids from Gona, Ethiopia." *Nature* 433:301–5.

Semendeferi, K., et al. 2002. "Prefrontal Cortex in Humans and Apes: A Comparative Study of Area IQ." *American Journal of Physical Anthropology* 114:224–41.

Semendeferi, K., and H. Damasio. 2000. "The Brain and Its Main Anatomical Subdivisions in Living Hominoids Using Magnetic Resonance Imaging." *Journal of Human Evolution* 38:317–32.

Senut, B., and M. Pickford. 2004. "The Dichotomy between African Apes and Humans Revisited." *C. R. Paleval* 3:265–76.

Sepler, F. 1990. "Victim Advocacy and Young Male Victims of Sexual Abuse: An Evolutionary Model." In *The Sexually Abused Male: Prevalence, Impact, and Treatment.* Vol. 1. Edited by M. Hunter. Lexington, MA: Lexington.

Seto, M., M. L. Lalumiere, and M. Kuban. 1999. "The Sexual Preferences of Incest Offenders." *Journal of Abnormal Psychology* 108:267–72.

Sevinga, M., T. Vrijenhoek, J. W. Hesselinks, H. W. Barkema, and A. F. Groen. 2004. "Effects of Inbreeding on the Incidence of Retained Placenta in Friesian Horses." *Journal of Animal Genetics* 82:982–86.

Sgroi, S. M., and N. M. Sargent. 1993. "Impact and Treatment Issues for Victims of Childhood Sexual Abuse by Female Perpetrators." In *Female Sexual Abuse of Children: The Ultimate Taboo.* Edited by M. Elliott. London: Longman Information and Reference.

Shakespeare. [1608] 1998. *Pericles.* Edited by Doreen Delvecchio and Antony Hammand. Cambridge, UK: Cambridge University Press.

Shalev, S. A., R. Carmi, A. Leventhal, and J. Zlotogora. 2003. "A Comprehensive Program for Prevention of Genetic Diseases among Arabs in Israel." *Harefuah* 142:792–94. In Hebrew.

Shelton, W. R. 1975. "A Study of Incest." *International Journal of Offender Therapy and Comparative Criminology* 19:139–53.

Shengold, L. 1989. *Soul Murder: The Effects of Childhood Abuse and Deprivation.* New Haven: Yale University Press.

———. 1980. "Some Reflections on a Case of Mother/Adolescent Son Incest." *International Journal of Psychoanalysis* 61:461–76.

Shepher, J. 1971. "Mate Selection among Second Generation Kibbutz Adolescents and Adults: Incest Avoidance and Negative Imprinting." *Archives of Sexual Behavior* 1:293–307.

Showers, J., E. D. Farber, J. A. Joseph, L. Oshins, and C. F. Johnson. 1983. "The Sexual Victimization of Boys: A Three-year Survey." *Health Values: Achieving High Level Wellness* 7:15–18.

Sicotte, P. 2001. "Female Mate Choice in Mountain Gorillas." In *Mountain Gorillas: Three Decades of Research at Karisoke.* Edited by M. M. Robins, P. Sicotte, and K. J. Stewart. Cambridge: Cambridge University Press.

Silk, J., S. C. Alberts, and J. Altmann. 2003. "Social Bonds of Female Baboons Enhance Infant Survival." *Science* 302:1231–34.

Simonds, P. 1974. *The Social Primates.* New York: Harper & Row.

Singer, K. I. 1989. "Group Work with Men Who Experienced Incest in Childhood." *American Journal of Orthopsychiatry* 59:458–72.

Singer, T., S. B. Seymour, J. O'Doherty, H. Kavbr, R. J. Dolan, and C. D. Firth. 2004. "Empathy for Pain Involves Affective But Not Sensory Components of Pain." *Science* 303:1157–62.

Slater, M. K. 1959. "Ecological Factors in the Origin of Incest." *American Anthropologist* 61:1042–59.

Sloane, P., and E. Karpinski. 1942. "Effects of Incest on the Participants." *American Journal of Orthopsychiatry* 13:666–73.

Smith, B. H., and R. L. Tompkins. 1995. "Toward a Life History of the Hominidae." *Annual Review of Anthropology* 24:257–79.

Smith, D., T. Meier, E. Geffen, D. L. Mech, J. W. Burch, L. G. Adams, and R. K. Wayne. 1997. "Is Incest Common in Gray Wolf Packs?" *Behavioral Ecology* 8:384–91.

Smith, H., and E. Israel. 1987. "Sibling Incest: A Study of the Dynamics of 25 Cases." *Child Abuse and Neglect* 1:101–8.

Smith, R. J., P. J. Cannon, and B. H. Smith. 1995. "Ontogeny of Australopithecines and Early Homo: Evidence from Cranial Capacity and Dental Eruption." *Journal of Human Evolution* 29:155–68.

Smuts, B., D. Cheney, R. Seyfarth, R. Wrangham, and T. Struhsaker. 1987. *Primate Societies.* Chicago: University of Chicago Press.

Sonkin, D. J. 1992. *Wounded Boys, Heroic Men: A Man's Guide to Recovering from Child Abuse.* Stamford, CT: Longmeadow.

Spencer, B., and F. J. Gillen. [1899] 1938. *The Native Tribes of Central Australia.* London: Macmillan.

Spencer, J. 1981. "Father–Daughter Incest: A Clinical View from the Corrections Field." *Child Welfare* 57:581–89.

Spencer, M. J., and P. Dunklee. 1986. "Sexual Abuse of Boys." *Pediatrics* 78:133–37.

Spiro, M. 1958. *Children of the Kibbutz.* Cambridge: Harvard University Press.

Spoor, F., B. Wood, and F. Zonneveld. 1994. "Implications of Early Hominid Labyrinthine Morphology for Evolution of Human Bipedal Locomotion." *Nature* 369:645–48.

Sroufe, L. A., and M. J. Ward. 1980. "Seductive Behavior of Mothers of Toddlers: Occurrence, Correlates, and Family Origins." *Child Development* 51:1222–29.

Stanford, C. 2001. "Avoiding Predators: Expectations and Evidence in Primate Antipredator Behavior." *International Journal of Primatology* 23:741–57.

———. 1999. *The Hunting Apes.* Princeton: Princeton University Press.

Stebbins, G. L. 1966. *The Basis of Progressive Evolution.* Chapel Hill: University of North Carolina Press.

Steed, J. 1991. "When Mothers Sexually Abuse Their Sons." *Toronto Star.*

Stephan, H. 1983. "Evolutionary Trends in Limbic Structures." *Neuroscience and Biobehavioral Reviews* 7:367–74.

Stephan, H., and O. J. Andy. 1977. "Quantitative Comparison of the Amygdala in Insectivores and Primates." *Acta Antomica* 98:130–53.

———. 1969. "Quantitative Comparative Neuroanatomy of Primates: An Attempt at Phylogenetic Interpretation." *Annals of the New York Academy of Science* 167:370–87.

Stephan, H., G. Baron, and H. Frahm. 1988. "Comparative Size of Brains and Brain Components." In *Neurosciences.* Vol. 4. Edited by H. Steklis and J. Erwin. New York: Alan Liss.

Stern, J. T. 1975. "Before Bipedality." *Yearbook of Physical Anthropology* 19:58–68.

―――. 1972. "Functional Myology of the Hip and Thigh of Cebid Monkeys and Its Implications for the Evolution of Erect Posture." In *Biblioteca Primatologica*. Vol. 14. Basil: Karger.

Stewart, K. 1981. "Social Development of Wild Mountain Gorillas." Ph.D. diss., Cambridge University.

Stewart, K., and A. Harcourt. 1987. "Gorillas: Variation in Female Relationships." In *Primate Societies*. Edited by B. Smuts, D. Cheney, R. Seyfarth, R. Wrangham, and T. Struhsaker. Chicago: University of Chicago Press.

Stocking, G., Jr. 1968. *Race, Culture, and Evolution: Essays on the History of Anthropology*. New York: Free Press.

Stokes, E. J. 2004. *Within-group Social Relationships among Females and Adult Males in Wild Western Lowland Gorillas (Gorilla gorilla gorilla)*. American Journal of Primatology 64:233–46.

Stone, L. 1977. *The Family, Sex, and Marriage in England, 1500–1800*. New York: Harper & Row.

Strabo. [circa 7 B.C.E.] 1930. *The Geography of Strabo*. 8 vols. Translated by Horace Jones. London: Heinemann.

Strait, D., F. Grine, and M. Moniz. 1997. "A Reappraisal of Early Hominid Phylogeny." *Journal of Human Evolution* 32:17–82.

Stringer, C. 2002. "Modern Human Origins: Progress and Prospects." *Phil. Trans. R. Soc.* 357:563–79.

Strum. S. 1987. *Almost Human: A Journey Into the World of Baboons*. New York: Norton.

Struve, J. 1990. "Dancing with the Patriarchy: The Politics of Sexual Abuse." In *The Sexually Abused Male: Prevalence, Impact, and Treatment*. Vol. 1. Edited by M. Hunter. Lexington, MA: Lexington.

Sugardjito, J., I. J. A. te Boekhorst, and J. A. R. A. M. van Hooff. 1987. "Ecological Constraints on the Grouping of Wild Orang-utans (Pongo pygmaeus) in the Gunung Leuser National Park, Sumatra, Indonesia." *International Journal of Primatology* 8:17–41.

Summit, R., and J. A. Kryso. 1978. "Sexual Abuse of Children: A Clinical Spectrum." *American Journal of Orthopsychiatry* 48:237–51.

Swartz, S. 1989. "Pendular Mechanics and Kinematics and Energetics of Brachiating Locomotion." *International Journal of Primatology* 10:387–418.

Swett, C., Jr., J. Surrey, and C. Cohen. 1990. "Sexual and Physical Abuse Histories and Psychiatric Symptoms among Male Psychiatric Outpatients." *American Journal of Psychiatry* 147:632–36.

Szalay, P. S., and E. Delson. 1979. *Evolutionary History of the Primates*. New York: Academic.

Takahata, Y. 1990a. "Adult Males' Social Relations with Adult Females." In *The Chimpanzees of the Mahale Mountains*. Edited by T. Nishida. Tokyo: University of Tokyo Press.

―――. 1990b. "Social Relationships among Adult Males." In *The*

Chimpanzees of the Mahale Mountains. Edited by T. Nishida. Tokyo: University of Tokyo Press.

Takahata, Y., M. A. Huffman, and M. Bardi. 2002. "Long-term Trends in Matrilineal Inbreeding among Japanese Macaques of Arashiyama B Troop." *International Journal of Primatology* 23:399–410.

Talbot, N., P. R. Duberstein, D. King, C. Cox, and D. Giles. 2000. "Personality Traits of Women with a History of Childhood Sexual Abuse." *Comprehensive Psychiatry* 1:130–36.

Talmon, Y. 1964. "Mate Selection on Collective Settlements." *American Sociological Review* 29:491–508.

Tattersall, I. 1998. *Becoming Human: Evolution and Human Uniqueness.* New York: Harcourt Brace.

Tattersall, I., E. Delson, and J. van Couvering. 1988. *Encyclopedia of Human Evolution and Prehistory.* New York: Garland.

Taylor, A. 1938. "Riddles Dealing with Family Relationships." 51:25–37.

Temerin, A., and J. Cant. 1983. "The Evolutionary Divergence of Old World Monkeys and Apes." *American Naturalist* 122:335–51.

Thakkar, R. R., P. M. Guitierrez, C. L. Kuczen, and T. R. McCanne. 2000. "History of Physical and/or Sexual Abuse and Current Suicidality in College Women." *Child Abuse and Neglect* 24:1345–54.

The Ante-Nicene Fathers. 1908. Vols. 2, 4. New York: Scribner's.

Thomas, J. N. 1980. "Yes, You Can Help a Sexually Abused Child." *RN* 43:23–29.

Thomas, M., and M. Stamertiow. 1993. "Mother/Son Incest: The Last Taboo." Presented at the Fifth Annual National Conference on Male Survivors: Advancing National Awareness of Male Victimization. Bethesda, MD.

Thornhill, N. W., J. Tooby, and L. Cosmides. 1997. "Introduction to Evolutionary Psychology." In *Human by Nature: Between Biology and the Social Sciences.* Edited by P. Weingart, P. J. Richerson, S. O. Mitchell, and S. Maasen. London: Erlbaum.

Thorman, G. 1983. *Incestuous Families.* Springfield, IL: Thomas.

Tilson, R. L. 1981. "Family Formation Strategies of Kloss's Gibbons." *Folia Primatologica* 35:259–87.

Tolson, F. 1993. *Be Silent No Longer: For Adolescent Male Victims of Sexual Abuse.* Edited by C. Pullen and P. Tedeschi. Denver: Men Assisting Leading and Educating [MALE].

Tooker, E. 1997. Introduction to Lewis Henry Morgan, *Systems of Consanguinity and Affinity of the Human Family.* Lincoln: University of Nebraska Press.

Toshisada, N., N. Corp, M. Hamal, T. Hasegawa, M. Hiraiwa-Hasegawa, K. Hosaka, K. D. Hunt, N. Itoh, K. Kawanaka, A. Matsumoto-Oda, J.C. Mitani, M. Nakamura, K. Norikoshi, T. Sakamaki, L. Turner, S. Uehara, and K. Zamma. 2003. "Demography, Female Life History, and Reproductive Profiles among the Chimpanzees of Mahale." *American Journal of Primatology* 59:99–121.

Trabelsy, T., and S. Golan. 1994. "No One to Care for a Nine-Year-Old Boy Who Has a Sexual Relationship with His Mother." *Yediot Aharonot* (Israel).

Tramer, M. 1955. "Über Das Inzest Problem" [The incest problem]. *Z. für Kinderpsychiatry* 22:1–23.

Trautmann, T. 1987. *Lewis Henry Morgan and the Invention of Kinship.* Berkeley: University of California Press.

Trevarthen, C. 1984. "Emotions in Infancy: Regulators of Contact and Relationship with Persons." In *Approaches to Emotions.* Edited by K. R. Scherer and P. Ekman. Hillsdale, NJ: Erlbaum.

Trivelpiece, J. W. 1990. "Adjusting the Frame: Cinematic Treatment of Sexual Abuse and Rape of Men and Boys." In *The Sexually Abused Male: Prevalence, Impact, and Treatment.* Vol. 1. Edited by M. Hunter. Lexington, MA: Lexington.

Trivers, R. L. 1972. "Parental Investment and Sexual Selection." In *Sexual Selection and the Descent of Man, 1871–1971.* Edited by B. Campbell. Chicago: Aldine-Atherton.

———. 1971. "The Evolution of Reciprocal Altruism." *Quarterly Review of Biology* 46:4:35–57.

Trocme, N., and D. Wolfe. 2001. *Child Maltreatment in Canada: Canadian Incidence Study of Reported Child Abuse and Neglect: Selected Results.* Ottawa: Minister of Public Works and Government Services.

Tsun, O. K. A. 1999. "Sibling Incest: A Hong Kong Experience." *Child Abuse and Neglect* 23:71–79.

Turner, J. H. 2000. *On the Origins of Human Emotions: A Sociological Inquiry into the Evolution of Human Affect.* Stanford, CA: Stanford University Press.

———. 1999. "The Neurology of Emotions: Implications for Sociological Theories of Interpersonal Behavior." In *The Sociology of Emotions.* Edited by D. Franks. Greenwich, CN: JAI Press.

———. 1998. "The Evolution of Moral Systems." *Critical Review* 11:211–32.

———. 1997a. "The Nature and Dynamics of the Social among Humans." In *The Mark of the Social.* Edited by J. D. Greenwood. New York: Rowman & Littlefield.

———. 1997b. "The Evolution of Emotions: The Nonverbal Basis of Human Social Organization." In *Nonverbal Communication: Where Nature Meets Culture.* Edited by U. Segerstrale and P. Molnar. Hillsdale, N.J.: Erlbaum.

———. 1996a. "The Evolution of Emotions in Humans: A Darwinian-Durkheimian Analysis." *Journal for the Theory of Social Behaviour* 26:1–34.

———. 1996b. "Cognition, Emotion, and Interaction in the Big-Brained

Primate." In *Social Processes and Interpersonal Relations*. Edited by K. M. Kwan. Greenwich, CN: JAI Press.

——. 1996c. "Toward a General Sociological Theory of Emotions." *Journal for the Theory of Social Behavior* 29:132–62.

Tuttle, R. 1986. *Apes of the World: Their Social Behavior, Communication, Mentality, and Ecology.* Park Ridge, NJ: Noyes.

Unga, E. 1991. "I Was Seduced by My Own Mother." *Woman's World* 8:12–13.

Ungar, P. 1996. "Dental Microwear of European Miocene Catarrhines: Evidence for Diets and Tooth Use." *Journal of Human Evolution* 31:335–66.

Ungar, P., and R. Kay. 1995. "The Dietary Adaptations of European Miocene Catarrhines." *Proceedings of the National Academy of Sciences of the United States* 92:5479–81.

Urquiza, A. J., and L. M. Keating. 1990. "The Prevalence of Sexual Victimization of Males." In *The Sexually Abused Male: Prevalence, Impact, and Treatment.* Vol. 1. Edited by M. Hunter. Lexington, MA: Lexington.

van den Berghe, P. 1990. *Human Family Systems: An Evolutionary View.* Prospect Heights, IL: Waveland.

——. 1980. "Incest and Exogamy: A Sociobiological Reconsideration." *Ethology and Sociobiology* 1:151–62.

van den Berghe, P. L., and G. M. Mesher. 1980. "Royal Incest and Inclusive Fitness." *American Ethnologist* 7:300–17.

Vanderbilt, H. 1992. "Incest: A Chilling Report." *Lear's.*

Vander Mey, B. J. 1988. "The Sexual Victimization of Male Children: A Review of Previous Research." *Child Abuse and Neglect* 12:61–72.

——. 1981. "Father–Daughter Incest: A Conflict Approach." Working paper. Department of Sociology, Clemson University, Clemson, S.C. Revised 1985.

Vander Mey, B. J., and R. L. Neff. 1986. *Incest as Child Abuse: Research and Applications.* New York: Praeger.

Vehara, S. 1988. "Grouping Patterns of Wild Pygmy Chimpanzees (Pan paniseos) Observed at a Marsh Grassland amidst the Tropical Rain Forest of Yalosidi, Republic of Zaire." *Primates* 29:41–52.

Veko, A., D. Lordkipanidze, G. P. Rightmire, J. Agusti, R. Ferring, G. Maisuradze, A. Mouskhelishvili, M. Niovadze, M. Ponce de Leon, M. Tappen, M. Tualchrelidze, and C. Zollikofer. 2002. "A New Skull of Early *Homo* from Dmanisi, Georgia." *Science* 297:85–89.

Vignaud, P. P. Duringer, H. T. Mackaye, A. Liklus, C. Blondel, J-R. Boisserie, L. de Bonis, V. Eisenmann, M-E. Etienne, D. Geraads, F. Guy, T. Lehmann, F. Lihoreau, N. Lopez-Martinez, C. Mourer-Chauviré, O. Otero, J-C. Rage, M. Schuster, L. Viriot, A. Zazzo, and M. Brunet, 2002. *Geology and Palaeontology of the Upper Miocene Toros-Menalla Hominid Locality, Chad. Nature* 418:152–55.

Vogel, G. 2004. "The Evolution of the Golden Rule." *Science* 303:1128–31.

Wahl, C. W. 1960. "The Psychodynamics of Consummated Maternal Incest: A Report of Two Cases." *Archives of General Psychiatry* 3:188–93.

Walker, A. 2002. "New Perspectives on the Hominids of the Turkana Basin, Kenya." *Evolutionary Anthropology* 11:38–41.

Walter, A. 2000. "From Westermarck Effect to Fox's Law: Paradox and Principle in the Relationship between Incest Taboo and Exogamy." *Social Science Information/Sur Les Sciences Sociales* 39:467–88.

Walter, A., and S. Buyske. 2003. "The Westermarck Effect and Early Childhood Co-socialization: Sex Differences in Inbreeding Avoidance." *British Journal of Developmental Psychology* 21:353–65.

Walters, D. R. 1975. *Physical and Sexual Abuse of Children: Causes and Treatment.* Bloomington: Indiana University Press.

Wang, T., S. N. Aitken, J. H. Woods, K. Polsson, and S. Magnussen. 2003. "Effects of Inbreeding on Coastal Firs Growth and Yield of Operational Plantations: A Model-based Approach." *Theoretical Applied Genetics* 108:1162–71.

Ward, C. V. 1993. "Torso Morphology and Locomotion in Catarrhines: Implications for the Positional Behavior of *Proconsul nyanzae.*" *American Journal of Physical Anthropology* 92:291–328.

Ward, C. V., M. G. Leakey, and A. Walker. 2001. "Morphology of *Australopithecus Anamensis* from Kanapoi and Allia Bay, Kenya." *Journal of Human Evolution* 41:255–368.

Ward, E. 1984. *Father–Daughter Rape.* London: Women's Press.

Washburn, S. L., ed. 1968. "Speculations on the Problem of Man's Coming to the Ground." In *Changing Perspectives on Man.* Edited by B. Rothbatt. Chicago: University of Chicago Press.

Wasserman, S., and K. Faust. 1994. *Social Network Analysis: Methods and Applications.* Cambridge: Cambridge University Press.

Watkins, B., and A. Bentovim. 1992. "The Sexual Abuse of Male Children and Adolescents: A Review of Current Research." *Journal of Child Psychology and Psychiatry* 33:197–248.

Watkins, W. S., A. R. Rogers, C. T. Ostler, S. Wooding, M. J. Bamshad, A. M. E. Braesington, M. C. Carroll, S. V. Nguyen, J. A. Walker, B. V. R. Prasad, P. G. Reddy, P. K. Das, M. A. Batzer, and C. B. Jorde. 2003. "Genetic Variation among World Populations." *Genome Research* 13:1607–18.

Watts, D. 1991. "Strategies of Habitat Use by Mountain Gorillas." *Folia Primatologica* 56:1–16.

Weber, A. W., and A. Vedder. 1983. "Population Dynamics of the Gorillas: 1959–1978." *Biological Conservation* 26:341–66.

Weich, M. J. 1968. "The Terms 'Mother' and 'Father' as a Defense against Incest." *Journal of the American Psychoanalytic Association* 16:783–91.

Weinberg, S. K. 1955. *Incest Behavior.* New York: Citadel.

Weiner, I. B. 1964. "On Incest: A Survey." *Excerpta Crimonologica* 4:137–55.

Weisfeld, G. E., T. Czilli, K. A. Phillips, J. A. Gall, and C. M. Lichtman. 2003. "Possible Olfaction-based Mechanisms in Human Kin Recognition and Inbreeding Avoidance." *Journal of Experimental Child Psychology* 85:279–95.

Welldon, E. V. 1988. *Mother, Madonna, Whore: The Idealization and Denigration of Motherhood.* London: Free Association.

Wellman, B., and S. D. Berkowitz. 1988. *Social Structures: A Network Approach.* Cambridge: Cambridge University Press.

Westerlund, E. 1983. "Counseling Women with Histories of Incest." *Women and Therapy* 2:17–31.

Westermarck, E. 1926. *A Short History of Marriage.* London: Macmillan.

———. [1891] 1922. *The History of Human Marriage.* 3 vols. New York: Allerton.

———. 1891. *The History of Human Marriage.* London: Macmillan.

Westermeyer, J. 1978. "Incest in Psychiatric Practice: A Description of Patients and Incestuous Relationships." *Journal of Clinical Psychiatry* 39:643–48.

Wheeler, P. E. 1993. "The Influence of Stature and Body Form on Hominid Energy and Water Budgets: A Comparison of *Australopithecus* and *Homo* Physiques." *Journal of Human Evolution* 24:13–28.

White, F. J. 1989. "Ecological Correlates of Pygmy Chimpanzee Social Structure." In *Comparative Socioecology.* Edited by V. Standen and R. A. Foley. Oxford: Blackwell.

White, L. A. 1949. *The Science of Culture.* New York: Grove.

———. 1948. "The Definition and Prohibition of Incest." *American Anthropologist* 50:416–35.

White, T., and G. Suwa. 1987. "Hominid Footprints at Laetoli: Facts and Interpretations." *American Journal of Physical Anthropology* 72:485–514.

White, T. D., G. Suwa, and B. Asfaw. 1994. "*Australopithecus Ramidus*: A New Species of Early Hominid from Aramis, Ethiopia." *Nature* 371:280–81.

Whitehead, P., and C. Jolly. 2000. *Old World Monkeys.* Cambridge: Cambridge University Press.

Whiten, A. 2002. "The Emotional Ape." *Science* 298:1720–21.

Wich, S. A., E. H. M. Sterck, and S. S. Utami. 1999. "Are Orangutan Females as Solitary as Chimpanzee Females?" *Folia Primatol.* 70:23–28.

Wiehe, V. 1997. *Sibling Abuse: Hidden Physical, Emotional and Sexual Abuse,* 2nd ed. Thousand Oaks, CA: Sage.

———. 1990. *Sibling Abuse: Hidden Physical, Emotional, and Sexual Trauma.* Lexington, MA: Lexington.

Wilder, J., S. Kingan, Z. Mobasher, M. Pilkington, and M. Hammer.

2004. "Global Patterns of Human Mitochondrial DNA and Y-Chromosome Structure Are Not Influenced by Higher Migration Rates of Females versus Males." *Nature Genetics* 36:1122–24.

Wildman, E. E., M. Uddin, G. Z. Liu, L. I. Grossman, M. Goodman. 2003. "Implications of Natural Selection in Shaping 99.4% Nonsynonymous DNA Identity Between Humans and Chimpanzees: Enlarging Genus Homo." *Proceedings of the National Academy of Sciences of the United States of America* 100, no. 12:7181–88.

Wilken, T. R. 2002. *Adult Survivors of Sexual Abuse*. Ottawa, CA: National Clearinghouse on Family Violence.

Willner, D. 1983. "Definition and Violation: Incest and the Incest Taboos." *Man,* new series 18:134–59.

Wilson, M., and R. Wrangham. 2003. "Intergroup Relations in Chimpanzees." *Annual Review of Anthropology* 32:363–92.

Wimmer, R., S. Kirsch, G. A. Rappold, W. Schempp. 2002. "Direct Evidence for the Homo-Pan Clade." *Chromosome Research* 10, no. 3:252.

Wirth, S., M. Yanike, L. M. Frank, A. C. Smith, E. N. Brown, and W. A. Suzuki. 2003. "Single Neurons in the Monkey Hippocampus and Learning New Associations." *Science* 300:1578–80.

Wolf, A. P. 2005. "Explaining the Westermarck Effect, or, What Did Natural Selection Select For?" In *Inbreeding, Incest, and the Incest Taboo*. Edited by A. P. Wolf and W. H. Durham. Stanford, CA: Stanford University Press.

———. 1972. "Childhood Association and Sexual Attraction: A Further Test of the Westermarck Hypothesis." *American Anthropologist* 70:503–15.

———. 1968. "Adopt a Daughter-in-Law, Marry a Sister: A Chinese Solution to the Problem of the Incest Taboo." *American Anthropologist* 70:873–85.

———. 1966. "Childhood Association, Sexual Attraction, and the Incest Taboo: A Chinese Case." *American Anthropologist* 68:883–98.

Wolf, A. P., and C. Huang. 1979. *Marriage and Adoption in China, 1845–1945*. Stanford, CA: Stanford University Press.

Wolf, A. P., and W. H. Durham, eds. 2005. *Inbreeding, Incest, and the Incest Taboo*. Stanford, CA: Stanford University Press.

Wolfe, F. A. 1985. "Twelve Female Sexual Offenders." Paper presented at Next Steps in Research on the Assessment and Treatment of Sexually Aggressive Persons (Paraphiliacs), St. Louis, MO.

Wolpoff, M. 1999. *Paleoanthropology*. Boston: McGraw-Hill.

Wolpoff, M., B. Senet, M. Pickford, and J. Hawks. 2002. "Sahelanthropus or 'Sahelpithecus.'" *Nature* 419:581–82.

Wood, B., and B. Richmond. 2000. "Human Evolution: Taxonomy and Paleobiology." *Journal of Anatomy* 196:19–60.

Wood, B., and D. Strait. 2004. "Patterns of Resource Use in Early Homo and Paranthropus." *Journal of Human Evolution* 46:119–62.

Wrangham, R. W. 1987. "The Significance of African Apes for Reconstructing Human Social Evolution." In *The Evolution of Human Behavior: Primate Models.* Edited by W. Kinzey. Albany: State University
of New York Press.

————. 1980. "An Ecological Model of Female-Bonded Primate Groups."
Behaviour 74:262–99.

Wrangham, R. W., and B. Smuts. 1980. "Sex Differences in Behavioural
Ecology of Chimpanzees in Gombe Natural Park, Tanzania." *Journal
of Reproductive Fertility,* suppl. 28:13–31.

Wyatt, G. E. 1991. "Child Sexual Abuse and Its Effects on Sexual Functioning." *Annual Review of Sex Research: An Integrative and Interdis-
ciplinary Review* 2:249–66.

Wyatt, G. E., and S. D. Peters. 1986. "Issues in the Definition of Child
Sexual Abuse in Prevalence Research." *Child Abuse and Neglect* 10:231–
40.

Yamagiwa, J. 1983. "Diachronic Changes in Two Eastern Lowland Gorilla Groups (Gorilla gorilla graueri) in the Mt. Kahuzi Region, Zaire."
Primates 25:174–83.

Yorukaglu, A., and J. L. Kemph. 1996. "Children Not Severely Damaged by Incest with a Parent." *Journal of the American Academy of
Child Psychiatry* 5:111–24.

Zastrow, C., and K. Kirst-Ashman. 1990. *Understanding Human Behavior and the Social Environment.* 2nd ed. Chicago: Nelson-Hall.

Zietkiewicz, E., V. Yotova, D. Gehl, T. Wambach, I. Arrieta, M. Batzer,
D. E. C. Cole, P. Hechtman, F. Kaplan, D. Modiano, J. P. Moisan, R.
Michalsky, and D. Labuda. 2003. "Haplotypes in the Dystrophin DNA
Segment Point to a Mosaic of Modern Human Diversity." *American
Journal of Human Genetics* 73:994–1015.

Zihlman, A., J. Cronin, D. Cramer, and V. Sarich. 1978. "Pygmy Chimpanzee as a Possibility for the Common Ancestor of Humans, Chimpanzees, and Gorillas." *Nature* 276:744–46.

Zlotnick, C., J. Mattia, and M. Zimmerman. 2001. "Clinical Features of
Survivors of Sexual Abuse with Major Depression." *Child Abuse and
Neglect* 25:357–67.

Zumpe, D., and R. P. Michael. 1996. "Social Factors Modulate the
Effects of Hormones on the Sexual and Aggressive Behavior of
Macaques." *American Journal of Primatology* 38:233–61.

INDEX

ABOUT THE AUTHORS

᳗

Jonathan H. Turner is Distinguished Professor of sociology at the University of California at Riverside. He is the author of twenty-nine books and the editor of a half dozen more. He has also published approximately one hundred and fifty chapters in edited books and articles for research journals. His primary interest is in developing general sociological theories about generic social processes. His substantive interests include the sociology of emotions, stratification, ethnic relations, interaction processes, social institutions, and biosociology. The present work builds upon two earlier works, *The Social Cage: Human Nature and the Evolution of Society* (with Alexandra Maryanski) and *On The Origins of Human Emotions: A Sociological Inquiry into the Evolution of Human Affect.* The goal of these and the present book is to understand important social processes, such as the cultural prohibition against incest, by reference to the evolutionary history of humans as an evolved ape as the ancestors of present-day humans built social structures and used culture to adapt to the environment.

Alexandra Maryanski is associate professor of sociology at the University of California at Riverside. She is trained in both anthropology and sociology with specializations in social institutions, social networks, Old World primates, and the interface between biology, culture, and social structure. She is the author (with Jonathan Turner) of two books, *Functionalism* and *The Social Cage: Human Nature and the Evolution of Society.* She has published more than thirty-five articles in journals and edited books

on kinship and the family, human nature, the evolution of language, hominoid evolution, early hominid social structure, primate social networks, and the biological foundations of human
societies. She is currently writing a book on Émile Durkheim and
his theory of religion.